The Effectiveness of the Different Learning Styles

Education and Learning

Dr. Sharon Campbell-Phillips

ISBN 978-93-5458-456-5
© Dr. Sharon Campbell-Phillips 2021
Published in India 2021 by Pencil

A brand of
One Point Six Technologies Pvt. Ltd.
123, Building J2, Shram Seva Premises,
Wadala Truck Terminal, Wadala (E)
Mumbai 400037, Maharashtra, INDIA
E connect@thepencilapp.com
W www.thepencilapp.com

DISCLAIMER: *The opinions expressed in this book are those of the authors and do not purport to reflect the views of the Publisher.*

Author biography

My name is Dr. Sharon Campbell-Phillips. I am from Trinidad and Tobago. I am very enthusiastic about community work and the development of others. I am also very passionate about conducting research and writing as it allows me the opportunity to share my knowledge with others and educate them as well as enhance and develop myself.

I am currently employed with the local government of Trinidad and Tobago where I work at the Division of Community Development. This Division is dedicated to developing communities so that persons' standard of living can be enhanced.

My writing career began when I was approached by a classmate from Bangladesh to collaborate and write professionally. I accepted the challenge and we began writing together. When I received my first publication, I was very excited and was motivated to continue writing, I am also a Doctor of Health Sciences.

CONTENTS

Preface

The mind of a person receives records via all the five senses. Most of the five, three senses which might be eyes, ears, and skin assist the maximum in informing her/his mastering style. Learning style is a set of characteristics, mindsets, and behaviors that outline our way of gaining knowledge. Gaining knowledge of style is a selected way wherein the thoughts receive and approach statistics. Its miles a quintessential idea that bridges the personality to cognitive dimensions of an individual. Studying style classifies different approaches wherein human beings learn the way they technique facts. By recognizing and understanding one's personal studying style, techniques better appropriate to mastering may be used. Hence the velocity and high quality of getting to know may be elevated. Know-how of one's learning style may be very important because it facilitates a person to be greater efficient and innovative, to boom achievement, to improve hassle solving talents, to make higher choices, and to research extra effectively. There is no pupil who makes use of solely one style or any other. Most of the students utilize a selection of modalities in gaining knowledge. It's far very important to increase their competencies to use as many learning styles as feasible which will achieve all the situations of mastering. In this book, we have discussed learning styles with their theories and educational implications leading us to have complete information approximately the application of these theories in the teaching-mastering method.

A learning fashion is a term used to describe the methods by which people acquire, interpret, and save facts. Every fashion can be broken down into a class-based totally on sensory desires: auditory, visible, and tactile. The presumption is that you may high-quality keep the statistics supplied to you if the situations of your learning style meet. Based totally on the concept that mastering styles exist, I keep in mind myself a visible learner. I prefer to write instructions and preserve my thoughts organized. I generate thoughts primarily based on analyzing examples or watching educational films. As an infant, my options had been lined frequently with auditory studying. I could without difficulty bear in mind matters that spoke to me. As our personalities broaden and the environment changes, so do our learning styles and mastering style evaluation is a good way to acquire facts approximately your number one studying style. A sequence of questions is asked to decide your sensory choices. Our gaining knowledge of the environment can play a position in how properly we can hold the records given to us. We may use specific studying styles primarily based on the state of affairs. A mastering fashion assessment gives an expansion of eventualities to assess the manner you analyze most of the time. The questions vary from the form of books you enjoy to what you do while you wait in line at a shop checkout. Consistent with the assessment, my gaining knowledge of style is forty% Auditory, 35% visual, and 25% Tactile. As an on the whole auditory learner, "you learn nice by way of listening to and listening" in addition to "hum or communicate.

Many humans recognize that all of us prefer unique gaining knowledge of styles and techniques. Mastering patterns institution, not unusual approaches that humans study. Every person has a mixture of learning patterns. Some humans can also locate that they have got a dominant fashion of learning, with some distance less use of the alternative patterns. Others may additionally discover that they use distinctive patterns in unique circumstances. There's no proper blend. Nor are your styles fixed. You could develop potential in much less dominant styles, as well as further broaden styles that you already use nicely.

Many people understand that all and sundry prefer special getting to know patterns and strategies. Studying patterns organization not an unusual methods that human beings examine. Anybody has a mix of studying patterns. Some people can also discover that they have a dominant style of gaining knowledge of, with some distance less use of the other patterns. Others might also locate that they use unique styles in specific circumstances. There may be no right blend. Nor are your styles constant. You may expand potential in less dominant styles, as well as further develop styles that you already use properly.

The use of more than one learning style and more than one intelligence for mastering is a highly new method. This technique is one which educators have simplest lately started to understand. Traditional education used (and keeps to apply) mainly linguistic and logical teaching methods. It additionally makes use of a limited range of studying and teaching techniques. Many colleges nevertheless rely upon study room and eBook-based totally teaching, lots of repetition, and forced tests for reinforcement and evaluation. A result is that we often label folks that use these getting-to-know styles and strategies as bright. Folks that use much less desired getting to know patterns often discover themselves in lower instructions, with numerous not-so-complimentary labels and occasionally decrease high-quality coaching. This may create positive and negative spirals that strengthen the perception that one is "clever" or "dumb".

By means of spotting and expertise your own getting to know patterns, you can use techniques higher appropriate to you. This improves the speed and first-class of your gaining knowledge.

The Seven mastering patterns

• Visible (spatial): You decide on the use of photos, images, and spatial information.

• Aural (auditory-musical): You select the use of sound and tune.

• Verbal (linguistic): You opt for the usage of words, both in speech and writing.

• Bodily (kinesthetic): You select the use of your frame, hands, and sense of contact.

• Logical (mathematical): You pick using good judgment, reasoning, and structures.

• Social (interpersonal): You opt to analyze in corporations or with other human beings.

• Solitary (intrapersonal): You opt to work by yourself and use self-have a look at.

Why getting to know styles? Apprehend the idea of studying patterns

Your gaining knowledge of patterns has greater influence than you could realize. Your preferred styles guide the way you research. Additionally, they alternate the manner you internally constitute stories, the way you recollect information, and even the phrases you pick. We explore greater of these features in this chapter.

Studies suggest that each getting to know fashion uses one-of-a-kind elements of the mind. by concerning extra of the mind all through gaining knowledge of, we don't forget extra of what we examine. Researchers the usage of brain-imaging technologies have been capable of find out the important thing areas of the mind responsible for every studying style.

• Visible: The occipital lobes in the back of the mind manipulate the visible sense. Both the occipital and parietal lobes control spatial orientation.

• Aural: The temporal lobes cope with aural content. The right temporal lobe is specifically vital for the track.

• Verbal: The temporal and frontal lobes, particularly specialized regions known as Brocaï and Wernicke regions (in the left hemisphere of these lobes).

• Physical: The cerebellum and the motor cortex (in the back of the frontal lobe) manage plenty of our physical movement.

• Logical: The parietal lobes, mainly the left aspect, power our logical thinking.

• Social: The frontal and temporal lobes take care of much of our social sports. The limbic machine (not proven apart from the hippocampus) also impacts each social and solitary pattern. The limbic device has plenty to do with emotions, moods, and aggression.

- Solitary: The frontal and parietal lobes, and the limbic machine, are also energetic with this fashion.

Introduction

The time period of getting to know styles is widely used to explain how beginners collect, sift through, interpret, arrange, come to conclusions about, and "save" statistics for similar use. As spelled out in VARK (one of the most popular studying patterns inventories), those styles are regularly classified by using sensory procedures: visual, aural, verbal [reading/writing], and kinesthetic. among the fashions that don't resemble the VARK's sensory recognition are reminiscent of Felder and Silverman's Index of studying patterns, with a continuum of descriptors for the way rookies method and arrange facts: energetic-reflective, sensing-intuitive, verbal visual, and sequential-global.

There are nicely over seventy distinctive learning pattern schemes; most of which might be supported through "a thriving industry dedicated to publishing gaining knowledge of-patterns checks and guidebooks" and "professional development workshops for teachers and educators".

Despite the variation in classes, the fundamental concept at the back of mastering patterns is the same: that every folk has a particular gaining knowledge of style (every so often known as a "preference"), and we study first-rate whilst facts is provided to us in this fashion. As an example, visually inexperienced persons could examine any situation count number high-quality if given graphically or through other styles of visible photos, kinesthetic newbies could analyze more efficaciously if they may contain bodily movements within the gaining knowledge of manner, and so forth.

Notwithstanding the popularity of learning patterns and inventories consisting of the VARK, it's important to recognize that there is no evidence to support the concept that matching sports to 1's gaining knowledge of fashion improves gaining knowledge of. It's not genuinely to be counted of "the absence of proof doesn't imply the proof of absence." On the opposite, for years researchers have attempted to make this connection via masses of research.

In 2009, mental technology inside the Public interest commissioned cognitive psychologists Harold Pashler, Mark McDaniel, Doug Rohrer, and Robert Bjork to evaluate the research on gaining knowledge of styles to decide whether or not there's credible evidence to help using learning patterns in coaching. They came to a startling however clear end: "even though the literature on gaining knowledge of styles is tremendous," they "discovered really no proof" helping the concept that "coaching is excellent provided in a layout that fits the choice of the learner." Lots of the ones studies suffered from weak studies layout, rendering them some distance from convincing.

Pashler and his colleague factor to a few motives to explain why studying patterns have won—and saved such traction, other than the sizeable enterprise that supports the concept. First, humans want to perceive themselves and others by using "kind." Such categories help order the social environment and provide short approaches of expertise every other. Additionally, this method appeals to the concept that freshmen need to be identified as "precise individuals" or, extra precisely, that variations amongst students need to be acknowledged as opposed to treated as quite a number in a crowd or a faceless magnificence of college students. Carried similarly, coaching to exceptional getting to know patterns shows that "all and sundry have the capacity to examine efficiently and without problems, if best coaching is customized to their individual getting to know patterns".

There may be some other motive why this method of getting to know patterns is so widely widespread. They very loosely resemble the concept of metacognition or the manner of considering one's questioning. as an example, having your students describe which look at strategies and situations for his or her last exam labored for them and which didn't is likely to improve their analyzing on the following examination. Integrating such metacognitive activities into the classroom unlike mastering styles—is supported through a wealth of research.

Importantly, metacognition is focused on planning, tracking, and evaluating any sort of thinking about wondering and does nothing to connect one's identification or capabilities to any singular technique to information.

There's, but, something you could take away from these unique procedures to studying not based totally on the learner, but as an alternative on the content being found out. To explore the endurance of the perception in studying styles, He factors out that the variations recognized through the labels "visible, auditory, kinesthetic, and reading/writing" are greater appropriately connected to the nature of the subject:

"There may be evidence that suggests that there are a few approaches to teach some subjects that are just higher than others, no matter the gaining knowledge of varieties of individuals. If you're considering teaching sculpture, I'm no longer positive that lengthy tracts of verbal descriptions of statues or sculptures might be a mainly effective way for individuals to find out about works of art. Evidently, these are physical gadgets and you need to test them, you might even need to deal with them."

Pashler and his colleagues agree: "An apparent factor is that the greatest educational approach is possible to differ across disciplines". In other phrases, it makes disciplinary sense to consist of kinesthetic sports in sculpture and anatomy guides, studying/writing activities in literature and history guides, visible activities in geography and engineering publications, and auditory activities in track, foreign language, and speech guides. Obvious or not, it aligns coaching and learning with the contours of the difficulty be counted, without prescribing the ability skills of the beginners.

Individuals analyze in distinct methods. 'Learning styles' is a time period used to specific person variations inside the procedures of getting to know. In accepting personal differences, we need to remember the idea of 'gaining knowledge of styles'. Expertise about the concept of mastering styles is of specific significance in selling mastering and learning studies. Gaining knowledge of a person is more inspired with the aid of his sorts of learning because everybody has the desired style for getting to know. Students can maximize their learning if they may be privy to their own fashion. Information of one's own fashion may even help the learner to study in his/her manner the usage of his/her satisfactory techniques for studying. Knowledge of getting to know patterns will help the trainer in handing over powerful presentations to diverse newbies within the class. Hence a teacher can decide what's best for the students. The trainer can also cope with the mismatch that could occur whilst manage the instructions. The gaining knowledge of types of students can be decided the use of numerous getting to know style inventories. This may help the trainer to get an idea about the learning sorts of the scholars inside the class and to put together as a result. A studying theory can be taken into consideration as evidence that describes how information is absorbed, processed, and retained at some stage in mastering. There are distinct learning theories that deliver a better concept of the cause in the back of coaching and mastering. The goal of education is to sell getting to know. To make getting to know a hit, the educators need to incorporate variety into their sorts of coaching to fulfill distinctive newbies. Teaching cannot achieve success without expertise in learning styles. Information of learning patterns facilitates the educators and also the inexperienced persons to become a success in the endeavor of coaching mastering system. This book shared gained knowledge of styles is presented in different sections. The first section gives an advent about studying patterns, segment two discusses the exceptional theories of gaining knowledge of styles and the 0.33 phase discusses the instructional implications of learning styles. The authors desire that the book may be very useful for instructors, college students, and additionally to the researchers in the discipline of schooling.

Chapter One Understanding Learning Styles Chapter Two Learning Styles in Theory and Practice Chapter Three Learning Styles, Mental Models and Problem-Solving Chapter Four Reflection and Learning Chapter Five Self-Regulated Learning Environment Chapter Six Learning Styles Dimensions Chapter Seven Visual and Verbal Learners Chapter Eight Sequential and Global Learners Chapter Nine Learning Styles and Academic Achievement Chapter Ten Learning and Diversity

Chapter One

Understanding Learning Styles

Education represents steady modifications. It isn't always a stagnant method, however one that evolves to satisfy the wishes of an ever-changing society. Media interest focuses no longer on the successes of schooling, however on the plain shortcomings. The growing variety of dropouts and graduates who enter the workforce unprepared have emerged as the public's issue. So once more, training is searching for methods to meet student wishes. Scholars getting to know styles is one method being explored. Gaining knowledge of fashion is a method of individualizing guidance at little or no fee. This has a look at investigated the matching of student studying styles and trainer coaching styles to improve scholar results. The attempts made to improve the quality of education are defined throughout the records of training. The ancient descriptions ill s trap te that trade and development had been a persistent procedure. Upgrades are discovered in curriculum revisions, diversifications of recent coaching methods, and new organizational styles for faculties. The past six many years have emphasized diverse instructional subject matters for school improvement. Especially, the final three many years have visible curriculum revisions in nearly all subject count regions. The modifications made within the 1960s have had a profound impact on American

 Education. Within the early Sixties, the emphasis for change was on science because of the post-Sputnik panic. The technology curriculum formulated a greater variety of path services and an extra scope for technology inside the general curriculum. Inside a quick time period, new curricula have been evolved in different problem regions—the new Math, project English, and social research. Those modifications have been made underneath the belief that if the right things had been taught, then college students might be capable of competing globally. Alas, subsequent research indicated that the "new things" were being discovered no extra efficaciously than the "vintage matters". With damaging research findings, the emphasis was modified for the latter 1/2 of the decade of the Sixties to instructional improvement via the use of different methods of providing material. Teaching machines, programmed texts, problem-fixing, and individualized preparation have been a number of the exceptional techniques attempted. In addition to lecture room presentation adjustments, new organizational patterns for schools were evolved. These styles included formal dependent school rooms, informal-unstructured classrooms, modular scheduling, open classrooms, and a faculty-within-a-school. Individualized instruction became additionally advanced in the form of modular scheduling, variable grouping, and non-guardedness. All attempted to enhance the pleasure of training. The individualized practice has been in addition delicate to encompass individualized packages. The idea for these special packages became the application of behavioral objectives.

This shape of individualization has acquired a lot of hobbies that targets are reproduced with the permission of the copyright owner. In addition, reproduction is prohibited without permission. Being pooled in banks to facilitate their use. Any other technique of individualized guidance is to use different instructional strategies with unique college students. Programmed guidance, laptop-assisted education, and unbiased observation are examples of such strategies. This fashion persevered to grow and increase within the past due 1960s and early Seventies. In my view Guided schooling (IGE), individually Prescribed preparation (IPI), software for mastering consistent with needs (PLAN), and getting to know for Mastery (LFM) have been created in this era. While all of the above strategies have added to the frame of know-how concerning individualized coaching, they've met with the most effective constrained fulfillment. The search maintains a way to improve pupil results this is generalizable to a variety of tutorial settings and wishes. Getting to know styles emerges as a key detail in the movement to make gaining knowledge of and preparation greater aware of the wishes of the person learner. Before individualized guidance techniques will be utilized appropriately, an evaluation of individual learner characteristics becomes wished. Instruments that measured analyzing ability, stage of mental improvement, socioeconomic history, pastimes, getting to know styles, and others have been evolved. Regardless of the ability to discover these traits for every man or woman, little evidence exists to verify any dating between college students possessing sure characteristics and unique instructional techniques. Isaac and Michael (1981) agreed that "in place of in search of Reproduced with permission of the copyright owner. Similarly, the replica is prohibited without permission. Fashionable principles of training making use of to anyone, seek empirically mounted ideas approximately a way to deal with people of unique sorts". Kemp (1971) reasoned that since research has shown that scholars examine different methods, the following era of studies efforts ought to determine why "some college students locate positive teaching strategies greater attractive and effective than others". The studies on learning style and coaching fashion has been an immediate result of this line of questioning. For the reason that mid-1970s, many studies efforts have studied getting to know patterns. Gregorc's (1979) style Delineator is a self-assessment of an in the four identification of one's studying style. The work of Dunn and Dunn (1975a) and Gregorc (1979) brought about the improvement of the getting to know patterns stock. Kolb's (1976) gaining knowledge of style stock is directed to secondary college students and adults. The national association of Secondary school Principals (NASSP) established a challenging force to review studying patterns. Their studies resulted inside the mastering style Profile. The know-how of studying patterns gives the teacher any other key to information college students. Interviews have additionally revealed that the instructional materials and techniques used by teachers have an immediate effect on many college students. If the technique is the preferred mastering mode, the learner commonly reacted favorably. If on the other hand, the methods were mismatched, the students "worked hard to analyze," "discovered some and ignored a few materials," or "tuned out." may want to it's that the maximum successful college students in a given study room manifest to own studying possibilities of the academics? We accept as true with this to be so. Gregorc & Ward (1977, p. 24) reproduced with the permission of the copyright proprietor. Similarly, a duplicate is prohibited without permission. Instructors are the unmarried most crucial detail inside the college; extra essential than the excellent of the facilities, the first-rate of the system and substances, or the extent of financing, Davies (1970). If teachers are the single most important element in schools, then the query has to be requested, "what is there about the teacher that determines why this is the maximum important unmarried detail?". Literature on studying and coaching styles suggests the suit or mismatch of styles between instructor and pupil may additionally decide how nicely they get alongside, with vital consequences for the studying technique. More and more studies are investigating the impact of matching students getting to know style and trainer teaching fashion on educational development. announcement of the problem the primary cause of this examine changed into to decide if matching pupil studying style and teacher teaching style would result in any difference in the success of college students within the classroom as measured by using the variety of students receiving credit score in 9th-grade international records classes. Mainly, the evaluation of the students' mastering fashion and instructor teaching style was decided. The overall performance turned into decided by using the final grade each scholar was assigned at the cease of a twenty-week semester. Unique goals of this look at were:

1. To decide whether or not college students whose fit among the auditory component of the learning style Pro

document and the auditory Reproduced with permission of the copyright proprietor. Further reproduction is prohibited without permission. A thing of the academics' gaining knowledge of fashion Profile is extra successful in passing the route than college students and instructors who do no longer suit.

2. To determine whether college students whose in shape among the visual element of the mastering fashion Profile and the visual thing of the lecturers' gaining knowledge of style Profile are extra successful in passing the course than students and teachers who do now not suit.

3. To decide whether or not college students whose healthy among each the auditory and visible components of the studying style Profile and each the auditory and visible components of the academics' mastering style Profile are greater a hit in passing the direction than college students and instructors who do now not healthy.

Importance of the take a look at the intention of educators is to maximize student studying. Individualizing training is one method used to meet this intention. Attempts to individualize instruction have produced many organizational modifications. A number of those changes encompass teaching machines, programmed texts, modular scheduling, open school rooms, variable grouping, and non-guardedness. Before new strategies can be implemented, extra understanding approximately the person student is wanted. They want to recognize how a pupil learns delivered approximately the improvement of studying fashion exams. Learning style consists of how a learner perceives, interacts with, and responds to the gaining knowledge of surroundings. It is tested in that pattern of conduct and overall performance via which and Reproduced with permission of the copyright proprietor. Similarly, reproduction is prohibited without permission. Person strategies educational reports. The expertise of scholar studying patterns provides teachers with vital information approximately character college students. Facts about mastering styles ought a direct implication on how situations remember to be offered. How concern remembers is supplied determines a teacher's teaching style. This observes examined if matching scholar gaining knowledge of style and teacher teaching fashion progressed scholar achievement in passing a route. On the district stage, consequences of this have a look at can provide records to help reduce the quantity of failing grades earned using 9th-grade college students. Implications of this examination also are generalizable to different districts for the subsequent reasons: 1. maximum high faculties have comparable organizational shape. 2. facts received from the identification of gaining knowledge of styles w unwell resource faculty personnel in growing individualized academic programs for students. Matching mastering patterns and coaching patterns is some other device for operating with at-danger College students. Capacity dropouts may enjoy success if instructors train college students' mastering styles. Matching learning patterns and teaching patterns is a model for guidance no longer dependent on grade level or difficulty. Definition of phrases on this takes a look at, the independent variable changed into the fit between students' learning style as measured via the learning style Profile and teachers' coaching fashion additionally measured via the gaining knowledge of style Reproduced with permission of the copyright proprietor. Similarly, a duplicate is prohibited without permission. Profile. The based variable turned into the wide variety of students receiving credit in ninth-grade international records classes. Ninth-grade world history became decided on for a look at for the following reasons. 1. World history is a required elegance for 9th graders. Via tenth grade, many college students reach the dropout age of sixteen years old. 2. at-threat college students need to satisfy success in required classes to stay in college. 3. Global history is a consultant of the cognitive needs of other required classes. 4. Class lists are pc generated for international history and represent a move phase of 9th graders in place of ability grouping observed in math training. The subsequent variables are defined operationally: fashion: A pervasive quality in the conduct of a man or woman. A pleasant that persists even if cognitive demands are modified. Mastering style: consistent with Keefe and Languis (1983), the NASSP project force has defined studying style as the composite of characteristic cognitive, affective, and physiological elements that function distinctly solid signs of the way a learner perceives, interacts with, and responds to the learning environment. It is verified in that pattern of behavior and overall performance via which a person methods instructional stories. Its basis lies within the structure of neural corporation and personality which each mold and is molded by using human improvement and the learning stories of domestic, faculty, and society. Keefe & Languis (1983, p. 2) Reproduced with permission of the copyright proprietor. In addition, the replica is prohibited without permission. For the functions of this have a look at, learning fashion become labeled as: (a) auditory, (b) visible, or (c) both. The studying style Profile Examiner's guide, Keefe & Monk (1986b) defines these phrases as follows: (a) auditory: perceptual response-initial response to information as an auditory response; (b) visible: perceptual reaction-preliminary reaction to facts as a visible reaction; and (c) each: auditory and visual perceptual responses are equal. Healthy/no fit: the use of the auditory and visible sub-scores of the getting to know style Profile, there may be an in the shape of styles when the student and teacher sub-scores are identical. If the scholar and instructor sub-scores do not agree, there may be no match of styles. Pass/fail: To get hold of c read it, as decided through district standards, a pupil must receive the report card grade of A, B, C, or D. Failure is determined through the file card grade E. coaching style: A dominant pattern of conduct and method of technique as used by teachers inside the schoolroom. This includes a trainer's non-public behaviors and the media used to transmit to or receive records from the learner. "Instructors tend to teach via the manner they research except there's an aware effort to do otherwise".

Learning patterns (LSs) have been described as the composite cognitive, affective, and physiological traits which are incredibly stable signs of how a learner perceives interacts with, and responds to the gaining knowledge of surroundings. Bruner has defined how humans assimilate knowledge about the environment thru four sensory modalities: visible (observing pictures, symbols or diagrams), auditory (listening, discussing), visible/iconic (reading and writing), and kinesthetic (the use of tactile sensory talents such as odor and touch). Many types of equipment had been advanced over the years to recognize how individuals learn such as the Vermunt's inventory, Kolbe getting to know fashion indicator, Meyer Brigg Indicator, Flemming's visible, Aural, examine/Write, and Kinesthetic (VARK) questionnaire, and so forth.[four,5,6] VARK is an acronym for visual, Aural, study/Write, and Kinesthetic. A few examples of the VARK studying fashion options (LSPs) are: visible (looking at and making pix, animations, graphs, tables, and many others.); aural (paying attention to and participating in speeches, discussions, and question-answer classes); study/write (analyzing and writing textual content related to the textbook, class notes, laboratory reviews, and so on.) and kinesthetic (conducting physical reports, manipulating objects, and many others., e.g. laboratories).

Gaining knowledge of techniques are precise mixtures or patterns of getting to know activities used throughout the learning system. The best of studying effects achieved relies to a sizable extent on the getting to know sports used by novices. those getting to know techniques may be broadly divided into a self-regulated approach in which the scholars perform most law sports themselves, and an externally regulated method wherein the students permit their studying method to be regulated through instructors/books or lack of regulation while college students are unable to alter their gaining knowledge of procedure by using themselves and additionally revel in insufficient support from external law as supplied by using instructors and getting to know the environment.

Recent research has made it pretty clear that distinct students have extraordinary LSs. LSPs are considerably exceptional in ladies and men. Study-write and kinesthetic inexperienced persons who undertake a deep technique mastering strategy carry out better academically than do the auditory, visible newcomers who appoint superficial observe strategies. Much work has been done on reading the person learning possibilities and the way academic strategies may be tailor-made to cater to the specific styles. However, individualization of educational techniques has not been proven to contribute significantly to examine results. Research has additionally shown that the best newbies are capable of adapt to the fashion which the mastering state of affairs requires. The academics can help students to broaden strategies for adapting to different situations, specifically while LSs do not healthy to a task. The focus of LSs can create a higher studying environment by enabling students to use suitable strategies.

The first-rate learning "style" for benefitting from coaching is to avoid depending upon any single style, or any fashion-like consistency in the method. It's been encouraged that newbies take a totally bendy approach to guidance so that you can optimize what they get out of each formal academic state of affairs this is useful in the long term, no longer just beneficial for dealing with the instructional situation inside the short-time period. Growing the power to reply productively to all varieties of educational conditions could be a laudable purpose for medical students. How pleasant to inspire this adaptability is yet to be decided.

therefore, the intention of this examination turned into to decide the impact of attention of LSs and motivating college students by way of externally regulated techniques to use blended methods of learning

Coaching and gaining knowledge are the principal components of the system of education. This device officially runs in school. The scholars getting to know takes region in a study room environment. So if the lecture room surroundings are powerful the gadget of education is successful otherwise no one can store it from destruction. Coaching/learning scenario immediately or circuitously depends upon studying patterns. Special theorists and educationists have defined gaining knowledge of styles in their personal way. They accept as true that this is a crucial concept to be studied. The idea of favor helps to understand that how the beginners are equal with each different, and how they range in terms of getting to know. There are numerous definitions of what studying fashion is. First off "learning style" idea was added by Rita Dunn in 1960. Currently in the training region, the concept of "studying style" has won brilliant effect too. in keeping with Kefee mastering styles, "are characteristic cognitive, affective and physiological tendencies that function highly strong signs of the way learners perceive, interact with and respond to the getting to know surroundings". Kolb describes gaining knowledge of styles as man or woman preferred ways even as they acquire and manner records. In addition, Grasha describes getting to know styles in a different way as "private traits that influence a pupil's potential to acquire statistics to interact with peers and the trainer, and otherwise to participate in gaining knowledge of experiences". Consistent with Felder and Silverman, mastering fashion is individual character strengths and options that they decide on whilst processing records. Accordingly, gaining knowledge of style is the manner which a character prefers even as obtaining, retaining, and retrieving facts. Global journal of training and psychological research (IJEPR) ISSN: 2279-0179 identify three, problem apart from the definitions of mastering styles there are distinctive models which depict that there are one of a kind mastering patterns and each learner has been desired mastering styles. That facilitates the learner in mastering conditions. Allow us to throw mild a number of the critical models. II.

Dunn and Dunn studying styles model

Dunn and Dunn getting to know styles model is one the famous model inside studying fashion models. This version represents that each biological and character developmental qualities possessed using an individual and the way someone learns new statistics and abilities are indicated using this atypical function of that character. The studying fashion model of Dunn and Dunn is s underneath: five learning fashion stimuli and some factors for each stimulus were diagnosed by way of Dunn and Dunn. These stimuli are environmental, emotional, sociological, physiological, and mental processing. Additionally, the factors which had been within the stimuli are sound, mild, temperature, and room design which are recognized as the environmental stimuli. Motivation, patience, responsibility, and structure had been recognized as emotional stimuli. Studying on my own, in a pair, with peers, with a teacher and such have been identified as sociological stimuli. Perceptual, consumption whilst mastering, power patterns at some stage in the day, and mobility needs are diagnosed as physiological stimuli. Worldwide or analytic, hemispheric and impulsive or reflective are identified as mental processing stimuli. Dunn and Dunn state that every learner responds otherwise in the direction of their surroundings. Sound is the sort of element. A few students want whole silence after they ponder on something. On the other hand, others need sound whilst getting to know. Moreover, they reply otherwise to the mild. Some college students want too much mild to suppose higher even as others decide on less illumination. Humans additionally react in a distinctive way to temperature. a few college students are more secure in the warm scenario at the same time as others pick cool places. Lastly, the layout of the room is important. a few learners are greater successful when they are in an informal bodily environment (carpeting, couch, or bed). However, some novices can study more efficaciously in proper surroundings (desks, tough chairs). Some college students favor research on their personal because they examine greater effectively whilst they may be on their own. a number of them prefer to examine organizations or some of them work with their friends or have interaction with a grownup. Additionally, a variety of responsibilities at the same time as getting to know may be desired through college students. All these elements are named as sociological stimuli. Difficulties and the perceptual issue is some of the rudiments of physiological stimuli. Some students choose pictures or maps as visual equipment, some of them select music and lectures as auditory sports, and the others prefer to be tactical or kinesthetically activity even as they learn statistics]. Even as concentration on something to research, intake aspect is vital for college students. a few students like to consume or drink something while others not. Furthermore, time of day whilst learners" power is the best also has a part in college students" gaining knowledge of. A fraction of the novices can concentrate on undertaking at one-of-a-kind times all through the day: Morning, afternoon, or evening. Except, a few college students who desire mobility need to move from region to area while managing an undertaking. International and analytic elements are inside psychological stimuli. International newcomers analyze better after they consciousness on the overall subject matter. Dunn states that those who decide upon the quick stories, illustrations, and graphics are international inexperienced persons" mastering choices. However, Dunn asserts that the data should be furnished to analytic freshmen successively once they research current records. Which will understand the complete image, those newbies ought to research all components of the data through bringing little portions collectively. Moreover left and right mind supremacy is related to the hemispheric element. Analytic novices have left mind supremacy while international freshmen own right brain supremacy. Except, impulsive freshmen choose to take a selection briefly whilst reflective beginners generally tend to utilize all alternatives and alternatives earlier than choice making.

Kolb's gaining knowledge of fashion model

Kolb evolved his getting to know fashion version over years basing it on the studies on various others, for example, Rogers, Jung, and Piaget. Kolb's mastering concept includes four unique studying styles, which can be based totally on a 4-level learning cycle. The mastering cycle tiers are ☐ Concrete experience (CE) - feeling ☐ Reflective statement (RO) - looking ☐ abstract Conceptualization (AC) - questioning ☐ energetic

Experimentation (AE). Kolb said that concrete reports lead to observations and reflections. Those reflections are immersed and translated into abstract ideas with implications for movement, which a person can actively test and experiment with. This permits the introduction of recent experiences and starts evolved a new cycle. Ideally, the method represents a gaining knowledge of cycle wherein all of the bases on gaining knowledge of, experiencing, reflecting, wondering, and performing are handled. The gaining knowledge of style definitions are representations of the aggregate of two desired patterns. Knowing someone's mastering fashion allows gaining knowledge to be orientated in step with the correct approach. each person responds to and needs the stimulus of all kinds of gaining knowledge of patterns to one extent or every other - it is a rely on the usage of emphasis that suits exceptionally with the given state of affairs and someone's mastering fashion preferences. The diverging learning style is studying via feeling and watching. The word diverges way to cut up or vary from something. These humans have a desire to look at in preference to do. They may be excellent at viewing concrete conditions from several special viewpoints. They prefer running in companies, get hold of personal feedback, collect facts and make use of creativeness to remedy issues. The assimilating learning fashion combines looking and wondering as methods to analyze. The phrase, assimilate, manner absorbing, and translating. This will imply that the assimilators like obvious causes rather than a sensible opportunity. For assimilators, ideas and ideas are greater vital than human beings. They would like clean motives and generally tend to like logically sound theories over ones that are based on practical value. These kinds of learners like readings, lectures, and exploring analytical fashions. The converging studying style is gaining knowledge by using doing and thinking. The phrase converges means to get in the direction of something. it can be seen as the convergers like to mix ideas and practice closer collectively. Humans with a converging learning style like to discover answers for realistic troubles. They decide upon technical responsibilities and are much less concerned with people and social or interpersonal problems. Convergers like to experiment with new thoughts, simulate and work with sensible applications. The accommodating learning style integrates doing and feeling as methods to learn. The word accommodation method adaptability may suggest that the accommodators like to conform the discovered matters into practice. Learners who choose accommodating mastering style love to do matters concretely. Accommodating learning fashion is predicated on intuition rather than logic. These newbies take a sensible and experiential technique to learned material. They opt to work in teams to complete duties. Grasha and Reichmann mastering style version.

Grasha and Reichmann's learning style model are based totally on the social interaction method. This version examines students'" responses closer to classroom sports rather than evaluating students" persona and cognitive traits [eleven]. for this reason, this version in particular makes a specialty of the social and affective dimensions of gaining knowledge of options in defining studying styles. According to this model, six studying styles are classified into three classes. Each category is organized on a bipolar continuum. Those gaining knowledge of patterns are aggressive-cooperative, avoidant-participant, and structured-unbiased. As Grasha emphasizes a student can possess extra characteristics of one studying fashion than some other style. Remark of those dominant traits is easy in class. Every learner has a dominant mastering style. However, everyone possesses multiple fashions further to his or her dominant studying style. Each learning style of the Grasha and Reichmann mastering style version become defined by way of Grasha. Competitive students need to be rewarded so they compete with their friends. Also, they prefer to carry out nicely above their classmates. For their class achievements, popularity is expected by those college students. Furthermore, they experience being at the focus of the eye. Some of their general study room choices are being a leader in a set in discussions, trainer-concentrated education, and activities that enable them to be advanced to their friends. Then again, collaborative students research through cooperating with their peers and instructors. Therefore, they opt to study by way of sharing. Therefore small organization tasks and discussions are those rookies" tendencies. College students who have avoidant learning fashion are unwilling to take part in lectures. They're no longer curious about what is going on in elegance either. Therefore, they do not select worrying teachers. Skip and fall grading systems and checks are not within their well-known getting to know school room choices. Unlike avoidant college students, individuals like to attend publications and lecture room activfulfillas much as possible. They're additionally enthusiastic to fulfill both the important and the elective necessities of the courses. Moreover, discussions and studying assignments are among their trendy classroom possibilities. Rookies with structured learning fashion want an authority inclusive of a trainer or a peer because they need clean commands and suggestions to do something. In other phrases, their source of shape is their instructors and friends. They simply examine what they want to learn. Furthermore, instructor-concentrated preparation is their standard study room choice. On the contrary, students, who have independent gaining knowledge of style, favor observing on their very own, depending upon their studying skills and they prefer impartial assignments as opposed to institution tasks. They prefer scholar-focused learning as their general lecture room desire. Dialogue studying styles in teaching/learning process, researches showed that a hit mastering is obtained by using conditions that are considered students" man or woman traits. Getting to know style is one of the personal traits that have an amazing effect on students" mastering. The getting to know patterns will genuinely fluctuate among college students in the classroom; Dunn and Dunn said they ought to attempt to make changes to their lecture room to be beneficial to every gaining knowledge of fashion. Some of these adjustments encompass room redesign, the development of small-organization strategies, and the improvement of contract hobby programs. Redesigning the lecture room includes finding dividers that can be used to arrange the room creatively, clearing the ground place, and incorporating pupil thoughts and ideas into the layout of the study room. Understanding how your baby learns pleasant allows you to teach extra successfully and additionally makes it a greater fun experience for both you and your toddler. Through locating out a pupil's favored gaining knowledge of style you will be able to become aware of viable demanding situations for a student on their specific direction or publications. Many students experience the realistic element of a vocational path but discover the behavior the course pretty tough. This may be when beside the point behavior can emerge. One of the motives for that is that idea tends to be taught in a visual and auditory way and consequently, the kinaesthetic learner finds it even extra of a mission than the alternative novices. Consequently, both teachers and college students have to be privy to learning patterns and instructors need to consider distinctive mastering patterns for the duration of their teacher and student can manage their own learning if they recognize what their mastering patterns are. Studying will increase if both college students and instructors understand how they examine and what their gaining knowledge of choices are. For that reason, identifying students'" studying patterns allows instructors to arrange their practice consistent with their students" character wishes. moreover, identifying newbies" learning styles helps their studying. also, inexperienced persons come to be more self-assured. similarly, „coaching to auto r college students" getting to know styles can assist college students to get more enthusiastic about the situation, discover and apprehend the statistics, enjoy grappling with the results, and most significantly, be greater willing to put what they have found out into practice". Besides, Lefever emphasizes that lively participation in the elegance, motivating towards getting to know and gaining knowledge of in a brief way and exact members of the family in a group may be realized by way of students if they're allowed to expose their learning options in elegance. Coffieldusingtes that students" studying patterns ought to be identified using teachers and academic designers by using assessing students" individual learning desires and designing unique getting to know and teaching interventions which encourage newcomers to demonstrate their patterns. Moreover, Reiff mentions that to put together a powerful curriculum students'" learning exposes must be taken into consideratiosuccessg fashion researches expose that students grow to be a greater success if they learn in a getting-to-know feared manner. But, teachers impose their own preferred getting-to-know styles to students during instruction. Their wishes harmony among getting to know kinds of students and their teachers" teaching patterns results in powerful learning. Consequently, consideration of inexperienced persons" learning fashion options is useful for each educational making plans and software improvement. Dunn (1990) cited that "students are not failing due to the curriculum. College students can research nearly any challenge remember whilst they may be taught with strategies and strategies responsive to their gain most effectively". Therefore, learners can examine most effectively if version mastering varieties of freshmen accommto date in their getting to know. To summarize the points indicated here to represent how getting to know patterns can be put into practice. These indications relate to expertise learning patterns, know-how getting to know, know-how the gaining knowledge of surroundings, information the function of the route and the curriculum, know-how the challenge and in several functions of resources and each of these can be applied to several getting to know contexts. The enjoyment of studying may be greater vi, talk to many students than the real completed product. At the full time, students, themselves must come to be conscious of their personal learning style. This is the primary and maximum crucial step to accomplishing a diploma of self-sufficiency in learning. Acknowledging getting to know patterns s therefore can assist to sell skills that increase beyond college, as an understanding of gaining knowledge of patterns can equip all students for lifelong getting to know. Many current studies have targeted mastering patterns. Itheseuctors or human beings involved in medical works need to gain from these studies. Instructors and scientists musmagnificentk at the study's results and apply the findings within the magnificent environment. If essential, they speak with other human beings to read this area. As noted earlier, technological trends offer us this possibility. In both pre-service and in-provider schooling, it very crucial that instructor applicants be educated as being aware of the getting to know patterns. The scholars should additionally assume accurately. They need to be critical and innovative in learning how to study. This form of focus not simplest supports mastering however additionally improves the students' self-seethe f-assurance. To increase the efficiency of getting to know patterns in the learning system, first off, it can be beneficial to provide an explanation for illustratively how students gain from getting to know patterns. Further, techniques-techniques and substances taking the studying kinds of students into attention may be used by the teachers. Teachers also can guide the mother and father in presenting learning conditions appropriate for the scholars" gaining knowledge of patterns. The motive of the usage of learning patterns is to locate the satisfactory approaches for both students to analyze efficaciously and instructors to educate successfully.

+Chapter Two

Learning Styles in Theory and Practice

Theories of studying styles advise that people think and study pleasantly in exclusive ways. Those aren't variations of ability but as a choice for processing sure kinds of facts or processing information in certain forms of manner. If accurate, learning styles theories could have vital implications for guidance because scholar success would be made of the interaction of guidance and the student's style. There's reason to assume that people view getting to know styles theories as broadly correct, but, in reality, scientific assistance for those theories is missing. We propose that educators' time and energy are higher spent on different theories that would resource instruction.

Gaining knowledge of patterns theories are various, however, each of those theories holds that people examine in distinct methods and that mastering may be optimized for a person by using tailoring training to his or her fashion. For example, one idea has it that a few humans examine fine using looking (visible inexperienced persons), a few by listening (auditory beginners), and a few by using moving (kinesthetic novices). For this reason, a first-grader gaining knowledge of to add numbers may advantage from a creation that respects her studying fashion: the visible learner may view units of items, the auditory learner might listen to rhythms, and the kinesthetic learner would possibly control beads on an abacus. How stunning it would be if this principle (or a similar theory) become authentic. Ideas that students had located elusive would all of sudden click, all due to a modest exchange in teaching exercise. But is the idea genuine? In reality, the notion of gaining knowledge of styles theories is extensive. A current assessment. Howard-Jones (2014) confirmed that over 90% of instructors in five nations (the United Kingdom, the Netherlands, Turkey, Greece, and China) agreed that people analyze better once they receive records tailored to their favored mastering patterns. Even though statistics on U.S. teachers are restrained, Ballone & Czerniak (2001), our experience has been that perception in the accuracy of such theories is big a number of the broader public. To check this impact, we conducted a quick survey on the use of Amazon Mechanical Turk. individuals (N ¼, 53.4% lady, mean age ¼ 35.2 years) rated on a seven-factor Likert-kind scale (1 ¼ strongly disagree and 7 ¼ strongly agree) their settlement with this statement: "There are steady differences among people in how they research from different studies: mainly, a few people generally research pleasant via seeing, some typically study great using listening, and a few commonly analyze exceptional via doing." The mean rating changed to 6.35 (SD ¼ 1.11).1 We discovered this strong notion even though literature reviews during the last thirty years have concluded that most proof does no longer guide any of the mastering patterns theories. The cause of this text is to (a) clarify what gaining knowledge of patterns theories declare and distinguish them from theories of potential, (b) summarize empirical studies about learning styles, and (c) provide hints for practice and implications supported via empirical studies.

What are the studying patterns Theories?

Researchers have described "mastering patterns" in numerous approaches, however, due to the fact we're involved primarily in applications to education (and now not, e.g., in how character dimensions impact gaining knowledge of), we focus on studying styles as (a) differential options for processing positive forms of information or (b) for processing facts in positive methods. The former definition might include getting to know styles theories that differentiate between visual, auditory, and kinesthetic inexperienced persons or between visual and verbal learners. Gaining knowledge of patterns theories based on choices for sure kinds of cognitive processing could encompass differences among intuitive and analytic thinkers or between activist, reflecting, or pragmatic thinkers. Several theoretical differences like these were around since the Fifties. Be aware that the definitions provided in advance distinguish gaining knowledge of patterns from abilities. the two are often careworn, but the distinction is vital. It is especially uncontroversial that cognitive potential is multifaceted (e.g., verbal potential and facility with the area have wonderful cognitive bases), and it is uncontroversial that people vary in these talents. For "styles" to add any price to an account of human cognition and learning, it should suggest something aside from what potential method. Even as patterns seek advice from how one does things, abilities issue how well one does them. The analogous difference is made in sports: two basketball players may also have equivalent capability however one-of-a-kind patterns at the court docket. One may additionally take dangers, whereas the alternative plays a conservative sport.

Predictions and records

Mastering patterns theories make truthful predictions. First, a learning fashion is proposed to be a regular attribute of a man or woman, consequently, a person's mastering style needs to be regular throughout conditions. Consequently, a person who was taken into consideration as an auditory learner might analyze fine through auditory approaches no matter the difficulty remember (e.g., technology, literature, or mathematics) or placing (e.g., school, sports exercise, or work). Second, the cognitive function has to be more effective when it's far constant with a person's desired fashion; for this reason, the visible learner needs to bear in mind better (or trouble-remedy better, or attend better) with visual materials than with different substances. Don't forget the first prediction. Without a doubt sufficient, it way that in case you're a visible learner nowadays, you shouldn't be an auditory learner day after today, or in case you're a visual learner on assignment X, you shouldn't be an auditory learner on venture Y. This bar—consistency—seems fairly low for a theoretical prediction, however, maximum learning patterns theories have failed to vault it. Even though there is a multitude of inventories and models for assessing gaining knowledge of styles, maximum is not reliable. And researchers are properly aware of this problem. In the latest survey of ninety-two getting to know patterns, researchers showed that troubles of reliability had been among their leader worries with the progress of their area. Concerning the second prediction—cognitive overall performance— one should draw a difference among proof that would assist the concept and proof of a studying pattern that might activate an exchange in academic practice. To assist the concept, one needs to look at a statistical interplay between the mastering varieties of individuals and the method of guidance. For instance, assume we tested "visible rookies" and "auditory novices." contributors in every group might be randomly assigned to a tutorial circumstance, where cloth would be offered either visually (e.g., a silent film) or auditorily (e.g., an audiotaped tale). Members should analyze better once they experience the material in their preferred modality. We need to pay attention to the predicted impact in visible learners and take into account more than auditory inexperienced persons when the movie is shown, and the alternative sample appears while individuals pay attention to the audiotape. However, all people learn pleasant with a visual presentation. realistic school room implications require a selected sample of records that now not only supports the concept but additionally indicates that coaching matched to getting to know patterns optimizes achievement for each organization. In other phrases, the two traces within the graph might have to cross, indicating (in this case) that the visible inexperienced persons discovered fine when watching the film, whereas the auditory beginners discovered satisfactory whilst taking note of the tale. Is there aid for either prediction—for instructional practice, or barring that, at the least that the principle is probably correct (even though it's no longer helpful)? No. numerous critiques that span decades have evaluated the literature on getting to know styles, and everyone has drawn the belief that there may be no feasible evidence to assist the idea. Even a current assessment supposed to be pleasant to theories of getting to know patterns didn't declare that this prediction of the idea has empirical support. The dearth of helping proof is specifically unsurprising in light of the unreliability of most units used to pick out beginners' patterns. There is an underlying venture to engaging in research on mastering styles: it's far not possible to show that something does now not exist. However unpromising the information these days, a brand new experimental paradigm might also eventually display that the principle changed into proper all alongside. Nevertheless, given our cognizance of educational application, we set an exclusive popular. We don't insist that the idea be validated definitively wrong. We are interested in study room exercise, and before a theory is authorized to influence study room exercise, there ought to be proof that the idea is correct. In reality, we want extra. We not best need to recognize that studying patterns exist however additionally need to understand that coaching to getting to know styles blessings students in a few ways.

Why do humans agree with studying styles Theories?
There are in all likelihood more than one motives why people trust learning styles theories are correct, and those reasons strike us as mainly applicable. First, humans often take things to be medical facts when they have no longer visible any of the proof that they assume needs to exist.

For instance, maximum educated people accept as true within the atomic theory of relying on, however, their knowledge of the helping proof is scant. It is simply something that "they" (i.e., scientists) have found out. Humans' perception is in addition reinforced by way of social evidence: so many other people agree with the atomic concept of remembering that it might seem oddly perverse to challenge it. furthermore, instructors are exposed to a plethora of materials that purportedly appreciate students' getting to know styles, substances that frequently claim a scientific foundation for his or her design. As soon as exposed to these types of apparently dependable (or at least not brazenly unreliable) resources, the confirmation bias may want to effortlessly support and maintain the perception. As an instance, suppose a trainer became assisting a scholar struggling with a concept. The instructor tries some exclusive ways of explaining it but to no avail. Sooner or later, she attracts a diagram, and the concept clicks. it is herbal for the trainer to finish, "Ah, this student must be a visual learner." but possibly any student might have benefited from the diagram as it changed into a powerful way to talk about that specific idea. Or possibly the scholar needed to listen to just one more rationalization. Many bills of the unexpected perception are possible, but the confirmation bias could lead to an interpretation that supports one's existing beliefs. A second possible reason for significant perception is the confusion between ability and style. As referred to earlier, most researchers agree that capability is multifaceted and that people vary in those abilities. From there, it's far a brief step to the idea that a weak spot in a single capacity can be supplemented with power in some other—as an instance, that a pupil having trouble in math might advantage from a lesson plan that played to his strength in music. This "change course" idea in reality seems like a fashion. Gardner's (1983) theory of multiple intelligences—which is an abilities theory—has been interpreted this way for decades, although Gardner (2013) has stated that this interpretation is inaccurate. The substitution concept is inaccurate, Gardner maintains, due to the fact recoding sincerely cannot take place, and that is a part of what makes different skills (or, in Gardner's theories, intelligence) one-of-a-kind. To do the math, you have to think mathematically. To use musical cognition to assume mathematically might be like looking to use a WMV document in Microsoft Excel. They're definitely incompatible. We agree with Gardner, but observe that it is at the least theoretically possible that there can be occasional exceptions. If one may want to examine fabric similarly properly in extraordinary methods, and if the ones exclusive methods match variations in human ability, then recoding for character students would now not only be possible however additionally be powerful. certainly, a few confined data are indicating that folks who trust they're higher with mental pics (or better with words) do such recoding on their very own and that this recoding can gain overall performance (e.g., Thomas & McKay, 2010). This isn't always an instance of getting to know patterns, alternatively, it's miles an example of potential performing as a style.

Why all of the Fuss?
So a load of proof fails to assist in getting to know

patterns. So what? Lots of theories are poorly supported and maximum does no longer benefit an editorial in the teaching of Psychology. The distinction here is that the concept has seeped into the famous culture, and plenty of human beings trust it, perpetuating its (ungrounded) effect on academic settings and products. Fortuitously, it seems most effective not often to influence how students examine. Less fortunately, mastering patterns theories, while invoked, are most often offered as a reason for poor lecture room performance. Most of us have had a student protest, "your teaching isn't compatible with my learning fashion," with the expectation that the instructor will make character inns that go past great education. Getting to know styles theories have to be debunked, and a high-quality place for this to take place is in our psychology lecture rooms. One ought to actually tackle it head-on, of direction, telling students approximately the idea and the shortage of evidence. But it moves us as an amazing possibility to have students suppose via the problem themselves. if they consider it, why do they accept it as true it? What does evidence appear to be in mental technology? What would proof for this unique concept look like? Ought to students acquire relevant proof inside the study room? Indeed, comparing studying styles theories might serve as a remarkable lecture room studies task. Take, for instance, the following lecture room eventualities.

Class activity scenario 1

With the purpose to explore demanding situations around research intended to evaluate the impact of styles on getting to know, the teacher can mild a schoolroom experiment. To do that, the teacher would possibly create a getting to know pastime that requires college students to identify their very own fine learning styles and then try and research new cloth (e.g., new vocabulary) through (a) their number one getting to know fashion or (b) an exclusive studying style. As an example, visual rookies and auditory newbies inside the class might be presented with new vocabulary. college students in each getting to know fashion institution would be randomly assigned to a studying condition, ensuing in some visual inexperienced persons and auditory novices accessing the brand new vocabulary visually (e.g., studying it in text) and some visual beginners and auditory novices accessing the brand new vocabulary auditorily (e.g., being attentive to a recording). All students would be assessed on the new vocabulary they found out, and class data might be graphed and analyzed. Elegance discussions may cognizance of expected consequences (e.g., higher overall performance on vocabulary learned through a number one fashion), real outcomes, elements that may have impacted outcomes (e.g., choice or previous understanding), limitations to the research, and the way the effects may additionally or may not translate into the schoolroom. Before starting this hobby, college students would need to finish a studying styles evaluation, and the trainer could need to put together a getting-to-know opportunity wherein records are to be had through every mastering fashion (e.g., textual content to read and audio of textual content). The instructor could also have to minimize influencing elements which include previous know-how or time spent on learning. Replicating this activity for studying other statistics (e.g., mathematics, the utility of concept, precise of story, and memorization of dates and activities) would allow college students to discover if mastering styles are steady throughout content material and, if now not, why.

Magnificence activity scenario 2

Any other pastime may explore the reliability of the evaluation of gaining knowledge of styles. As an instance, do external elements, inclusive of studies previous to taking the assessment, influence the final results? If students have these days completed activities or had experiences that undoubtedly impacted outcomes, would they be greater or much less possibly to pick out an answer based totally on that enjoyment or memory? As an example, if a person recently listened to an audible worldwide Positioning device (GPS) to discover a place, could that man or woman be more likely to select an audible technique of transport for directions over the use of a map, even if they don't forget themselves to be a visual learner? Could a horrific experience with an auditory GPS, however an awesome revel in studying a map, spark off a self-diagnosed auditory learner to choose an extra visible approach for guidelines? If recent stories count, does that change the reliability of the measure? Class exploration and dialogue can address these factors.

Differences and Commonalities in educational

practice

The wish underlying learning styles theories is that a knowledge of student variations will enhance instruction. However then, too, we expect that there are some factors of the thoughts that don't differ, which are commonplace throughout college students, and that honoring those fundamental capabilities will improve preparation. There is anxiety in applying these two forms of expertise in the lecture room. On one hand, obsession with scholar individuality will result in paralysis: If each student is specific, how can instructors draw on their stories with other students to enhance the training of this precise scholar? If every pupil, in particular, there is no purpose to assume that what worked earlier than will work now. Then again, if instructors awareness totally of what they trust is true of all students, then instructors are likely to pick out one set of "fine practices" and stubbornly follow those practices to all students. To many, studying styles provide a middle ground—a middle floor between identically treating each student and treating each scholar uniquely. The proposed solution has been to create classes of novices based on their specific gaining knowledge of styles. Categorization approach using a few, easily discovered capabilities to infer that other capabilities are gifts. as an example, through gazing at some perceptual capabilities of an item—it's miles round, red, and shiny—we categorize it as an apple and as a result can correctly infer different non-observable residences: It has seeds inside, it's miles safe to eat, and so on. Further, learning patterns additionally categorize. By gaining knowledge of some properties (e.g., solutions on a questionnaire), teachers hope to deduce other characteristics (e.g., how the student will respond to exceptional varieties of education) that may be used to improve the academic system. The point of this text, but, is that such categorization ultimately fails. More extensively, the history of psychology suggests very restrained fulfillment in finding any useful categorization scheme for college kids. By way of ways, the maximum a hit sort of categorization is one this is already painfully obvious to educators: differences in previous knowledge and capacity should be respected. Psychology has had a great deal more fulfillment describing commonalities among students than it has had in describing categorization schemes for variations. Researchers have compiled a reasonably magnificent list of homes of the thoughts that scholars share. And even though going from lab to school room isn't always honest, there is proof that scholars gain while educators deploy study room methods that capitalize on those commonalities. As an instance, we recognize that spacing learning over time and quizzing (amongst other techniques) improve reminiscence. We know that teachers can adjust the classroom environment to lower trouble behaviors. In mathematics, there is a specific developmental progression through which teachers can high-quality train numbers and operations. In reading, phonics practice blessings most children. For that reason, psychologists have made some fantastic contributions to education. On the subject of gaining knowledge of patterns, however, the maximum we deserve is a credit score for attempts and endurance. Getting to know styles theories have not panned out, and it is our responsibility to ensure that students know that.

Declaration of Conflicting hobbies

The authors declared no capability conflicts of the hobby with appreciation to the studies, authorship, and/or booklet of this newsletter.

Half of the topics noticed an opposite-coded model (There aren't consistent differences amongst human beings in how they examine. The opposite-coded mean turned into 5.22 (SD ¼ 2.19), which was considerably decrease than the rating for the usual query, (311) ¼ 5.65, $p < .001$. We suspect that this difference becomes due to some members Willingham et al. Inside the fashionable model, only a few topics (2.1%) indicated that they notion the gaining knowledge of patterns principle is incorrect (as mentioned by deciding on 1 or 2 for their reaction). within the reverse-code circumstance, 20.4% of individuals chose a score indicating disagreement. We suspect those subjects desired to accept as true with studying patterns principle but got burdened using the wording (i.e., disagreeing with a negative statement).

Creation

The range of college students engaged in better training continues to increase. College students come to colleges with various ethnic and cultural backgrounds, from a large number of educational packages and institutions, and with differing mastering patterns. Coupled with this increase in diversification has been a boom in distance schooling programs and expansions in the forms of academic media used to supply facts. These changes and advances in technology have led many educators to rethink conventional, uniform instruction strategies and strain the importance of considering scholar studying styles inside the design and transport of route content material.

Mismatches between a teacher's style of coaching and a pupil's method of getting to know have been mentioned as potential mastering limitations within the classroom and as a cause for the use of diffusion of teaching modalities to deliver instruction. The idea of the use of a menu of teaching modalities is based on the premise that at least some content material could be offered in a way perfect to each form of learner inside a given classroom or direction. Some research has targeted profiling learning sorts so that teachers have a higher knowledge of the cohort of students they may be educating. These records can be used to guide the selection of guidance modalities employed inside the schoolroom. confined studies have additionally centered on describing and characterizing composite mastering patterns and styles for students in diverse concentrations of taking a look at (e.g., medicine, engineering). This evaluation will describe the capability of software and boundaries in assessing mastering patterns.

Mastering patterns

A benchmark definition of "gaining knowledge of patterns" is "function cognitive, affective, and psychosocial behaviors that function highly stable indicators of how freshmen understand, interact with and reply to the mastering surroundings. Ten studying patterns are taken into consideration by many to be one thing of success in higher education. Confounding research and, many times, software for studying fashion theory has begotten the myriad of techniques used to categorize getting to know patterns. No single typically normal technique presently exists, however rather several capability scales and classifications are in use. Maximum of those scales and classifications are greater comparable than dissimilar and attention on environmental preferences, sensory modalities, character sorts, and/or cognitive patterns. Loss of a conceptual framework for each studying style theory and dimension is a commonplace and significant grievance in this place. In 2004 the UK learning and capabilities studies center commissioned a report meant to systematically observe present studying style models and units. Within the fee record, Coffield et al recognized numerous inconsistencies in mastering style models and devices and counseled educators concerning their use. The authors also outlined an advised studies timetable for this place.

Instead, many researchers have argued that expertise in gaining knowledge of patterns may be of use to each educator and student. college participants with an understanding of learning patterns can tailor pedagogy so that it best coincides with gaining knowledge of patterns exhibited by most people of college students. Four alternatively, students with knowledge of their own options are empowered to use diverse techniques to enhance gaining knowledge of, which in flip may additionally impact average educational pleasure. This potential is mainly essential and useful when a trainer's teaching fashion does now not fit a pupil's getting to know fashion. Compounding the issue of mastering styles in the schoolroom has been the movement in lots of collegiate environments to distance and/or asynchronous education. This shift in instructional modality is inconsistent with the getting to know fashions with which older college students and adult freshmen are accustomed from their number one and high faculty education. Three, thirteen, and fourteen as a substitute, environmental effects and greater good sized availability of technological advances (e.g., non-public virtual assistants, virtual video, the sector huge web, wireless internet) may also make younger generations of college students extra comfy with distance gaining knowledge of.

Learning styles gadgets

As formerly stated, numerous models and measures of studying patterns were defined inside the literature. Kolb proposed a model related to a 4-level cyclic shape that starts evolved with a concrete enjoy, which leads to a reflective remark and finally an abstract conceptualization that allows for energetic experimentation.18 Kolb's version is associated with the studying style inventory device (LSI). The LSI makes a specialty of learner's preferences in phrases of concrete as opposed to abstract, and movement as opposed to a mirrored image. Inexperienced persons are ultimately defined as divergers, convergers, assimilators, or accommodators.

Honey and Mumford advanced an alternative instrument known as the mastering fashion Questionnaire (LSQ).6 presumably, the LSQ has progressed validity and predictive accuracy in comparison to the LSI. The LSQ describes 4 distinct forms of newbies: activists (examine usually using experience), reflectors (learn from reflective statement), theorists (research from exploring associations and interrelationships), and pragmatics (analyze from doing or trying things with practical effects). The LSQ has been greater broadly used and studied in control and commercial enterprise settings and its applicability to academia have been questioned.6 An alternative to the

LSQ, the Canfield getting to know style inventory (CLSI) describes studying patterns alongside 4 dimensions.19 those dimensions consist of situations for getting to know, area of the hobby, mode of mastering, and situations for overall performance. Analogous to the LSQ, the applicability of the CLSI to instructional settings has been puzzled. Moreover, some confusion surrounding the scoring and interpretation of certain result values also exists.

Felder and Silverman introduced a learning fashion evaluation instrument that become specially designed for school room use and was first implemented in the context of engineering education. The tool includes forty-four short objects with a desire among two responses to every sentence. Learners are labeled in four dichotomous regions: desire in phrases of type and mode of statistics perception (sensory or intuitive; visible or verbal), techniques to organizing and processing records (lively or reflective), and the fee at which students develop toward knowledge (sequential or international). The device related to the version is called the Index of studying Survey (ILS). The ILS is based totally on a 44-item questionnaire and outputs a preference profile for a pupil or an entire class. The choice profile is based on the four previously defined studying dimensions. The ILS has several blessings over other gadgets such as conciseness and simplicity of management (in both a written and automated format). No published information exists almost about the use of the ILS in populations of pharmacy students or pharmacists. Cook defined a take a look at designed to take a look at the reliability of the ILS for figuring out mastering styles among a population of inner medicinal drug residents. The researchers administered the ILS two times and the studying style type Indicator (LSTI) once to one hundred and eighty-six residents (eighty-six men, fifty-two girls). The LSTI has been formerly as compared to the ILS via several investigators. Cook dinner located that the Cronbach's alpha ratings for the ILS and LSTI ranged from 0.19 to 0.69. They preliminarily concluded that the ILS scores have been reliable and valid among this cohort of residents, especially inside the energetic-reflective and sensing-intuitive domain names. In a separate observation, cook et al tried to evaluate convergence and discrimination among the ILS, LSI, and some other computer-based tools referred to as the analysis of the Cognitive patterns (CSA). eleven The cohort studied consisted of family remedy and internal medicine residents as well as first- and 1/3-year clinical students. 80-9 contributors finished all three units, and responses have analyzed the usage of calculated Pearson's r and Cronbach's α. The authors discovered that the ILS active-reflective and sensing-intuitive rankings in addition to the LSI lively-reflective rankings have been legitimate in figuring out learning styles. However, the ILS sequential-global area didn't correlate properly with different gadgets and can be improper, at least on this given population. The authors recommended the usage of caution while interpreting rankings without strong information of assembling definitions and empirical evidence.

Several different contraptions designed to measure character indexes or psychological sorts might also overlap and describe studying patterns in nonspecific fashions. One example of such a trademark is the Myers-Briggs Index.6 while some relation between personality indexes and learning styles can also exist, the usage of devices supposed to explain persona to signify getting to know fashion has been criticized by several authors. Consequently, the usage of those markers to degree learning patterns isn't recommended. The concept of emotional intelligence is any other popular manner to represent intellect and getting to know capacity but similarly should no longer be misconstrued as an effective approach of describing gaining knowledge of patterns.

Way of life

Several authors have proposed correlations between the way of life and gaining knowledge of styles. This is predicated on the concept that way of life impacts environmental perceptions which, in turn, to some diploma determine the manner wherein information is processed and organized. The garage, processing, and assimilation strategies for records contribute to how new expertise is learned. Subculture additionally plays a function in conditioning and reinforcing gaining knowledge of patterns and partially explains why teaching methods utilized in positive components of the world can be useless or much less powerful when blindly transplanted to every other locale. Teachers must be aware of this phenomenon and the influence it has on the form of studying patterns that might be found in classrooms. That is in particular genuine in lecture rooms which have a big contingency of global students. Such lecture rooms are getting an increasing number of not unusual as increasingly schools to expand their internationalization efforts.
The technological age may also be influencing the learning kinds of more youthful students and rising generations of

newcomers. Millennial technology has been described as more technologically superior than their generation X opposite numbers, with higher expectations for the usage of computer-aided media inside the classroom.15, sixteen,26 more youthful students are acquainted with greater visual images related to diverse laptop- and TV-primarily based video games and recreation systems. Additionally, video generation is increasingly becoming "transportable" in the manner of cell computing, MP3 gadgets, non-public virtual video players, and other technology. All of those advances have made visual pix extra pervasive within industrialized international locations.

Making use of getting to know patterns to the lecture room

As magnificence sizes increase, so do the kinds and numbers of pupil mastering styles. Also, as formerly noted, internationalization and adjustments inside the media tradition may have an effect on the spectrum of classroom gaining knowledge of styles as properly. Given the range in gaining knowledge of styles that may exist in a lecture room, a few authors cautioned that students have to adapt their mastering styles to coincide with a given instruction style.6,27 This permits instructors to dictate the techniques used to teach in the schoolroom. This approach additionally allows instructors to "train from their strengths," with little attention to other external elements including the learning fashion of students. Even as handy, this unilateral method has been criticized for placing all of the obligations for aligning teaching and mastering on the scholar. Whilst most people of data is offered in formats that can be misaligned with getting to know patterns, students may spend greater time manipulating fabric than they do in comprehending and applying the statistics. Additionally, a unilaterally designed schoolroom may strengthen a "do nothing" method among faculty members. Instead, a teaching style-mastering style mismatch would possibly venture college students to regulate, grow intellectually, and study in more integrated approaches. However, it could be tough to predict which students have the baseline potential to regulate, specifically whilst giant gaps in the expertise of a given challenge exist already or when the learner is a beginner to the topic being told. This might be particularly tough within professional curricula in which path load expectancies are sizable.

First-class practice most likely entails a teaching paradigm that addresses and contains multiple dimensions of getting to know patterns that construct self-efficacy. educating in a manner that encompasses multiple mastering styles gives the teacher the possibility to reach a greater volume of a given class, while additionally hard students to increase their range of mastering styles and aptitudes at a slower tempo. This could keep away from misplaced getting-to-know possibilities and avert useless frustration from each trainer and pupil. For many teachers, multi-fashion coaching is their inherent approach to gaining knowledge, whilst different instructors extra usually hire unilateral styles. Studying might be higher facilitated if instructors were cognizant of both their teaching styles and the learning kinds of their students. Information and appreciation of a given man or woman's teaching style call for self-reflection and introspection and ought to be a factor of a nicely maintained teaching portfolio. Main modifications or changes to teaching styles might not be important with a purpose to efficiently create a schoolroom environment that addresses multiple learning patterns or goals character ones. However, school participants need to be careful to no longer over ambitiously, arbitrarily, or flippantly design publications and activities with an array of coaching modalities that aren't carefully connected, orchestrated, and added.

Beginner learners will probably be extra a success when classrooms, either through design or using risk, are tailor-made to their gaining knowledge of style. however, the closing intention is to instill inside students the talents to understand and react to diverse patterns so that gaining knowledge is maximized irrespective of the environment.28 that is a vital ability for an impartial learner and students in any professional route.

Particular consideration of getting to know styles is probably given to asynchronous publications and other courses wherein a sizable part of the time is spent online. As technology advances and study room sizes in lots of establishments grow to be an increasing number of big, asynchronous preparation is becoming extra pervasive. Normally, students who have grown acquainted with technological advances might also opt for asynchronous publications. Online systems may also inherently affect studying on a single measurement (visible or auditory). maximum researchers who've as compared the getting to know types of college students enrolled in online versus traditional publications have located no correlations among the gaining knowledge of styles and getting to know consequences of cohorts enrolled in both direction kind. Johnson et al compared getting to know fashion profiles to student pride with both online and face-to-face study groups. Forty-eight university college students participated in the analysis. Studying patterns were measured using the ILS. Students had been surveyed about their delight with numerous observed group codecs. Those effects have been then correlated to actual overall performance on course examinations. Active and visible learners tested a great preference for face-to-face take a look at organizations. As an alternative, college students who have been reflective rookies demonstrated a desire for online organizations. Probably due to the small pattern size, none of these variations finished statistical significance. The authors suggest that these results are evidence for guides employing hybrid coaching styles that attain as many distinctive college students as possible. Prepare dinner et al studied one hundred and twenty-one internal medication residents and additionally observed no affiliation ($p > 0.05$) among ILS-measured gaining knowledge of patterns and options for studying codecs (e.g., internet-primarily based versus paper-based totally gaining knowledge of modules). Ratings on evaluation questions related to studying modules administered to the residents have been additionally no longer statistically correlated with learning patterns.

Prepare dinner et al tested the effectiveness of adapting internet-primarily based getting to know modules to a given learner's fashion. The investigators created two versions of an internet-based instructional module on complementary and alternative medications. One model of the modules directed the learner to "active" questions that supplied freshmen immediate and comprehensive feedback, whilst the other model worried "reflective" questions that directed inexperienced persons back to the case content material for answers. Eighty-nine citizens had been randomly matched or mismatched primarily based on their active-reflective learning styles (as decided via ILS) to either the "energetic" or "reflective" take a look at the model. Posttest rankings for both query kind among mismatched subjects did not differ significantly (p = 0. ninety-seven), suggesting no interaction between mastering patterns and query sorts. The authors concluded from this small study that mastering styles did not affect getting to know effects. They have a look at turned into limited in its loss of assessment of baseline know-how, motivation, or different traits. Additionally, the issue of the assessment may not have been sufficient to differentiate a difference, and/or "mismatched" novices may also have robotically adapted to the facts they received irrespective of a kind.

Studies OF PHARMACY students

No posted research has systematically examined the gaining knowledge of forms of pharmacy college students. Pungent et al collected some getting to know patterns statistics as a part of a take a look at designed to evaluate how first-year pharmacy students' studying styles motivated alternatives closer to specific sports-related to hassle-based learning (PBL). One hundred sixteen first-year college students finished Kolb's LSI. Studying styles have been then matched to responses from a survey designed to assess scholar alternatives closer to diverse components of PBL. most people of college students had been categorized by using the LSI as being accommodators (36.2%), with a reasonably even distribution of patterns among closing students (19.8% assimilators, 22.4% convergers, 21.6% divergers). there has been a proportional distribution of mastering patterns among a convenience sample of pharmacy college students. Divergers have been the least glad about the PBL approach of practice, whilst convergers proved the most powerful choice for this method of learning. The investigators proposed that the subsequent step is probably to correlate learning styles and PBL choices with real instructional achievement.

Constrained research correlating mastering styles to getting to know outcomes has hampered the software of mastering style principle to actual lecture room settings. Complicating studies is the plethora of different studying fashion size gadgets available. Despite these boundaries, efforts to better define and make use of studying fashion principle is a place of growing research. Higher information and expertise of learning styles may additionally turn out to be increasingly critical as classroom sizes increase and as technological advances continue to mildew the varieties of college students entering better education. while studies on this region keep developing, school members have to make concentrated efforts to train in a multi-style style that each reaches the greatest quantity of students in a given magnificence and challenges all college students to grow as newcomers.

Learning patterns: an outline of theories, fashions, and measures

Even though its origins had been traced lower back lots in addition, research in the location of getting to know fashion has been active for—at a conservative estimate—

around 4 decades. During that length, the depth of interest has varied, with recent years seeing a particularly marked upturn inside the wide variety of researchers operating inside the region. Also of note is the style of disciplines from which the research is emerging. An increasing number of, studies inside the place of studying fashion are being conducted in domains outdoor psychology—the field from which among the significant concepts and theories originate. These domains encompass clinical and health care training, management, industry, vocational schooling, and a good-sized variety of settings and ranges inside the subject of education. It is of little surprise that applications of these concepts are so huge-ranging given the centrality of mastering—and how first-class to do it—to almost every issue of life. as a result of the amount of research, the range of the disciplines and domain names wherein the research is conducted, and the varied ambitions of the studies, the topic has emerged as fragmented and disparate. This is nearly genuinely the way it needs to seem to practitioners and researchers new to the region, with its complexities and convolutions hard to realize and assimilate. As such, it's miles possibly timely to offer an account of the significant themes and problems surrounding mastering fashion and to don't forget the devices to be had for the size of favor. This paper targets to offer such an account, trying to make clear commonplace areas of ambiguity and especially problems surrounding measurement and appropriate units. It pursuits to carry collectively vital components of the place in one of this manner as to permit for a broader appreciation of getting to know the style and to tell concerning feasible tools for size. It's far expected that such an account will sell research in the discipline by way of imparting it as more accessible and with the aid of growing a more appreciation for the area across disciplines and in researchers and practitioners new to the area.

For some time now instructional research exploring the issue of educational achievement or achievement has prolonged—rightfully so—beyond "simple" troubles of intelligence and previous educational fulfillment. There are several gaining knowledge of related standards, inclusive of belief of educational management and fulfillment motivation that has been a focal point of interest while attempting to perceive elements affecting learning- related overall performance. One idea specifically which has provided a few treasured insights into mastering in both instructional and other settings is getting to know fashion. There's the popular reputation that the way wherein individuals pick to or are inclined to method a mastering state of affairs has an impact on overall performance and achievement of mastering consequences. even as—and perhaps because—getting to know fashion has been the point of interest of any such tremendous wide variety of research and practitioner- based totally studies within the region, there exist a variety of definitions, theoretical positions, models, interpretations, and measures of the construct. To a point, this will be considered a natural consequence of extensive empirical investigation and is to be expected with any usually growing concept which proves beneficial in gaining expertise of this sort of essential and prevailing endeavor as mastering. However, the extent of ambiguity and debate is such that even the assignment of selecting the proper device for investigation is a laborious one, with the unifying of subsequent findings within an existing framework problematic, at satisfactory. This paper does not searching for to acquire an absolute clear up and converge upon the precise version and measure of getting to know fashion, however is a substitute to tell via description and assessment. It's far meant as a useful resource for researchers and professionals who desire a vast appreciation of the location of getting to know the style and who may additionally, formerly, have been working with in- depth information but, perhaps, simplest a slender cognizance of the sector. Using and Cheema (1991) have previously referred to that researcher inside the area of cognitive fashion/studying fashion frequently present handiest a very restricted (if any) account of the style of theories and devices which exist for the measurement of favor.

Even as educators in all fields have become increasingly aware of the critical significance of expertise in how people analyze, it's far equally essential that any tries to integrate learning fashion into instructional programs are made from a knowledgeable function. John Yerxa, training Officer with the branch of standard practice and the Adelaide to Outback GP schooling Programme, feedback: "certainly being aware that there may be exclusive approaches to method teaching and getting to know can make a distinction". Even as there can be some reality in such remarks, they're now not useful in a drive toward research- and practitioner- primarily based pastime which famous precise focus of learning style principle and empirical evidence. This paper pursuits to provide an available evaluation of theories, instruments, and empirical work inside the discipline of mastering style.

Key Terminology … And some essential troubles

Defining the important thing terms in this place isn't always an honest assignment. The phrases "gaining knowledge of fashion", "cognitive fashion" and "learning approach" are—understandably—often used imprecisely in theoretical and empirical accounts of the topic. The phrases getting to know the style and cognitive style are, on a few occasions, used interchangeably, whilst at different times they may be afforded separate and wonderful definitions. Cognitive style is described with the aid of Allport (1937) as a character's typical or recurring mode of trouble fixing, wondering, perceiving, and remembering, while the term studying fashion is adopted to mirror a subject with the utility of cognitive fashion in a studying situation (driving & Cheema, 1991). Using and Cheema (1991) go on to describe the cognitive style in phrases of a bipolar dimension (wholist–analytic) whilst getting to know fashion is visible as encompassing some of the additives which aren't jointly one-of-a-kind. it is also probable that cognitive fashion—at the very least—can be appeared as one enormous issue of getting to know fashion. Hartley (1998) offers the following definitions: cognitive patterns are the methods in which one-of-a-kind individuals ordinarily technique-specific cognitive duties; studying styles are the methods in which people normally approach exceptional gaining knowledge of tasks. A third key time period within the vicinity, getting to know techniques, Hartley (1998) defines as the techniques students adopt while reading. Hartley (1998, p. 149) continues: "one-of-a-kind techniques may be selected by using beginners to address extraordinary obligations. Getting to know styles is probably extra automatic than gaining knowledge of strategies which are non-compulsory." This final point, which tries to differentiate between style and method, reflects a habitual problem within the place.

The "country- or- trait" debate associated with such a lot of human psychological traits (consisting of personality) is, now not tremendously, applicable right here. Mastering fashion may be considered as solid over the years (structural)—a traitor as changing with every revel in or scenario (technique)—a country. Perhaps the extra achievable view is that a fashion may additionally nicely exist in a few shapes, this is it could have structure, however, that the shape is, to a few diplomae, attentive to studies and the needs of the situation (system) to allow exchange and to permit adaptive behavior. The "motherboard/software program" and "hard/smooth" wiring analogies have additionally been used to describe the interface of style (motherboard/tough wiring) and approach (software/smooth wiring). Investigating the difficulty of stability in studying style lavatory (1997) did locate evidence to aid consistency in studying fashion over time, but was important of contemporary techniques of analysis and recommended warning in drawing any company end regarding balance.

One final time period worthy of definition here is "preferences". Several authors talk to the favoring of one approach of coaching over another (together with organization work over impartial- look at) as mastering options. The primary possibilities are pretty properly integrated within some of the models mentioned and are regularly dealt with explicitly by way of the extra intricate models of gaining knowledge of style.

Characterizing learning style: Simplifying topics

The preferred manner in which an individual approaches a task or learning scenario—their studying/cognitive fashion or technique or approach—has been characterized in numerous one-of-a-kind methods primarily based on a ramification of theoretical models. Before reviewing those models and characterizations, it can be helpful first to recollect present attempts at simplifying and categorizing modern-day systems alongside key dimensions.

Curry's Onion model

The use of how studying/cognitive fashion is measured to endorse a layer- like model of gaining knowledge of behavior, Curry (1983, 1987) utilizes an onion metaphor to demonstrate internal and outer layers of the construct. Initially proposing three layers, Curry later consists of "social interplay" as a fourth layer. "Instructional desire" refers back to the man or woman's desired preference of mastering the environment. It's far defined because the outermost layer, the most observable layer, and the layer maximum inclined to steer, making it the least solid degree of size. Units mentioned as measuring academic choice consist of the studying choice stock. Social interaction offers the following layer and pertains to the man or woman's choice for social interaction for the duration of learning. Reichmann and Grasha's (1974) pupil learning style Scale defines freshmen in step with their type and level of interplay (independent/dependent, collaborative/competitive, and participant/avoidant). The

0.33 and greater stable layer is "information processing style" and is defined because of the individual's intellectual technique to the processing of information. Devices related to the dimension of this deposit are Kolb's getting to know style stock. Cognitive desire stock and inventory of gaining knowledge of approaches. The very last layer defined is "cognitive character fashion". This appears the sturdiest issue, described as an "especially everlasting persona measurement ... obvious best whilst a character's behavior is determined throughout many exclusive mastering conditions".

Using and Cheema's fundamental Dimensions

Having identified in extra of 30 labels used to explain a ramification of cognitive and getting to know styles, driving and Cheema (1991) endorse a vast categorization of a style consistent with two fundamental dimensions representing how records are processed and represented: wholist–analytic and verbalizer–imager.

The wholist–analytic measurement represents the manner wherein people tend technique data, either as a whole (who list) or damaged down into components (analytic). Quoting Nickerson, Perkin, and Smith (1985), using and Cheema describe the wholist–analytic dimension the use of typically related terms: analytic—deductive, rigorous, restrained, convergent, formal, crucial and artificial; wholist—inductive, expansive, unconstrained, divergent, casual, diffuse and creative.

Taxonomy of gaining knowledge of fashion fashions

The verbalizer–imager size describes the diploma to which people generally tend to symbolize records as words (verbalizer) or as pictures (imager).

They advise some of the fashions of cognitive fashion which can be subsumed beneath those dimensions (or households).

Driving and Cheema (1991) make the point that many of the patterns recognized do not function closely in empirical work and that attention has centered on most effective a small range of styles. They conclude that at the same time as there's quite a little research comparing the various styles, they can as a minimum be placed into the two huge categories of wholist–analytic and verbal–imagery. The two fundamental cognitive styles exist independently and aren't contingent upon each other; an Imager may be located at both cease of the wholist–analytic measurement. Driving (1991) has evolved the evaluation of the Cognitive pattern (CSA) as an evaluation tool integrating the two dimensions.

Cognitive- centred, activity (learning)- focused and persona- concentrated methods

Using Grigerenko and Sternberg's (1995) discussion of favor- based ideas and studies, Rayner and riding (1997) do not forget mastering fashion inside the framework of character-centered, cognitive- targeted, and learning- focused approaches. There's a simplest confined dialogue of persona- focused processes given, consistent with Rayner and riding, its restrained effect within the place and the life of only a single version (Myers Briggs fashion model) which explicitly incorporates personality as a prime thing.

Cognitive- concentrated processes cognizance at the identity of patterns primarily based on the man or woman distinction in cognitive and perceptual functioning. The dialogue of cognitive-centered approaches attempts to combine the earlier work of driving and Cheema (1991), categorizing models in keeping with wholist–analytic and verbal–imager concepts. The dialogue revisits models considered in advance using and Cheema and extends to include several extra fashions inclusive of riding's (1991) Cognitive style evaluation (CSA). The CSA is a computerized evaluation tool that identifies a man or woman's function alongside both the wholist–analytic measurement and the verbalizer–imager measurement. The CSA is an example of a version and instrument of gaining knowledge of style which incorporates the two proposed fundamental dimensions of fashion.

Studying- focused techniques are prominent on the basis that there is a more hobby in the impact of favor on studying in an educational placing, and the development of latest mastering- relevant constructs and concepts, often born out of the utilization of evaluation gadgets. Rayner and using's subsequent dialogue of getting to know- focused processes are framed around the distinction among procedure- based fashions, desire- based fashions, and cognitive competencies- primarily based models. Procedure models are described in phrases of perceiving and information processing, with Kolb's Experiential gaining knowledge of model representing one such method. Desire fashions recognition on people's options for the learning scenario and encompass favored time of day for observing, temperature, mild, the choice for organization/impartial take a look at. Cognitive talents- based tactics are characterized through the choice to apply cognitive- focused models of favor to a getting to know the state of affairs. Those tactics focus on subject- dependency, perceptual modality, and memory.

Further critiques are furnished with the aid of De Bello (1990) and Swanson (1995). De Bello affords a systematic review of eleven of what he considers "main fashions", selected in step with the following standards: constitute an ancient angle; have influenced others; replicate person practitioners' tries to pick out style; relate to concurrent problems in education; are studies oriented or are well known in the subject. De Bello gives a complete account of those fashions reviewed with an evaluative element, making this a useful guide for the choice of appropriate models for work in the location. Swanson's overview uses Curry's onion version as a framework for categorizing models and measures consistent with the mentioned issue layers of studying style. Swanson's article additionally gives a tremendously uncommon assessment of the outcomes of lifestyle and ethnicity on getting to know style.

Curry's (1987) assessment is concerned with the psychometric properties of measures of getting to know fashion. Her article examines 21 measures of favor, focusing on issues of reliability and validity, troubles which remain raised as a count number of difficulty within the region.

Even as each of these critiques offers a slightly special angle on the subject, the impetus for every one of them is the want to rationalize an area affected by a confusing array of terms, definitions, fashions, and measures.

Theories, fashions, and Measures

The subsequent dialogue of getting to know style models and gadgets is—as is regularly the case—in no way exhaustive. It is, however, pretty complete and consists of descriptions of most of the models as a minimum mentioned in current and extensive review papers. The choice system in reality did now not center on figuring out fashions that differed from each other in any such way as to provide opportunity views. Instead, the goal is to make a point of mentioned overlaps among special fashions so that you can make express the need for rationalization in research and exercise and encourage readers to discover in addition similarities. Even as it'd, conceivably, be viable to compile an exhaustive listing of contraptions, this would possibly encompass many derivatives and adaptations along with some of the devices without an empirical base and an absence of reliability and validity facts.

Model

Subject- dependence/subject- independence is largely an individual's capability to dissemble in perceptual responsibilities—likened to spatial intelligence and is related to the potential to dissemble in non- perceptual problem fixing responsibilities. Evidence that discipline- dependence changed into additionally relevant to intellectual ability in addition to more than a few different psychological skills, consisting of experience of self, has brought about the construct being given the broader label of "differentiation". As a style, is related to a general preference for getting to know in isolation (discipline- independence) instead of integration (field- dependence). Subject- impartial learners are characterized as running with an inner body of reference, intrinsically prompted with self- directed dreams, structuring their personal mastering, and defining their very own take a look at techniques. Subject- structured learners then again are characterized as depending greater on an external body of reference, are extrinsically inspired, reply higher to certain defined performance goals, have a want for structuring and guidance from the teacher, and a preference to have interaction with different beginners. These traits will in reality have implications for the desired learning scenario and therefore getting to know the consequences.

Even though it has stimulated a wonderful deal of studies inside the discipline of education especially, Witkin's concept is criticized on the subsequent grounds: to generalize overall performance on perceptual obligations to personality and social behavior is an over- extension of the concept and that area- independence—due to its excessive correlations with measures of intelligence is a degree of capacity as opposed to fashion and therefore is of little fee within the field of cognitive fashion.

Model and measurement
Impulsivity- reflexivity has measured by the use of the Matching familiar Figures take a look at (MFFT) which requires familiar line drawing of items to be matched towards numerous possibilities. Individuals who make brief responses after brief scanning of the alternatives are labeled "cognitive impulsive" whilst individuals who scrutinize every opportunity earlier than creating a final choice are labeled "cognitive reflective".

Of be aware right here is the association said among field- dependence/subject- independence   and impulsivity- reflexivity with some of the studies reporting huge correlations among MFFT and EFT scores. Reflective is pronounced as extra area- independent and impulsive as extra area- established, indicating a full-size overlap inside the two constructs.

Convergent style is characterized through the technology of the one frequent accurate answer from the "to be had" information and divergent fashion as a propensity to supply several potentially suitable answers to the hassle.

Dimension

Assessment of convergent questioning is the greater sincere of the two, using general intelligence tests, more than one- desire gadgets, in addition to being inferred from an overall performance at the EFT and MFFT. Due to the fact, the variety of potentially accurate solutions is used as an index of divergent wondering, checks along with makes use of objects check and the results take a look at our usual methods of assessment.

There are some counseled implications right here: that positive concern regions can also encourage, and therefore praise, convergent over divergent thinking (that is, technology- related disciplines); that there needs to be a like- for- like fit among teacher and scholar in terms of favored style that, because of the inherent shape and recurring in most formal educational settings, divergent questioning proves unpopular with instructors and is discouraged. There has been an association drawn between divergent wondering and subject- independence (which is considered to be more creative), given that individuals scoring high on divergent thinking also score excessive on-field independence.

Using the diploma of complexity with which the character perceives the challenge, Holzman, and Klein (1954) introduced the fashion measurement leveler–sharpener. The leveler tends to oversimplify their perceptions of the assignment, assimilating elements and reducing complexity. In comparison, the sharpener fails to assimilate efficiently but alternatively introduces complexity, treating every piece of element or occasion as a novel. Assimilation is therefore the size defining this unique cognitive style, with levelers and sharpeners being placed at the extremes of the continuum.

The "failure to assimilate" function is validated by using the Schematizing check which requires the character to decide the size of a series of squares of light which get step by step bigger. The tendency is to underestimate the dimensions of preceding squares judged towards the current large squares. At the same time as levelers show a particular sensitivity to this effect, sharpeners make greater accurate estimations attributable to failing to assimilate modern-day and past occasions (squares of light).

While there may be relatively little work making use of the leveler–sharpener cognitive fashion (driving & Cheema, 1991), using and Dyer (1983) were able to perceive similarities between this style and area- dependence/independence.

Interestingly, Pask (Pask, 1972; Pask & Scott, 1972) makes the point that whilst each business functions thru an extraordinary method for learning—in the long run—each business attain a similar degree of knowledge. Serialists perform a step- by way of- step technique to gaining knowledge of, selecting to deal most effectively with small amounts of statistics or cloth at anybody time earlier than going on to hyperlink these steps and reap information. Holists alternatively will utilize sizable amounts of records from the beginning, trying to achieve knowledge via identifying and specializing in the most important patterns or developments inside the records. The serialists understand the studying undertaking in phrases of a series of unbiased discrete subjects and issues and awareness on developing links between them, but for holists, the focus is on the mission as an entire. Pask determined the relative characteristics of serialists and holists as serialists—step- by using- step, logical linear progression, slender recognition, careful and vital main to a tendency to fail to spot the assignment from an international attitude; wholists—broad-angle and international techniques resulting in an inclination to make hasty selections based on insufficient facts or evaluation.

Pask and Scott (1972) devised a chain of problem- solving duties that allowed individuals to adopt either a step- via- step or worldwide technique to fix the project. People adopting a step- via- step approach to test easy hypotheses had been labeled as serialists whilst holists have been the ones folks that tried to attain a faster solution through testing extra complex hypotheses.

Riding and Cheema (1991) factor out that despite being widely established, the dimension is based on simplest a fairly small pattern and has no longer benefited from any empirical work inspecting its association with different learning patterns. Notwithstanding this feedback, Pask (1976) did record that holists scored better at the Analogies test and Divergence check than serialists, suggesting feasible similarities with the convergent- divergent style measurement.

The statement that individuals have a recurring propensity to process statistics both verbally or imaginably emanates from the dual coding concept and can have crucial implications for studying. The verbalizer–visualizer cognitive size is classified through assessments examining people's ability to generate records no longer present but based upon the presence of a spontaneous picture. People capable of responding fast are considered visualizers and people with slower response quotes verbalizers. Proof exists to assist the perception that, even as the ability to exchange among modes exists, some people rely closely on one or different modes. The truth that individuals have choices for either visible or verbal notions has implications for studying. Alesandrini (1981) stated that the tendency for visualization turned inversely associated with technology and verbal analytical potential, while the normally mentioned finding is that verbalizer's research satisfactory from textual content- based fabric and visualizers from pictorially offered fabric. This suggests that a mismatch between learner and mode of presentation will adversely affect overall performance.

Gregorc (1982) describes four different and observable behaviors: summary, concrete, random, and sequential inclinations. A combination of these inclinations is indicative of character fashion. Those dispositions are, Gregorc believes, reflective of in- born predispositions however individuals want to be able to function outdoor their herbal style. Four mastering patterns are recognized:

concrete sequential, providing direct, step- by- step, orderly, sensory- based learning; concrete random, proposing trial and blunders, intuitive and unbiased procedures to learning; summary sequential, presenting analytic, logical strategies and a preference for verbal coaching; and abstract random, presenting a choice for holistic, visual, experiential, and unstructured gaining knowledge of.

The style Delineator is a forty-item self- report inventory related to the rank ordering of sets of phrases. The layout is just like that of Kolb's (1976) mastering styles stock and it's been recommended that observation and interviews ought to be used alongside the instrument to assist within the identity of gaining knowledge of style and preferences (De Bello, 1990). The degree identifies an individual's mastering fashion in keeping with Gregorc's version.

The assimilator–explorer cognitive fashion defines style in phrases of a man or woman's propensity to clear up problems via both novel or familiar techniques. The style changed into developed around trouble- fixing behavior and has a close affiliation with the use of creativity.
A- E fashion has measured the usage of a thirty-two- item self- file questionnaire evolved using Kauffmann and Martinsen (1991) in which people are scored in keeping with their stage of apparent choice for novelty (denoting explorers) or familiarity (denoting assimilators) in cognitive feature.

Grounded in an assumption that cognitive fashion is related to creativity, problem-solving and decision- making techniques, as well as factors of persona, Kirton (1994), argued that fashion develops early in existence and stays stable over both time and state of affairs. Kirton brought an adaption–innovation measurement along which cognitive fashion might be measured with adaptors characterized using the choice to do matters higher and innovators using the choice to do things in another way.

A- I is assessed using the Kirton Adaptor–Innovator stock (KAI), a thirty-two- item self- record device developed to be used with a grownup populace with each place of job and life enjoy. Visible as a degree of trouble- solving fashion and creativity, the KAI is in common use in the field of control and training.

The Cognitive fashion Index becomes evolved through Allinson and Hayes (1996) so one can operationalize cognitive style to be used inside the vicinity of control. It specializes in the measurement of intuition versus analysis which, Allinson and Hayes argue, represents a superordinate dimension of cognitive style. Hemispheric asymmetry underlies the size, with proper mind orientation characterized by using intuition with a tendency for fast choice-making based on feeling and the adoption of an international angle. Left mind orientation is characterized by analysis wherein decisions are a result of logical reasoning focusing on detail.

The CSI is a 38- object self- report questionnaire that provides a rating suggestive of both an intuitive or analytic nature.

Kolb's Experiential Learning Model (ELM) and studying styles inventory (LSI) (gaining knowledge of- targeted Processed- primarily based method/information

Processing style)

Kolb (1976, 1984) proposes a four- degree hypothetical learning cycle. Individuals will display a preference for or will deal with a few stages better than others and learning is visible as a non-stop, interactive method. The four ranges of the ELM are described as: concrete enjoy (CE; experiencing) which favors experiential learning; summary conceptualization (AC; questioning) in which there's a preference for conceptual and analytical thinking to acquire knowledge; active experimentation (AE; doing) involving lively trial- and- error mastering; and reflective statement (RO; reflecting) in which vast attention is given to the mission and capacity answers before there may be any strive at movement. The four getting-to-know orientations shape two orthogonal bipolar dimensions of mastering. the first size is comprehension—the greedy of facts from revel in—and is constituted by the bipolar orientations CE–AC. the second size defined is transformation—the processing of grasped facts—and is constituted with the aid of the closing orientations AERO. Relative positioning alongside those dimensions defines the gaining knowledge of styles described by way of Kolb as convergence, divergence, assimilation, and accommodation. The character who adopts a convergent method uses summary conceptualization to pressure energetic experimentation. Movement is based on an abstract understanding of the venture and projected strategies for the successful completion of the challenge. Divergers combine reflective remarks with concrete experience to devise a frequently innovative solution. Divergers are often defined as innovative learners due to their propensity to recall more than one capability strategy for getting to know and hassle solving. Assimilators are involved commonly with the rationale in their observations, favor abstract conceptualization, and reflective statements. As such, assimilators are searching mainly to refine summary theories in place of developing possible strategies and answers. Lastly, Kolb defines the accommodator. Using lively experimentation and urban revel in, these individuals have a clear choice for hands- on studying. The accommodator has been described as inclining prompt movement and a mentioned capability for adapting to diverse situations.

Initially evolved as a nine- object self- record scale (Kolb, 1976), the revised LSI is a twelve- object self- document questionnaire. Respondents are required on each of the items to rank four-sentence endings corresponding to each of the four mastering patterns. LSI ratings mirror a man or woman's relative emphasis at the four mastering orientations and allow categorization in step with the corresponding learning fashion. Aggregate ratings measure a person's desire for abstractness over concreteness (AC–CE) and action over the mirrored image (AERO).

Assertions that the patterns outlined with the aid of Kolb might be related to pupil performance have been borne out in some of the studies in which, for example, convergers perform better on conventional examinations related to concrete solutions. Despite such support, research inspecting the psychometric houses of the LSI has raised concerns concerning its reliability and validity.

Kolb's emphasis on experiential mastering and the developmental nature of gaining knowledge suggests a capability for alternate in style. Research that has examined balance and change the use of the LSI gift a combined image. Low check- retest reliability records and modifications in fashion type suggested through Sims et al. (1986) are countered by way of reports of quite high test- retest reliability of 0.99 observed by Veres, Sims, and Locklear (1991). Even though additionally reporting high check- retest reliability records, bathroom (1997) is cautious approximately them, believing that besides the point statistical techniques may be covering individual adjustments in fashion in favor of institution effects.

Honey and Mumford's (1992) description and the dimension of learning fashion are grounded in Kolb's experiential mastering version, with patterns carefully similar to those defined through Kolb. The studying styles Questionnaire (LSQ) was evolved to be used with control trainees and has been proposed as an alternative to Kolb's LSI. The four getting-to-know patterns measured by way of the LSQ are activist (Kolb's lively experimentation); reflector (Kolb's reflective statement); theorist (Kolb's summary conceptualization; and pragmatist (Kolb's concrete enjoy).

Even though developed to be used with management trainees, the LSQ has been used in several settings which include schooling. However, worries concerning the psychometric qualities of the LSQ had been raised. Duff and Duffy (2002) record a failure to guide the lifestyles of either the bipolar dimensions or learning styles proposed through Honey and Mumford and observed the LSQ has the handiest modest stages of internal consistency. Given that their pattern turned into undergraduate students, Duff and Duffy finish the LSQ isn't always an acceptable opportunity to the LSI and that its use within the area of higher training is premature.

Vermunt (1992) describes the concept of gaining knowledge of style in phrases of processing strategies, along with an attention of the goals and goals of the studying exercise used to determine what's learned; law techniques, which serve to screen getting to know; intellectual models of mastering, encompassing the learner's perceptions of the gaining knowledge of the system; and studying orientations, defined as private objectives, intentions, and expectations based totally on beyond enjoy of studying. based totally on these strategies and orientations, Vermunt derives four learning patterns: undirected, in which there may be a problem in assimilating mastering material, dealing with the extent of fabric and prioritizing the importance of components of the fabric; replica, wherein very little effort is made to apprehend but alternatively statistics are reproduced to finish the undertaking or achieve the minimal required standard; application directed, that is characterized by the software of getting to know the material to concrete situations a good way to gain expertise; and finally, which means directed mastering, which entails attempts to benefit deeper information of mastering fabric and to draw on current and related know-how to reap vital know-how. Vermont's mastering styles stock (LSI) changed into evolved as a diagnostic tool for use in a higher education context.

The diploma to which every one of the four styles is favored is classed using Vermunt's LSI. The LSI incorporates twenty subscales and one hundred and twenty objects regarding take a look at strategies, reasons, and intellectual fashions. People respond to statements alongside a five- point scale in step with the degree to which the declaration is descriptive in their behavior or the volume to which they consider the announcement.

Based on earlier work by using Marton and Saljo (1976) Entwistle, Hanley, and Hounsel (1979) evolved a device for assessing mastering style which focuses on the extent of engagement or depth of processing carried out at some stage in studying. The proposed version centers around four modes of the orientation of the learner: which means orientation; reproduction orientation; accomplishing orientation; and holistic orientation. tendencies toward precise mixtures of orientations become aware of people as conforming to one of the following gettings to know styles: deep (purpose to recognize, concerning thoughts, use of proof, and lively learning); surface (goal to breed, unrelated memorizing, passive getting to know, and fear of failure); strategic (have a look at a corporation, time control, alertness to assessment needs, and aim to excel); and apathetic (lack of path and shortage of hobby).

Chapter Three

Learning Styles, Mental Models, and Problem-Solving

Mastering demanding situations engage questioning. Instructors will consider and finally design, hard scenarios so one can stimulate their pupils to generate more than a few viable solutions. In turn, students will consider how they will meet the challenges. The mental model principle informs instructors' knowledge approximately thinking: it explains how mental fashions rise from the idiosyncratic methods of developing the speaking and relationships important to manual questioning. Intellectual fashions are functional cognitive systems that have a technique/product nature. In addition, they have numerous functions that permit them to shop statistics and enact techniques to generate effects.

The concept explains how pupils engage within the questioning technique to assimilate reminiscence, new facts, and customized techniques to locate solutions to demanding situations. Whilst faced with a novel project, pupils retrieve, restructure and/or create, and save useable mental models according to their perceived relevance to generate an acceptable final result.

Expertise mental version idea
The phrase "version" has resulted in a few vexations by

using researchers of cognitive concept due to peoples' fact that they understand what the word means while used in the designation mental version. all and sundry is aware of what a version is! To eliminate any ambiguity about the phrase, "version" right here serves two grammatical purposes: a noun in which it's far "a representation in 3 dimensions of a proposed shape", and as a verb "to form an element in imitation of devising a model of a phenomenon or machine". Intellectual models, being "models" are bimodal as a product produced thru cognition by using individuals to create an illus action or shape of a phenomenon or technique to a problem, and as a process in which a motion of retrieval, restructuring, or creation happens to shape and reform those representations of the structure of a phenomenon or option to a trouble. Consequently, the time period modeling modeling" may be used to explain the process that people adopt when they create or retrieve, intellectual to devise greater beneficial or subtle mental fashions to solve problems. Confusion also exists in people's beliefs that a "version", in its purest shape, maybe a reproduction of the reality of a phenomenon in an environment. Mental models are not simply reproductions: they have a dynamic lifestyle this is separate from the reality they version after they had been produced via the person. When a mental version is seen as useful. Its miles are saved, using the character, in long-term reminiscence where it can be associated or linked to many other mental fashions and cognitive systems such as schemes. But, the intellectual model now exists within its personal fact and no longer relies on the replication of its source phenomenon. Novel hassle conditions are of interest to educators because they require inexperienced persons to map expertise and skills from recognized problems to new occasions. Norman (1988) recognized that cognitive representations, along with schemata, could not explain what came about whilst individuals come upon new or novel problems. Schema concept turned into visible to be rigid due to schemata's reliance on static propositional representations and it did no longer account for the negotiation of irregular regular encounters with the environment. Mental fashions use both propositional representations and schema to expect effects and in doing so, assist the functionality of quick-time period memory. Solving complex troubles can be limited by way of operating reminiscence because it cannot hold all the components, such as which particular expertise and which software of skills is important to solve the hassle. Halford (1993) argued that mental models reflect the shape of the phenomenon in the environment whether or not it is a state of affairs, task, idea, or trouble with which a man or woman is confronted. He hypothesized that if we can efficaciously, or incorrectly, understand the phenomena then we generate a respective accurate, or incorrect, intellectual version. In other words, people can keep intellectual fashions, this is, representations of phenomena which they efficaciously or incorrectly understand but for which they see a few prices in preserving. Norman (1983) additionally highlighted this erroneous and wrong nature of mental models thereby suggesting a reason for and person's retention of erroneous records. Senge (1992) advised that intellectual fashions had a multifarious nature and explained that we "can't convey all of the complicated information of our world in our thoughts". He argued that ". . . we do no longer have intellectual fashions . . . we're our mental fashions" as "they're inextricably woven into our private lifestyles records and experience of who we're". The essence of intellectual version idea and its interest to instructors is its ability to explain how students have interacted with the arena. Gentner and Stevens (1983) and van der Veer and Peurta-Melguizo (2002) defined this interplay by using linking mapping with an intellectual model's feature as an overall performance control mechanism. This mechanism permits us to predict, interpret, and communicate. Craik (1943), the grandfather of the mental version principle, defined them as "representations in the mind of actual or imaginary situations" and used the concept to explain how people explain, recognize and remedy predicted events. In precise, intellectual fashions are cognitive structures that can be based on new understandings, previous know-how, present ideas, and past reviews that we use to interpret and give an explanation for events in our world. Williamson (1999) proposed that intellectual fashions are malleable and require a few accommodations through the person or learner and that this may now not usually be easy to do, particularly if they are anchored with the aid of deeply held beliefs. Social and cultural relationships that anchor a mental version can be very robust due to their being based totally on reviews, personal perceptions, and superstitions which could connect to positive feelings and/or reports. Therefore the educational, social, and cultural relationships that exist to create mental models can, in the end, make the mental model tough to control and modify if it is wrong. However, human experience also can serve to make learning richer and, therefore, remembered.

Methodology to parent intellectual version capabilities

They have a look at that changed into undertaken to research mental version capabilities changed into an empirical qualitative have a look at, based in an Australian number one college commencing in February 2005 and finishing in October 2006. The method becomes focused on the records processing concept and connected with the introspection mediating process tracing paradigm. This technique supplied a significant conceptual framework to offer the model to "appearance within the minds of newcomers to explore what takes place whilst getting to know occurs" and while students are sporting out duties that contain hassle solving. This attention turned into important because a determination of the in-action intellectual models utilized by students when they were solving troubles could determine the capabilities of intellectual models that guide the system. The context for the has a look at changed into robotics, which is an optional aspect of the Queensland generation Syllabus. It presents a wealthy, multi-disciplinary environment wherein to interact center years students in designing, building, programming, and activating robots to complete set duties. This examination illuminated the dynamic nature of intellectual fashions through a longitudinal method that included a selection of investigative devices. The examine worried a binary recognition each on the journey markers where information become gathered thru Likert Scale questionnaires, semi-dependent interviews, stimulated recall interviews, teach again episodes, journals and awareness organization interviews, and at the fascinating glimpses of the human reviews afforded alongside the way. The research examined how one instructor and her college students' intellectual models can tell teaching, getting to know, and actual evaluation practices. There has been twenty-four year six pupil members and one trainer within the have a look at. Four college students were anonymously chosen to take part in the extra in-intensity elements of the examination consisting of stimulated remember sessions and semi-structured interviews. All interview information was analyzed using pattern coding that allows you to lessen facts to attainable gadgets to permit both the willpower of the intellectual fashions being studied and pass-participant evaluation of common intellectual models. So whilst mental fashions are inner systems they may be exteriorized when brought about using interplay with a website gadget that includes robotics. The ensuing interactions, within the domain and with different participants, are physical and those performances may be discovered.

How the capabilities of intellectual fashions can assist in problem-fixing

People assemble idiosyncratic models that may not be correct or beneficial to remedy problems yet are retained due to their notion that they may be useful. The individuality of a retained intellectual model retained arises from how it displays that individual's interactions with the surroundings. Intellectual fashions also comprise reflections of troubles, events, and testimonies that can be imaginary. Such fanciful ruminations arise from our consistent interaction with the sector and mirror our individualistic capability to increase the relationships and communicate essential to guide know-how. The functions of intellectual fashions that allow problem environments to be explored were set up through longitudinal observe and encompass how intellectual fashions help us: o explain; o predict; o manipulate movement and thought; o diagnose; one hundred fifty-five o talk; and, o bear in mind. The explanatory function allows expertise and choice of techniques due to the fact intellectual fashions "facilitate cognitive and physical interactions with the surroundings, with others, and with artifacts". Honestly placed, if you want to recognize their international via comprehending what reasons, affect, controls, or prevents phenomena, people construct models of it. But, now not everything contained in an intellectual model is entire or accurate because, as Norman (1983) advised, an individual's intellectual models are fashioned via non-public attributes along with their historical past experiences, expertise in extraordinary domain names, and, often, their unscientific or superstitious ideas. Additionally, we neglect aspects or store them poorly in lengthy-term memory, and intellectual fashions that are not used regularly turn out to be stagnant, regularly needing re-evaluation and modification if they are to remain useful and purposeful as a way of explaining phenomena. The predictive function enables hassle solving in novel situations. This act isn't always continually an honest, logical, or tidy process due to mental fashions containing intellectual snapshots, analogies, assertions, propositions, relations, abstractions, superstitions, and beliefs, in addition to the related conceptual, declarative, and procedural information for that state of affairs. Intellectual models permit an individual to predict how a device will work or trouble will be solved and this feature serves to distinguish mental fashions from different cognitive structures that don't account for novel situations that individuals encounter. If a mental version is correct and complete then its predictive energy should be greater and people can examine the plausibility of feasible solutions. The look for answers to lecture room challenges generally requires students to concurrently run and hyperlink diverse intellectual fashions as they predict possible effects. The control function offers a platform from which to make selections and control behavior due to the fact individuals recall alternatives while confronted with preference. Mental fashions are "what people truly have of their heads and what guides their use of things. "Individuals can be aware of running intellectual fashions although they can also be run unconsciously or automatically. If an instructor is introducing a new concept that students are struggling to recognize, they could retrieve and run intellectual models containing ideas, standards, and/or techniques from past instructions that were a success. The instructor's retrieval of successful studies suggests that mental models can be controlled to conform to the environmental phenomena and subsequently enable successful mapping of the new knowledge to existing mental fashions. The jogging of mental fashions enables even bad performances to be managed because against different cognitive structures which include schemata and scripts intellectual models have the ability to deal with novel conditions. The study room experiences, documented via Henderson and Tallman's (2006) studies, were both "liberating and stultifying" for the trainer and student. The difference is because of manage: both the man or woman controls their mental modeling through retrieving and/or adapting them whilst they are identified to be ineffectual to facilitate an effective answer or the character is controlled by using an unadaptable mental version and can't make progress to a solution. The diagnostic feature of mental fashions allows students to increase metacognitive cognizance. The term "perturbation" turned into used to explain the contradictions felt with the aid of newbies whilst new information became needed to hyperlink with earlier information to create a modified intellectual version. The customized intellectual version might comprise the brand new reports and principles to conquer the perturbed nation. some steerage can be vital for the learner to move through perturbation into a kingdom of equilibrium and this want for guidance displays Vygotsky's (1978) area of Proximal improvement in which it is essential to take college students "a little past" what they know or experience comfy doing alone. The diagnostic characteristic of intellectual fashions for students, therefore, is based on an understanding, or metacognitive awareness, that they'll be running with an intellectual version that doesn't allow them to assimilate new standards. Without this guided assistance. The conversation function permits others to look and apprehend the externalization of a man or woman's intellectual fashions. Intellectual models facilitate the conversation strategies of writing, analyzing, speaking, and listening whilst thinking via hassle-fixing situations. While college students proportion or talk their mental fashions to others in magnificence it involves oral discourse that requires dialogue where the social negotiation of a transitory mental version which can mutually be held with the aid of the contributors takes place. This sharing frequently necessitates a "collaborative critiquing of one's own and others' intellectual models". Mental fashions are communicated via a language and other character and cultural nuances such as facial expression, frame posture, and vocal sunglasses which all need to be 'translated' so that communication is a success. Written discourse may be complex as nicely and involves some form of writing where textual content or symbolic script is used to express what is thought. Mental fashions have a reminiscence function. They are temporary and permanent due to their life in each running memory and lengthy-time period memory. However, it would appear that multiple intellectual models or components of mental models could be run simultaneously. How individual links the associated parts of the mental fashions which might be run depends on the community of associated understandings that they instantiate while the mental version is created and stored. Sooner or later, how properly a man or woman accesses or retrieves the required mental version, or component thereof, will depend upon the efficacy of the storage method and the relevance of relationships perceived. Mental modeling can be inspired by many elements, which include a scholar's meta-capability and their capacity to effectively use their running reminiscence.

The mental model Mode: a diagram of the functionality

Whilst intellectual fashions are inner representations they're externalized via some motion. When students adopt problem fixing in number one classrooms they're required to carry out certain behaviors important to create or discover an answer. Whilst the learning areas, within which the scholars are operating, might differ the intellectual modeling required to finish the venture should show similarities. The intellectual model Mode (MMM) has been designed to explain the mental modeling that individuals undertake whilst they may be addressing hassle-fixing situations. The model has the features that mental models serve whilst a character encounters a hassled state of affairs. The subsequent discussion makes use of the domains of design and era and arithmetic to demonstrate the features of intellectual modeling. It pursuits to establish the validity of the MMM to assist instructors who are presenting design or mathematical challenges for pupils in the primary. One of the distinctions between trouble fixing in layout and era and arithmetic is the belief of complexity in the hassle to be solved and the creativity afforded the scholar in search of an answer. Layout and technology problems can be contextualized in most 'normal' situations and while complex concerns need to be made the solutions available can be pretty creative and specific. The solutions can be new. In arithmetic, troubles are maximum typically used to introduce new mathematical knowledge to be able to contextualize the information and tactics so that scholars can see how arithmetic can be carried out in 'regular' conditions. The answers usually require a few strategic processes, together with building a table to organize data or the assessment of capabilities, and are maximum generally genuine. This new as opposed to proper binary might not be mutually distinctive however gives and cause the delineation of the styles of problems addressed in each of the learning regions. Mental modeling using the MMM in arithmetic can contain a spread of procedures to get to the same solution. students encountering a hassle to clear up, which includes how many pencil holders will be required for his or her year three classroom given x variety of kids, y range of tables, and z wide variety of pencils, will need to retrieve the declarative understanding approximately numerical values and operations from long-time period reminiscence necessary to provide an explanation for what methods the problem entails. They may then diagnose their capability to remedy the problem. This metacognitive method is vital because Johnson-Laird (2006) recommended that in most cases the incapacity to clear up a problem is due to a loss of the expertise required to accomplish that. Once the scholar has installed that they do have the essential information they make predictions or check solutions. If operating with some other scholar, they'll proportion their transitory intellectual model predictions through oral, and perhaps written, communique. The student will determine whether, or no longer, to modify their chosen answer and adopt the transitory intellectual model or preserve, and eventually store, their personal. They will need as a way to explain their answer and how it meets the standards installed inside the hassle and if it does — it's far most in all likelihood proper. Design and era offer pupils opportunities to create novel solutions to ordinary troubles. Casakin (2011) mentioned the get admission to and retrieval system that students adopt after they layout. This system, not diverse from that used by scholars to resolve issues in mathematics, engages the student in retrieving the conceptual, declarative, and procedural knowledge required to switch to unique trouble. The retrieval procedure relies upon how a scholar explains the trouble in mild in their idiosyncratic ways of interacting with the arena. If pupils, within the months that lecture room above who established what number of pencil holders had been required have been ultimately given a quick to design and cause them to, then it is possible that a spread of beliefs, values, and intentions could inform the following answers. A trainer, who had uncovered the scholars to a rich sort of materials, joining techniques, and ethical design considerations, might anticipate disparate designs. The MMM \ facilitates explain the techniques that scholars undertake whilst designing wherein a constant cycle of explaining, diagnosing, and predicting could occur as the student implemented the layout system to satisfy the requirement of the short. The MMM offers instructors a shape that explains the thinking methods that their pupils will use when meeting studying challenges. If scholars are encountering problems in negotiating a problem, then some a part of the MMM might not work effectively to improve gaining knowledge of. Newell and Simon (1972) explored the idea of hassle space, which defined all feasible sequences of the intellectual operations that scholars needed to address whilst solving a problem. This concept implies that teachers want to recollect this area and enact their own intellectual modeling, transacting the gap to make certain that all expertise required for pupils to solve the trouble is available. Johnson-Laird (2006) indicates that "imagination facilitates us to cause and reasoning allows us to assume" and this has importance for instructors who're designing the demanding situations to interact with students in number one school rooms. First, instructors should be creating the mastering environments that reveal pupils to rich problem states that permit them to intellectual version. Intellectual modeling, in design and technology or mathematics, ought to allow pupils to construct upon the repertoire of abilities, reminiscences, strategies, and know-how required to cope with novel troubles. hassle states, irrespective of getting to know areas, want to provoke robust intellectual modeling that engages both the reasoning that helps to explain, diagnosing and predicting capabilities vital to problem solve and the imagining that promotes our idiosyncratic interactions with the world that create the relationships important to shop intellectual models in our long time memory. Providing great possibilities to flex hassle-fixing techniques seems to be a key to fulfillment in mastering to satisfy challenges. similarly to have the possibility to trouble resolve, Joacobse and Harskamp (2009) advise that pupils also be given a few initiatives for the approaches they will use thereby encouraging cognitive flexibility and adaptability. Intellectual version theory, via the MMM, enables the instructor to reveal the effectiveness of cognitive tactics used by pupils when they may be given such initiative. it can also assist to explain why students repeat the same errors. Johnson-Laird (2006) said that the maximum potential cause of a pupil's preference for an inaccurate anticipated solution lies in her lack of ability to consider all alternative answers and those methods may retain unless the scholar is helped to relinquish them. The intellectual model Mode affords a manner to give an explanation for constructive and ingenious wondering in classrooms and allows clearer expertise of what honestly takes place while we meet challenges.

Influence of college students getting to know styles at the

effectiveness of educational interventions

To be an effective self-regulated learner, students actively have to persuade and adjust all studying strategies of the cognitive, metacognitive, and motivational dimensions. One of these multilayered law of studying permits upgrades in processes of the cognitive, metacognitive, and motivational issues of mastering. Zimmerman's (2008, 2000, 1998) and Pintrich's (2000) models of self-law proportion those key-additives and orchestrate their sub-strategies in cyclic-reflective expertise to precise phases of self-regulated gaining knowledge. studying styles are seemed like one of the essential elements to be taken under consideration while designing guidance and studying environments: "training designed to deal with an extensive spectrum of gaining knowledge of styles has continuously proved to be extra effective than traditional coaching, which makes a specialty of a slender range of patterns". However, the scientific knowledge of the concept of studying style is as a substitute inconsistent. Getting to know-fashion fashions variety from holistic approaches to precise models that focus on positive dimensions of learning, i.e., statistics accumulating, processing, and retrieval.

Mastering patterns in concept and educational exercise

The sector of instructional psychology contains numerous mastering fashion models, all aiming at the development of getting to know. Getting to know fashion checks could contribute to the learner's intrapersonal know-how as a part of his/her declarative meta-understanding. Hence, intrapersonal information is described as know-how about the own thinking, reminiscence, and corresponding dispositions. Therefore, by knowing approximately precise choices a learner unifies, he/she at the least fulfills a primary prerequisite to self-regulate his/her gaining knowledge of manner and/or environment in a way that fits his/her individual studying choices. However, assessing gaining knowledge of styles could not only make contributions to the newcomers' meta-information and ultimately create the premise for the development of his/her manipulate mechanisms in a self-regulated getting to know surroundings. Even before newbies take part in a (self-regulated) mastering surroundings, getting to know styles might be an essential aspect. As aforementioned, numerous id-models advocate to assess the real learning forms of the goal-institution as a central aspect of the beginners' characteristics. Analogous to self-regulation mechanisms of learners that may occur in the stages of self-regulated studying, academic designers ought to do not forget the main gaining knowledge of types of their target institution while designing training. Theoretically, this has to result in an optimization of the designed preparation via improving its suitability for the target institution/learner. The relevance of gaining knowledge of styles for academic designers as well as the sector of self-regulated getting to know and in accordance research, hence, appears to be unquestionable. But, a significant wide variety of various understandings of learning style definitions, theoretical positions, models, and measures may be diagnosed. This ends in an increasing loss of clarity about what a studying fashion is and the way it enables preparation and (self-regulated) studying techniques. Cassidy (2004) states: "as a consequence of the number of studies, the disciplines and domains wherein the studies are conducted, and the numerous aims of the research, the subject has grown to be fragmented and disparate". To cope with gaining knowledge of styles, first, fundamental information for the idea is obligatory and to be supplied in order of no longer to contribute to similarly dilution of the concept. Hawk and Shah (2007) remember gaining knowledge of styles now not as a state. The authors point out that mastering styles and mastering style models all share the basic assumptions that "students study in one-of-a-kind ways", the idea of "learning style is a part of the broader idea of persona", and "studying fashion falls into the categories of dispositional trends and characteristic diversifications wherein there are variations throughout individual humans but there are groupings of people who have commonplace or similar learning style traits". Relating to Hawk and Shah's (2007) characterizations as a simple premise, and interchangeable use of the terms "gaining knowledge of style" and "cognitive fashion" seems to be feasible. some fashions include completely cognitive aspects of collecting, processing, and retrieving records, while different models encompass constructs dependent on the age-suitable assessments administered, e.g., environmental stimuli (sound, light, temperature, seating, and so on.) that function no direct relation to cognitive procedures. Driving and Cheema (1991) further intricate on the now not nicely defined usage of mastering fashion and cognitive style: "even as cognitive fashion is a bipolar measurement, getting to know fashion entails many factors and are normally now not 'both-or' extremes. One both has and does now not have the detail in one's fashion, similarly, the absence of one element does not necessarily mean the presence of the other element".

Although terminological shortcomings in mastering/cognitive fashion studies have been made explicit for several many years and the gain of taking such styles under consideration when designing instruction appears to be obvious – at the least from a theoretical perspective – scientists still argue approximately its sensible efficacy. Regarding numerous empirical studies on mastering patterns, consequences nonetheless draw an unclear photo approximately the "authentic" relevance of the idea. An in-intensity literature review revealed numerous contradicting effects of research on gaining knowledge of patterns. The subsequent investigations and reviews all help the advantage that arises from thinking about mastering styles when designing training. The scope of the instructions observed in those research gives a huge range from conventional training conditions to hypermedia mastering environments. In comparison, other research and opinions disagree with the aforementioned. Analogous to the contradicting research, the investigated getting to know environments and instructional settings also vary from the conventional study room to multimedia getting to know environments. As a consequence, as already stated, the photograph approximately the "actual" relevance of mastering styles stays unclear. Positive results of taking mastering styles under consideration while designing practice are nevertheless questionable.

Index of studying patterns (ILS)

The Index of studying styles was "designed to capture the most important mastering fashion differences among engineering students and provide a great foundation for engineering instructors to IADIS international convention on Cognition and Exploratory mastering in digital age formulate a coaching method that addresses the studying wishes of all students". The model shares commonalities with other popular mastering fashion approaches, e.g., studying fashion stock. In regards to the theoretical assumptions made above, the ILS is explicitly stated no longer to encompass 'either-or categories' of its bipolar dimensions. All scales are to be understood as continua, which means that a scholar's cognitive choice to getting to know on a given ILS scale can be both pretty properly balanced, fairly, or strongly distinctive for one of the alternative pole of the dimensions. The four bipolar ILS dimensions may be defined as follows:

• Energetic – Reflective. Energetic freshmen tend to collect and apprehend statistics great if they have interaction with it actively and strive things out, e.g., using debating, bringing something to software, or via coaching-lower back. Reflective newbies favor considering new things respectively statistics for themselves first. The motto of active inexperienced persons is "let us try to see how it works", even as reflective novices pursue the principle "permit me first think carefully about it".

• Sensual – Intuitive. Sensing inexperienced persons tend to do properly in gaining knowledge of records and to observe set up approaches and procedures whilst fixing troubles. They're more goal-orientated, cautiously and patiently, however keep away from complex issues or surprises. Intuitive inexperienced persons on the other hand choose to discover exclusive possibilities and relationships and modern strategies. They can better grasp new ideas, work commonly faster and greater revolutionary and feature much less trouble with abstract standards and mathematical expressions. But, they tend to keep away from rote getting to know, repetition, exercises, and fixed schemes.

• Visual – Verbal. Visible learners do not forget greater of what they have got seen, e.g. images, diagrams, flow charts, movies, demonstrations, and so on. Alternatively, verbal newcomers prefer linguistically primarily based on gaining knowledge of this is written and spoken records or declarations. however, it needs to be stated at this point, that no matter the deviation of someone, the mixture of visual and verbal facts is maximum conductive.

• Sequential – worldwide. Sequential newcomers tend to understand higher by way of studying in logical linear steps, where every step is the logical outcome of the previous step. In comparison, international newcomers rather generally tend to make massive steps and collect extraordinary material and facts quasi-random and without the popularity of contexts and relationships, however, all at once, they apprehend the complete context.

Mental fashions as a foundation for reading hassle solutions

A mental version is an idiosyncratic representation of a reality or a component, of ideas or extra typically an ideational framework about something interesting inside the international. Mental fashions, as varieties of representations, rely on language and use symbolic pieces and approaches of expertise to construct a heuristic for a scenario. The principle of intellectual fashions follows the constructivist assumption that human information is always fragmentary and therefore regarded as dynamic, due to the fact it's far continuously multiplied and/or changed. For this reason, intellectual fashions characteristic as internal models of the out of doors global and convey subjective plausibility. About trouble solving tactics, research display a robust correlation between powerful mental modeling and the answer to complex problems. Consistent with Dörner's (1976) issues are characterized by way of three components: 1.) an unsatisfying actual nation, 2.) a preferred target state, and three.) a barrier that presently inhibits the intellectual transformation of the actual to the target kingdom. The larger this barrier is the extra complex the problem it seemed. The definition of trouble fixing processes clarifies the importance of intellectual fashions for successful hassle solving. Funke (2003) states that problem-solving questioning is characterized by way of filling the gaps inside a movement plan that can't be done robotically. For that purpose, a mental model is constructed which bridges the manner from the initial to the intention kingdom. Ifenthaler (2010, 2008) describes the externalization of inner cognitive structures as a deliberate communication technique of mental models. Every time the statement of information illustration is vital, externalization is necessary because direct access is not viable. As a result, strategies to degree expertise representations result from the conscious conversation of mental fashions, e.g., through thinking aloud, text writing, building graphs, information, or idea maps. This outcome in the differentiation among internal knowledge representations and external, so known as re-representations. The re-representations are communicated on the idea of the mental representations and ok sign and symbol systems. Therefore, the answer to a phenomenon in question is represented by using an individual mental model, and consecutively the representation of this model because of a conversation method allows the research of person problem answers.

Perfection – a Pendant to reflection

Professional self-regulated learners are stated to be powerful in actively influencing and adjusting all mastering procedures of the three key additives of gaining knowledge of cognition, metacognition, and motivation. Metacognitive methods are attributed to play a superior function, due to the fact metacognition can function as a device to modify the additional dimensions of getting to know and consequently optimize their particular components in regards to the goals set. Zimmerman's model of self-law (2008, 2000, 1998) indicates cyclic-reflective know-how of self-regulation. Three stages are recognized analogous to an input-output device, where each result of an action collection affects the following. At the start of a studying cycle stands the forethought segment. Pintrich (2000) provides "making plans and activation" to the label of that preliminary degree of every self-regulated learning cycle. In standard, it can be characterized as a practical section, accompanied using the actional and submit-actional phase. Consequently, the mastering segment of movement is enclosed using a preparatory and a publish-processing phase. In phrases of metacognition, the differentiation among prospective and retrospective monitoring may be carried out to the encircling phases, represented by way of mental constructs: mirrored image is primarily characterized to refer to something experienced, for that reason suiting the postnational segment, whereas reflection is relating to future activities and based totally on prospective thoughts, hence suiting the practical segment. The latter, subsequently, is to be understood because of of of of the pendant mirrored image. Regarding what Dewey (1933) described when introducing the concept of the mirrored image – human beings examine more from reflection on their very own experience than from the enjoy itself – reflection may be characterized as reflection's inverted counterpart: a tool for optimizing next enjoy, respectively problem-fixing and mastering methods. Consequently, reflection includes the activation of principal learning relevant structures (e.g., content material understanding, strategies, values, hobby, and so forth.) which are prospectively regarded to be useful for future performance.

Activates as an Educational Intervention in Self-Regulated learning Environments

Outside educational interventions must be used at the right time and the proper quantity, so that the self-regulatory gaining knowledge of procedure isn't disturbed, but rather supported. Academic designers want to develop studying environments imposing the proper degree of outside- and strength of mind which poses no longer an easy project. Consequently, studies have gained a large hobby in investigations of call for-orientated help and help interventions (scaffolds). One unique shape of scaffolds is shaped by using instructional cues, so-referred to as activates. Within the context of self-regulated getting to know they appear as effective because they function as a "brief-time intervention" and only constitute a minimal external control mechanism. Davis (2003) and Ifenthaler (2012) differentiate among varieties of prompts: accepted and directed. Ordinary activates comply with the principle "forestall and suppose". A widespread spark-off encourages learners to break the modern-day gaining knowledge of or trouble fixing procedures for a moment and reflect. Right here, the object of reflection is left absolutely open. There aren't any unique issues highlighted or instructed by way of the activation. Directed activates, on the other hand, follow the precept "prevent and reflect on consideration on. Davis (2003) states that the more particular directed prompts should be greater powerful than widespread, unspecific activates if they have been correctly applied within the mastering or problem-solving surroundings. It's far assumed here that folks who do not have the necessary know-how and capabilities required for the preferred deliberations – reflective or reflective – need further coaching at the side of the setoff. Directed activates include such an instruction, as an example, in form of complete sentences. Ifenthaler (2012) alternatively discovered common activates to be more efficient in comparison to directed prompts, due to the fact they leave a positive amount of autonomy for self-regulative acting. Still, Ifenthaler (2012) agrees with Davis' (2003) argument that directed activates can be more green for newbies that do not have already got a selected set of earlier know-how and skills.

Cognitive processing

Cognitive processing aimed toward identifying a way to acquire a purpose is referred to as hassle solving. In problem fixing, the hassle solver seeks to plot a technique for remodeling trouble from its modern-day nation right into the desired country when a solution is not right now apparent to the trouble solver. Therefore, the hallmark of problem-solving is the discovery of a brand new method for addressing a problem. This definition has three parts: (1) hassle solving is cognitive—that is, it happens internally inside the mind (or cognitive system) and should be inferred in a roundabout way from conduct; (2) hassle fixing is a process—it includes the manipulation of understanding representations (or sporting out intellectual computations); and (three) hassle solving is directed—it's miles guided via the desires of the trouble solver.

The definition of trouble fixing covers a huge range of human cognitive sports, such as educationally relevant cognition—figuring out how to manage one's time, writing an essay on a selected subject matter, summarizing the primary factor of a textbook phase, solving an arithmetic phrase hassle, or figuring out whether a scientific idea is legitimate by using conducting experiments.

A problem takes place whilst a hassle solver has a goal however, to begin with, does no longer realizes a way to achieve the intention. This definition has three components: (1) the present-day state—the problem begins in a given nation; (2) the purpose kingdom—the problem solver needs the trouble to be in a special country, and hassle solving is required to transform the problem from the contemporary (or given) state into the aim country, and (three) barriers—the hassle solver does now not recognize the best solution and a powerful answer approach is not obvious to the hassle solver.

In keeping with this definition, a hassle is personal, so that a situation that could be a problem for one character may not be a hassle for every other person. As an example, "3 + 5 = ___" is probably trouble for a six-12 months-old child whose motives, "let's examine. I'm able to take one from the 5 and deliver it to the three. That makes four plus 4, and I realize that 4 plus four is eight." but, this equation isn't always a problem for a grownup who is aware of the ideal answer.

Types of issues

Routine and non-routine troubles. It's far standard to differentiate between habitual and non-routine troubles. In habitual trouble, the problem solver knows an answer method and best wishes to hold it out. As an instance, for most adults the hassle "589 × 45 = ___" is recurring if they recognize the method for multicolumn multiplication. Recurring troubles are from time to time known as physical activities, and technically do not healthy the definition of the problem stated above. While academic activity intends to sell all of the aspects of hassle fixing (such as devising a solution plan), then non-routine issues (or sporting events) are appropriate.

In a non-routine hassle, the problem solver does no longer start starts realizing a way for fixing the hassle. as an instance, the subsequent problem (pronounced using Robert Sternberg and Janet Davidson) is non-routine for the majority: "Water lilies double in the vicinity every twenty-four hours. At the beginning of the summertime, there's one water lily on the lake. It takes sixty days for the lake to be absolutely protected with water lilies. On what day is the lake half of included?" in this trouble, the problem solver must invent a solution approach primarily based on working backward from the ultimate day. Based on this method, the hassle solver can ask what the lake might appear like on the day earlier than the final day, and finish that the lake is half-covered on the fifty-ninth day.

Nicely defined and ill-described problems. It's also standard to differentiate between well-described and sick-described issues. In a well-defined hassle, the given state of the trouble, the purpose kingdom of the problem, and the allowable operators (or actions) are every without a doubt certain. as an example, the subsequent water-jar hassle (adapted from Abraham Luchins) is an example of a properly described trouble: "I can give you three empty water jars; you could fill any jar with water and pour water from one jar into any other (until the second jar is complete or the first one is empty); you could fill and pour as in many instances as you like. Given water jars of size 21, 127, and three devices and an infinite delivery of water, how can you purchased precisely 100 gadgets of water?" that is a nicely-defined hassle due to the fact the given state is truly precise (you have empty jars of length 21, 127, and 3), the purpose nation is simply specified (you need to get 100 devices of water in one of the jars), and the allowable operators are really distinctive (you could fill and pour in step with unique methods). properly-defined problems can be either habitual or non-routine; in case you do now not have preceding enjoy with water jar issues, then finding the answer (i.e., fill the 127, pour out 21 once, and pour out three twice) is a non-routine hassle.

In sick-described trouble, the given state, goal state, and/or operations aren't really targeted. As an example, within the hassle, "Write a persuasive essay in want of year-round schools," the aim kingdom isn't clean due to the fact the standards for what constitutes a "persuasive essay" are vague and the allowable operators, such as the way to get entry to resources of records, aren't clean. Most effective the given state is obvious—a blank piece of paper. Unwell-described troubles may be habitual or non-routine; if one has extensive experience in writing then writing a quick essay like this one is a recurring hassle.

Procedures in problem fixing

The procedure of problem-solving may be damaged down into two main phases: trouble representation, in which the problem solver builds a coherent mental representation of the problem, and trouble solution, in which the trouble solver devises and incorporates out a solution plan. hassle representation can be damaged down similarly into trouble translation, wherein the hassle solver translates each sentence (or photograph) into an inner mental representation, and trouble integration, in which the hassle solver integrates the statistics right into a coherent intellectual illustration of the trouble (i.e., a mental version of the state of affairs defined within the hassle). Trouble answer can be damaged down similarly into answer planning, wherein the trouble solver devises a plan for how to resolve the trouble, and answer execution, wherein the problem solver consists of out the plan using conducting solution behaviors. although the four strategies of hassle fixing are listed sequentially, they'll arise in many different orderings and with many iterations within the path of solving the trouble.

As an instance, don't forget the butter problem described by way of Mary Hegarty, Richard Mayer, and Christopher Monk: "At fortunate, butter charges sixty-five cents according to stick. this is cents less consistent with a stick than butter at Vons. if you want to shop for four sticks of butter, how lots will you pay at Vons?" inside the trouble translation phase, the problem solver can also mentally constitute the first sentence as "lucky = 0.65," the second sentence as "fortunate = Vons - 0.02," and the third sentence as "4 × Vons = ____." In trouble integration, the trouble solver may additionally construct a mental quantity line with fortunate at zero.65 and Vons to the proper of fortunate (at 0.67); or the problem solver can also mentally combine the equations as "4 × (fortunate + 0.02) = ____." A key insight in problem integration is to understand the proper relation between the fee of butter at fortunate and the price of butter at Vons, specifically that butter prices greater at Vons (even though the keyword within the problem is "less"). In solution planning, the trouble solver may additionally destroy the problem into parts, consisting of: "First add 0.02 to 0.65, then multiply the result through four." In solution executing, the hassle solver contains out the plan: 0.02 + 0.65 =0.67, 0.67 × 4 = 2.68. In addition, the hassle solver should display the hassle-solving procedure and make adjustments as wished.

Teaching for hassle solving

A venture for educators is to educate in methods that foster meaningful getting to know rather than rote learning. Rote instructional techniques sell retention (the capacity to solve problems which might be equal or fantastically similar to the ones offered in instruction), however, no longer trouble fixing transfer (the capacity to apply what changed into learned to novel troubles). For example, in 1929, Alfred Whitehead used the time period inert know-how to refer to mastering that cannot be used to solve novel issues. In contrast, meaningful academic techniques sell both retention and transfer.

In a classic example of the difference between rote and meaningful learning, the psychologist Max Wertheimer (1959) described two approaches of coaching college students to compute the area of a parallelogram. Inside the rote technique, students learn to measure the bottom, measure the peak, and then multiply base instances' peaks. Students taught with the aid of the $A = b \times h$ approach are capable of finding the place of parallelograms formed like the ones given in training (retention trouble) however common parallelograms or different shapes (a switch hassle). Wertheimer used the time period reproductive questioning to refer to trouble solving wherein one blindly consists of out a formerly found out manner. In comparison, inside the significant technique, students analyze by way of slicing the triangle from one quit of a cardboard parallelogram and attaching it to the alternative quit to shape a rectangle. as soon as students have the perception that a parallelogram is only a rectangle in cover, they could compute the vicinity because they already recognize the manner for finding the location of a rectangle. Students taught through the insight method perform well on both retention and transfer issues. Wertheimer used the time period effective questioning to consult problem fixing wherein one invents a brand new method to fixing unique trouble.

Educationally applicable Advances in trouble fixing
Latest advances in instructional psychology factor to the role of domain-particular information in problem-solving–

which includes know-how of specific strategies or problem types that observe to a specific subject. Three critical advances were: (1) the coaching of hassle-solving methods, (2) the nature of professional problem solving, and (3) new conceptions of individual variations in hassle-fixing capacity.

The teaching of trouble-fixing processes. A crucial boost in educational psychology is cognitive approach training, which incorporates the coaching of hassle-fixing techniques. For example, in undertaking Intelligence, essential college children successfully discovered the cognitive techniques wished for fixing issues much like the ones discovered on intelligence checks. In Instrumental Enrichment, students who had been categorized as mentally retarded learned cognitive approaches that allowed them to reveal massive improvements on intelligence checks.

Expert hassle fixing. Another critical improvement in educational psychology issues differences between what experts and beginners realize in given fields, such as medication, physics, and computer programming. as an instance, professional physicists tend to save their know-how in huge incorporated chunks, whereas novices tend to shop their know-how as isolated fragments; expert physicists tend to attention to the underlying structural characteristics of physics phrase issues, while beginners awareness of the surface functions; and professional physicists tend to work ahead from the givens to the aim, whereas novices work backward from the purpose to the givens. Studies on knowledge have implications for expert schooling as it pinpoints the varieties of domain-precise understanding that specialists need to research.

Character differences in trouble-solving capability. This 1/3 develop issues new conceptions of intellectual ability primarily based on variations within the manner humans technique information. For instance, humans may range cognitively–including their choices for visible as opposed to verbal representations, or for impulsive as opposed to reflective methods to trouble solving. Rather, people can also vary within the pace and performance with which they carry out precise cognitive processes, along with creating a mental contrast or retrieving a piece of data from reminiscence. as opposed to characterizing intellectual capacity as an unmarried, monolithic capability, the latest conceptions of highbrow capacity consciousness at the role of a couple of differences in records processing.

Chapter Four

Reflection and Learning

Getting to know via mirrored image

Maximum of us go through existence viewing our reviews as isolated, unrelated activities. We also view those happenings in reality as the experiences they are, no longer as opportunities for studying. Psychologists consult with this kind of life view as an "episodic hold close of fact" and it isn't a dependency we want to pass along to kids. As an alternative, we want students to get into the addiction of linking and building which means from their experiences. Such work calls for reflection.

Mirrored image has many aspects. For example, reflecting on work enhances its meaning. Reflecting on stories encourages perception and complex getting to know. We foster our own growth whilst we manipulate our gaining knowledge of, so some reflection is first-class performed alone. Reflection is likewise more suitable, however, whilst we ponder our studying with others.

Reflection entails linking a cutting-edge enjoy to previous learnings (a technique referred to as scaffolding). Reflection additionally entails drawing forth cognitive and emotional records from numerous resources: visual, auditory, kinesthetic, and tactile. To reflect, we ought to act upon and procedure the data, synthesizing and evaluating the information. Ultimately, reflecting additionally method applying what we've found out to contexts past the unique conditions in which we learned something.

Valuing mirrored image

The art of coaching is the artwork of helping discovery. Instructors who sell reflective lecture rooms ensure that scholars are absolutely engaged within the procedure of making that means. They organize coaching so that scholars are the producers, no longer simply the customers, of know-how. To first-class guide youngsters within the conduct of reflection, those instructors technique their position as that of "facilitator of that means making."

Inside the role of facilitator, the instructor acts as a middleman between the learner and the gaining knowledge of, guiding every student to method the getting to know hobby strategically. The trainer enables each scholar to screen character progress, assemble which means from the content material discovered and from the system of mastering it, and apply the learnings to different contexts and settings. Mastering turns into a continual procedure of enticing the mind that transforms the mind.

Unfortunately, educators do not frequently ask students to mirror their mastering. Thus, whilst students are asked to reflect on an assignment, they may be stuck in a quandary: "What am I presupposed to do? How do I 'reflect'? I've already finished this task! Why do I need to reflect on consideration on it anymore?"

In reaction to our questions, college students who are inexperienced with mirrored images provide easy answers such as "This turned into a clean task!" or "I surely enjoyed doing this challenge." If we want students to get in the dependency of reflecting deeply on their work—and if we need them to apply the behavior of thoughts which includes applying past expertise to new situations, considering thinking (metacognition), and ultimately open to non-stop learning—we ought to teach them techniques to derive rich meaning from their studies.

Putting the Tone for mirrored image

maximum lecture rooms can be labeled in one in all two ways: active and a piece noisy, with college students engaged in arms-on work; or teacher-oriented, with students taking note of a presentation or quietly operating on man or woman obligations. Every of these teaching environments sets a tone and an expectation. As an instance, when college students work actively in businesses, we ask them to apply their "six-inch" voices. When we ask them to attend to the teacher, we additionally request that they turn their "eyes front." once they work for my part at their desks, we ask them no longer to trouble other rookies.

Instructors must signal a shift in tone once they ask students to mirror their gaining knowledge. Reflective instructors help students remember the fact that the scholars will now appear again as opposed to passing forward. they may take a ruin from what they have been doing, step far from their work, and ask themselves, "What have I (or we) learned from doing this activity?" some instructors use music to signal the change in thinking. Others ask for silent wondering before college students write about a lesson, a mission, or other study room project.

Inside the reflective lecture room, instructors invite college students to make meaning from their reviews overtly in written and oral form. They make an effort to invite college students to reflect on their learnings, to compare meant with real consequences, to assess their metacognitive strategies, to analyze and draw causal relationships, and to synthesize meanings and follow their learnings to new and novel situations. Students recognize they may now not "fail" or make a "mistake," as the ones phrases are normally defined. Instead, reflective students understand they can produce non-public insight and analyze from all their reviews.

Guiding pupil reflection

It is a reflective method to mentally wander through wherein we were and to attempt to make a few experiences out of it. Maximum lecture rooms are oriented more to the prevailing and the future than to the past. Such an orientation method that students (and instructors) locate is simpler to discard what has befallen and to transport on without taking inventory of the seemingly isolated reports of the beyond.

Teachers use many techniques to guide college students via a length of reflection. We offer several right here: discussions, interviews, wondering, and logs and journals.

Sometimes, encouraging mirrored images is as easy as inviting college students to think about their thinking. Students understand meaning-making is an essential purpose when the mirrored images will become the subject of dialogue. As an example, behavior discussions approximately students' trouble-fixing processes. Invite students to share their metacognition, reveal their intentions, detail their techniques for solving the trouble, describe their mental maps for monitoring their hassle-solving method, and replicate the method to decide its adequacy. in the course of those forms of rich discussions, college students learn how to listen to and explore the implications of every other's metacognitive strategies. The form of listening required at some point of such discussions also builds the habits of mind associated with empathy, flexibility, and patience.

Interviews

Interviews are another way to guide students to share reflections about their studying and their boom inside the behavior of thoughts. A teacher can interview a student, or students can interview classmates. Set apart time at the end of gaining knowledge of collection—a lesson, a unit, a college day, or a college year—to question every different approximately what has been learned. Manual college students to search for ways they can observe their learnings in future settings. Interviews also offer instructors and students opportunities to version and exercise an expansion of behavior: listening with expertise and empathy, questioning and speaking with readability and precision, and wondering and posing troubles.

Wondering

Well-designed questions—supported via a lecture room surroundings grounded in to agree with—will invite college students to expose their insights, understandings, and applications of their learnings and the behavior of mind. Right here are viable questions to pose with each pupil:

- As you replicate in this semester's work, which of the habits of thoughts were you maximum aware of to your own learnings?
- What metacognitive techniques did you use to display your performance of the habits of mind?
- Which addiction of thoughts will you focus on as you start your next mission?
- What insights have you gained because of using these conduct of mind?
- As you consider your destiny, how may that behavior of mind be used as a manual to your existence?

Logs and Journals

Logs and journals are every other tool for student mirrored images. Periodically ask students to reread their journals, comparing what they knew at the start of a studying sequence with what they know now. Ask them to choose giant learnings, envision how they might observe those learnings to future conditions, and decide on a motion plan to consciously regulate their behaviors.

Modeling reflection

Students want to stumble upon reflective role fashions. Many instructors locate such fashions in novels in which the characters take a reflective stance as they remember their moves. a selection of novels and films use the design element of reflection because of the way to inform a tale. as an example, in Marcel Proust's Swann's manner, the main man or woman is tormented by the odor of a "petite madeleine" that reminds him of his past. Proust makes use of this device to dig into the people beyond. In Mem Fox's Wilfrid Gordon McDonald Partridge, Wilfrid discovers that existence's meaning can come from the retrieval of effective memories. The reminiscences absolutely are given which means, however, through making them express to a person else.

Even though fictional function modeling is beneficial, students also need to peer adults—parents, teachers, and directors—to replicate their practice. Perhaps you can offer an instance out of your personal work. We offer here an excerpt from Bena Kallick's journal reflecting on a workshop consultation. She sent her mirrored image to the workshop members. Here's the excerpt:

Reflecting on the day, I am still mad at myself for not listening more carefully to your needs for the afternoon consultation. I desired to percentage a number of my mind with you. First, I discover that I can use the conduct of thoughts as one lens for reflection. As I reconsidered yesterday, there had been four behavior that I centered on: listening with understanding and empathy, wondering flexibly, coping with impulsivity, and last open to continuous studying.

Listening with expertise and empathy. One of the strengths in my work is my ability to live immersed within the work of others. I want with a purpose to listen to the surface text of the work, pay attention to the subtext of the individual (the context of the schoolroom, the persona of the instructor, the intentions and values that are expressed as the character gives the work), and make sure that my comments and critique are in track with the person that I hope may be capable to make use of them. I felt that our institution became tuned to the work that changed into presented and that I was able to model that degree of listening. As a result, I think that the presenters were capable of listening to their own work extra deeply.

The opposite 1/2 of my listening, but, became no longer as attuned. Patricia attempted to signify that we make time to proportion our own work in the afternoon, however, due to the fact I lunched with Michelle and became involved with some of the problems and issues she turned into running on, I misplaced some of my attitude in which the organization turned into. As a result, I jumped in with the plan to observe the possibility for "logo x" rubrics. Even though I solid the afternoon for the opportunity of your working on your personal rubrics, I located that nearly every person either labored on the general rubric (with electricity and commitment) or started to do their personal work for the study room. I idea that most people were using the time productively, and so I did no longer listen carefully to Patricia's issues. I ought to have lunched with Patricia and David, talked through what becomes in my head for the afternoon, and listened at that point for their examination of the organization and its wishes.

Wondering flexibly. I constantly pleasure myself on the degree to which I'm willing to shift plans and reply to the institution's instant needs. That power, but, also can end up a weak point—and I suppose that came about the day before today. Whilst Dan advised that we flow to developing outcomes that would work throughout the disciplines, I immediately went there without checking with the organization. Maybe that occurred due to the fact the question is of highbrow hobby to me right now and I also desired to work on it. I have been suffering from the way to expand a rubric that might be sufficiently rigorous and, at the identical time, descriptive sufficient to provide a fixed of standards for college kids that might show them what changed into anticipated irrespective of concern. Clean standards could address a query together with "Why can we want to jot down nicely if I'm in a technology class?" To me, these criteria are a giant part of building a mastering culture. I was exploring the usage of the standards when it comes to the conduct of mind—I will expand this notion extra absolutely in a moment.

Coping with impulsivity. Nicely, this is wherein the habits intersect and from time to time feel contradictory. I moved in no time with Dan's inspiration. I might say that I did not manage my impulsivity. Can you be both bendy and manipulate your impulsivity at an identical time? I suppose the way to do this is to check your movements. I have to have done so with the institution in preference to assuming I knew wherein to go. Had I managed my impulsive act thru a short take a look at the afternoon schedule, we would have long passed down the equal path, or a specific one, and as a minimum made the decision collectively.

Ultimate open to continue gaining knowledge of. I started out considering Evonne Goolagong. (She's a sincerely excellent tennis participant). What I continually renowned approximately her changed into her grace, agility, and widespread flexibility. She had all the strokes, and often what got in her manner of triumphing become that she did no longer make the proper preference of stroke for the event.) I suppose I'm at a point in my profession wherein I have many selections in my repertoire for each teaching scenario. Occasionally I do not take the time to think thru that's the proper preference for the event. I'm finding it easy to excuse impulsive behavior by considering it as bendy behavior. Due to the fact I am an "in the moment" teacher, I want to be aware of this extra than I've been lately. I'm grateful to you the day passed for reminding me of the importance of this dynamic for me to remain the instructor I imagine I would love to be!

After this specific reflection, Kallick labored with the academics to lay out their next session to better meet everyone's wishes. Sharing elements of the mirrored image delivered them to another degree of information as they worked together in a getting-to-know network. Reflection can bring the equal spirit of the network to your lecture room, too.

College students also examine a lot after they see examples of reflection from other students' journals. You may need to cull an expansion of examples to percentages. Here is a reflection from a set magazine written with the aid of college students from the Communications Academy at Sir Francis Drake high college in San Anselmo, California:

Today our group spent the maximum of the time reading articles and the ballot data pamphlet. We got all participated and had been open and informative. Our purpose seems to be the execution of the actual set of criteria for our venture.

We're passing around our notable magazine to write down what we want to do or improve on for ourselves. I want to work on analyzing. I locate myself analyzing sufficient to slip with the aid of however now not sufficient to be absolutely knowledgeable inside the subject. It takes plenty of time, so I want to locate some of that, too. I need it so that it will answer the questions I have requested with precision and accuracy. My stretch intention would be to do everything assigned to be finished and on time. If I start to slack off, simply kick my lower back into the vicinity …

I want to be greater patient. I also experience I speak lots and do not suggest to. I need to attempt to concentrate with expertise and empathy.

The scholars at University Heights faculty in New York town are required to reflect on the conduct of mind they've adopted after they gift their portfolios to a panel of judges. The subsequent excerpt is a reflection from one pupil:

Through "wondering seriously and questioning," we look at questions, myths, and even validated information. From that, we gain intelligence (getting to know from evidence, now not opinion) and reviews to find what we agree with to be the fact. …

I discovered the significance of training. Lack of understanding is a weak spot. It fogs the mind and blurs the human eye. The handiest information can clean our visions of this weakening lack of thought.

I found out the value of our pleasure. In my opinion, folks that were pressured to serve without pay were not slaves. They were captives to slaves of greed.

Now that I have this bolstered knowledge, I have to use it in my existence. However, the success of that challenge can simplest be judged with the aid of me. Best I recognize what is happiness and splendor in this mind and it will take me an entire lifetime to apply what I have found out to my life.

Developmental troubles

The work of educators at Croton simple school in Croton-on-Hudson, NY, suggests how the satisfaction of students' reflections changes as youngsters expand their studying and writing abilities. Whilst kindergartners were requested to reflect orally, they gave rich descriptions in their work. But as they evolved their writing capability and were encouraged to write their personal reflections, the reflections became much less descriptive. This variation puzzled the teachers till they found out that students are extra worried approximately spelling, punctuation, and other aspects of editing after they first learn to write. Due to the fact, students do no longer have a superb deal of fluency with their writing, they're greater restricted in what they describe.

In assessment, when assembly with the instructor, the kindergartners elaborated on what they wrote approximately their work. And once college students became greater fluent with their writing skills, they were capable of constituting their reflective mind more effortlessly.

Teaching college students how to replicate

First of all the students at Croton standard frequently offered stereotypical remarks together with "This changed into amusing!" or "I selected this piece of labor because it is my satisfactory." instructors realized that they needed to spend time teaching college students how to mirror. They requested college students, "What does a reflection appear like while it simply tells you something approximately they enjoy?" After significant discussion—and after considering fashions of a mirrored images from college students and posted authors—the students began to understand what turned into known as for. The mirrored image was not a time for testimonials approximately how suitable or horrific the experience turned into. As a substitute, the mirrored images become the time to don't forget what turned into discovered from the enjoyment. Reflection was a time to explain what college students saw of their very own work that modified, needed to alternate, or may need to be described so any other person may recognize its meaning.

The academics then summarized key statements that students made about their work when requested the query "What would I trade to make my work better?" college students from kindergarten thru second grade made comments such as those:

- I would upload to the picture.
- I'd use what I know to show extra within the image.
- I might upload what is lacking.
- I would be more careful.

Students in third and 4th grade made comments like these:

- I might correct.
- I might proofread.
- I might take note of conventions.
- I might amplify greater.
- I'd live to the issue.

Students' levels of reflection

Kindergarten
- Describes what is drawn.
- Specializes in the drawing.
- Feedback on realism.
- Shows interest (what scholar actually loves).
- Mentions use of color.
- Mentions use of letters.

- will pay attention to what letters spell.

1st Grade
- Specializes in conventions.
- Needs papers to have a neat appearance.
- Talks approximately what changed into favored in the drawing.

2nd Grade
- Makes a specialty of details.
- Focuses on hues.
- Indicates development of a concept.
- Pertains to content material of tale (how scholar feels approximately the content of what changed into written).

3rd–fifth Grade (gaining knowledge of-to-examine degree)
- Responds extensively to dictation.
- Starts evolved to write down through self.

Teachers used these terms to describe 3rd and 4th-grade students' writing as the lecturers pondered upon it:
- Makes use of humor.
- Talks approximately genre or form of writing.
- Attends to fashion (makes use of communication).
- Describes properly sufficient for a reader to photo what changed into written.
- Makes a specialty of the script.
- Focuses on the description.
- Offers data.
- Is thrilling.
- Works tough.
- Is thrilling.
- Attends to the reader.
- Is apparent.
- Does no longer drag writing out.

- Uses descriptive words.

Via this enjoyment, the academics realized that the questions they requested would possibly limit college students' responses. They reminded themselves that the cause of reflection is threefold:

- To assist college students to become more aware of their writing—what makes writing work and what does no longer.
- To help students take more duty for his or her writing—to recognize that writing must be understood through a target market and to learn how to expect a reader's reaction via self-assessment.
- To see a boom in writing over the college months and to be able to talk approximately that boom with college students' dad and mom.

Instructors emphasized to students that the reason for mirrored image turned into now not to develop a cautiously crafted piece of writing, however, to increase the ability for metacognition.

Sentence Stems

Sentence stems can stimulate reflections. Use them in conferences (in which mirrored images may be modeled), or positioned them on a sheet for students who pick out writing to leap-begin their reflections. Here are examples of viable sentence stems:

- I selected this piece of writing because …
- What absolutely surprised me about this piece of writing became …
- After I study my other portions of writing, this piece is

unique because …
- What makes this piece of writing strong is my use of …
- Right here is one instance from my writing to reveal to you what I imply.
- What I want to without a doubt work directly to make my writing higher for a reader is

Student choices

Students may additionally choose genuinely to explain what is going on within the writing in their personal manner. While college students set their goals, they may use their reflections as a basis for guiding their learning adventure. College students would possibly accumulate work at some point of the month as a part of a portfolio manner. Every sector could review the work in their series folders and pick one or portions to go into their portfolio. When they make those selections, they can take the opportunity to reflect on the reasons for his or her alternatives and to set goals for their next sector's work.

Building the Voices of mirrored image

The remaining motive of coaching reflection is to get students into the dependency of reflecting on their very own movements and constructing meaning from those studies. When they broaden the conduct of thoughts associated with reflection, they may hear each an inner and an external voice.

Voice of mirrored image.

Inner Voice

The inner voice of reflection is self-expertise. Self-understanding is tough to explain in detail, however, we will outline it as each what and the way we're wondering.

Self-understanding includes ways of thinking that won't be seen to us consciously. Given our tradition, students have an issue understanding that they want to have interaction in "self-speak." To help college students broaden the inner voice of reflection, they may be asked to do the following:

• Write a letter to themselves detailing what they found out from an enjoyment.

• Send themselves a letter of advice, reminding themselves of what to look out for the following time they do something.

• Interview themselves.

• Make a list of connections they see between their work and others' work. Consist of friends' work along with work that has been studied inside the lecture room.

• Report the stairs they undergo to clear up a problem. Guide them to touch upon how useful those steps were.

External Voice

College students listen to an external voice of mirrored image in others' comments, suggestions, exams, evaluations, and feedback. Outside sharing of reflections is vital due to the fact this sort of reflection multiplies the gaining knowledge of for every character. As students evaluate the learning events that have taken region, they give their learning new which means. The opportunity to share frequently validates a scholar's internal conversation. Right here are recommendations for assisting students to develop the capability for sharing their reflections:

• Sit down in a circle. Ask each person to percentage one reflection on the day's sports.

• Organize small-institution reflections wherein college students proportion their minds. Then ask a reporter to give the mind of the one to the whole magnificence.

• Invite students to percentage hassle-fixing strategies. Ask them to attend to what number of one-of-a-kind methods they can efficiently solve a hassle.

• Ask students to a percentage as a minimum one instance wherein they observed their group the usage of the behavior of thoughts.

At some stage in those study room experiences, teachers have the possibility to model the behavior of thoughts themselves. They can display evidence of top listening talents, explore for clarity and information, ask thoughtful questions, and percentage metacognitive wondering. Through enjoy and non-stop modeling, the class starts to learn how to use the conduct of mind in reflective conversations, which strengthens the transfer to the internal voice of mirrored image.

Documenting Reflections

Many teachers report reflective conversations as a manner of assessing progress with the habits of mind. As an instance, as referred to in chapter eleven, some instructors create a notebook tabbed with every pupil's call. They also preserve sticky labels near to hand. While a pupil makes a vast remark that indicates proof of using a dependency of mind, the teacher jots down the important thing phrases from the comment on a label and sticks the label on the tabbed page for that pupil. This file offers a rich source of records for a convention or a scholar file.

You would possibly also remember studying student journals and noting how pupil reflections are growing. Keep a document for each scholar with notes about whether the student has moved from superficial to in-intensity reflections. Signs of in-depth reflections include making unique reference to the gaining knowledge of occasion, imparting examples and elaboration, making connections to different getting to know, and discussing adjustments based on insights from this revel in.

Growing the habits of mind related to continuous increase and improvement calls for the capability to be self-reflective. As students replicate their studies, they benefit from critical evaluation statistics approximately how they understand the efficacy in their thinking.

A lot of us grow up contemplating errors as awful, viewing mistakes as proof of fundamental incapacity. This terrible questioning sample can create a self-pleasant prophecy, which undermines the mastering system. to maximize our mastering it is crucial to invite: "How are we able to get the maximum from every mistake we make?"

The reflective practitioner

Due to the current and future jobs marketplace described above, in which workers want to evolve to suit converting roles, continuous gaining knowledge is needed. Learning to study is consequently a crucial skill along with accepting responsibility for one's personal mastering and development. This is applicable at the same time as at university or college but also inside the global of work. Billett's research illustrates how the evolving courting among self and work influences powerfully the development of self-identity, self-consciousness, and personal agency. The mirrored image is part of this development and the improvement of reflective abilities assists with the procedure of understanding how to learn, and the recognition of the individual's centrality to their own learning. Reflecting on learning achievements can empower the learner to make shrewd selections about a way to flow beforehand with their gaining knowledge of desires. Working in the direction of turning into a reflective practitioner enhances what a worker can convey to their process position, in addition to the improvement of their destiny profession plans.

Employees can hone their reflective abilities as a way to seriously appraise what has been experienced through practice. This in turn allows them to improve ongoing exercise, by the usage of the records and knowledge they are gaining from enjoying. Billett (2011) reiterates the strength of experiential gaining knowledge of and emphasizes the breadth of its attainment, to consist of, work-primarily based getting to know (WBL), ships, and work placements (which can be a part of a piece incorporated getting to know program which include co-operative learning).
Studies indicate that this is best when it involves others and for this reason the hazard to collaborate and proportion ideas about modifications, changes, and new methods of running. Reflecting critically, and sharing the consequences of this, maybe horrifying and might motive emotions of vulnerability among the ones exposing their thoughts and findings; running in groups and networks with fellow people or other students can provide the aid and more than one enter had to assist address this and offer proof that the manner is worthwhile, even supposing it feels daunting in the beginning discusses this requirement for open-mindedness and willingness to listen to others and act upon criticism. The important thing

factor to consider is that even though lots of this questioning and hobby round reflection stem from academia this doesn't need to be educational questioning, it desires to be greater than theoretical or hypothetical. What makes a reflection on practice this sort of powerful tool is the combination of greater scholarly theorized thinking with practitioner's real-world reports and gaining knowledge of. The synergy created via the mixture of resources is based on exceptional factors. Brockbank and McGill (1998) sum this up in terms of an interplay between a practitioner's reports, feelings, and emotions, with their activities and achievements. Ideally, reflective practitioners will harness and combine the highbrow and the emotional with their operational practices. In preference to a one-dimensional reaction, this catalyst will produce an ongoing manner in which thinking, appearing, questioning, and collaborating are delivered together in a supportive combination, creating nuanced, clever responses and advanced effects.

These programs are designed to apprehend and renowned administrative center getting to know (i.e. applicable in subject place and the degree to the cutting-edge route of taking a look at) and have titles consisting of work-based studies; professional research; negotiated learning course and so forth. This means applicable studying already collected faraway from formal schooling can be documented and awarded credit score through established techniques and therefore assist the student to develop. that is one way to create suitable routes to HE-level qualifications for busy employees who need, or want, to have a look at and might provide them a time (and money) saving device; they will probably be required to undertake much fewer modules (therefore much fewer prices) and complete a long way much less campus attendance than a conventional full-time student. The popularity of earlier studying is broadly practiced internationally. Universities and faculties use procedures that facilitate a "credit score declare" (HE awards and qualifications include a certain wide variety of instructional credit). College students can be supplied with assistance in making this declare – however only the pupil knows the info of their beyond learning and therefore to achieve success in this declare college students should look lower back and significantly mirror on their past mastering. This self-audit is essential if the student is to gain the most credit viable. Challenge such activities helps active reflection on work sports. Adopting this reflection as an inherent part of continuously comparing, reviewing, and enhancing their performance, pleasure and results might be the appropriate outcome. it can be useful for students to method this talents audit as a non-public education needs analysis (TNA), something many work-primarily based rookies are familiar with. Combined with their growing educational skills, essential mirrored image encourages work-primarily based students to exchange practices in the place of business, for this reason improving their private overall performance, however also the general performance of their employer. Such organizational traits awareness at the getting to know that naturally takes place at work, and emphasize that each one range of worker are work-based beginners. It isn't a decrease stage or derogatory term however instead an illustration of lifelong learning. Many work-primarily based novices discover that, as learner employees, they're already the use of vital reflection in an intuitive manner without realizing and this will be very empowering for them because it affords a sturdy place to begin to enhance this competencies-set.

Teaching reflective competencies

coaching reflective abilities in academia has progressively grown in importance from robust beginnings in professions consisting of nursing it has become more obvious how useful the practice turned into for work-primarily based learners usually. Coaching reflective skills is starting to seem across the curriculum, with many exclusive forms of college students being requested to compile reflective essays, reviews, journals, logs, diaries, or portfolios as part of their assignments in UK universities. Assistance with this reflection is regularly observed in student handbooks, as part of induction days, by way of allowing access to past college students' successful reflective work and thru stated periods containing studying theories and styles, meta-cognition, self-analysis of strengths and weaknesses, and the writing of private statements

Hooked up WBL programs (which include the ones mentioned above) have long blanketed energetic reflection within the core modules; beginners might usually compile a series of brief narrative statements (500-1,000 words) wherein they purposefully replicate upon their studying approaches in the course of extraordinary work and take a look at activities. these statements are often converted into a "Portfolio of lively mirrored image", which incorporates their revel in of numerous modules, their cutting-edge and beyond sports, and their plans − all located inside a framework of private and professional improvement. Those activities will facilitate the improvement of reflective practitioners who can percentage their essential reflections and evaluation, together with their better-degree ideas, with their work colleagues. The goal of those modules is to create practitioners for whom it's miles the "norm" to constantly mirror, plan and broaden; mechanically revisiting the way wherein activities are conducted, rather than assuming that the "old manner is the nice".

Instructions given to students to assist them to mirror what they have done and learned, and on how they intend to build on that getting to know, regularly include illustrations of around layout based totally on the work of Kolb (1984) and Gibbs (1998). Kolb's (1984) model is based on his experiential gaining knowledge of theory and used extensively in schooling and training to inspire contributors to reflect on each concrete story and summary concept. This means that emotions and senses are used in addition to notion methods. Furthermore, interest is given to thinking about records, however additionally doing something with the information. Reflection is consequently no longer passive however leads to active experimentation, creativity, and development. Kolb shows that reflective commentary transforms concrete studies into getting to know reports. As practitioners forestall, suppose, replicate and remember they ask themselves questions inclusive of: "How am I able to use this information?" and "How will it help with my daily work responsibilities and beautify my work role?" The experimentation level assessments out new thoughts to help decide how and where the brand new mastering can be used practically. Kolb's cycle ought not to be used within the cyclical way it is usually reproduced, with each step, from revel into experimentation being accompanied. The cycle is non-stop and can be joined at any level. The mirrored image is extra iterative and messy than a neat circle shows. there may be a positive circularity to shifting thru the degrees of evaluation, studies, and mirror however it's miles ahead moving loop of inquiry – in place of a "closed off" or "fenced in" circle. To save you an emphasis on searching returned (despite this being wished) some prefer the term "reflecting forwards", which foregrounds the developmental nature of the manner.

Gibbs (1988) in addition developed the concept of a reflective cycle to inspire newcomers to systematically think about the stages of enjoyment or hobby. The headings he recommended to inspire debate around making feel of a situation, and its outcomes, which includes, what else might have been performed, what might be achieved special/better next time, and so forth, are description, emotions, assessment, evaluation, conclusion, movement plan.

One of the most crucial things that tutors of labor-based totally newcomers can do is increase excellent listening abilities. They need to concentrate and also respond accurately. This reaction might encompass prompts and encouragement in place of commands. There's no factor forcing ideas, plans, and priorities on a piece-based scholar, who is aware of their own place of business higher than you do. A dating built on respect and reciprocal getting to know needs to be fostered, instead of a greater conventional learner/teacher dating in which the teacher claims to keep the information that they may (or may not) filter out to the "empty" pupil.

Revealing factors of task activities, mind and ideas may be unnerving however as a scholar's self-belief and self-focus grow they may come to be greater willing to percentage factors in their exercise with their train. This can imply that the train in flip will need to increase their very own coaching techniques to encompass understanding a way to tease out crucial facts from their students. The crucial elements of this "teasing out" manner are the facets of the pupil's practice that align with the current course of the examination. Those facets need to be notion about, mentioned, and labored on the way to make future upgrades, via deliberate moves.

Simply mastering approximately idea and then trying to observe it afterward is increasingly more criticized. If tutors percentage their expertise and information of idea with the scholar-practitioners, they may be at once helping them to enhance their work exercise via showing the capacity of mixing know-how, studies, and understanding of the concept and running toward filling what Schon termed the "concept practice hole". Eraut (1994) stated that HE prioritizes clinical over expert knowledge and deemed "off the shelf" theories as not useful. The idea needs to be used and interrogated, which will transform and liven up it. That is mainly pertinent to work-primarily based novices who similarly locate "off the shelf" college publications not at all useful and rather require a miles extra tailor-made and man or woman, but collaborative studying experience.

While enjoy, studying, concept and practice are merged there is far more capability for innovation than viewing any of the factors one by one. Gray (2001, p. 24) suggests that reflecting actively and usefully is a process that generates the improvement of "a dynamic synergy and dialectic among academic learning and work-primarily based practice". The results are well worth the show walking their delicate tightrope among provoking students into wondering, searching returned, and being vital, whilst helping, encouraging, and guiding rather than telling. The traditional notion of information as being finite and capable of being owned or held by one celebration and exceeded directly to some other is more and more challenged. College students do now not come to university as empty buckets waiting to be stuffed up with what the lecturer knows already. Information is co-produced in all sorts of venues and all styles of ways and those WBL tutors' techniques grow to be the exact opposite of "filling empty buckets" fashion coaching and will instead be in comparison to a midwife role – with the show helping the scholar to provide beginning to what's already in them. Steerage may include such suggestions:

• Mirror strategically on wherein you have discovered via past stories;

• Remember that the hobby and the studying procedure are entwined – not separate entities;

• Replicate not simply on your contemporary study however more typically alongside your existence path;

• Make the maximum of your programs' guided self-audit – deal with it like a TNA;

• establish wherein exactly you're – in terms of profession, private development, and learning;

• acknowledge what you are already good at – as an instance "writing reports" – this feeds into academic writing, greater than you would possibly assume – so do no longer convince yourself that you recognize not anything about academia;

• Reflection makes you recognize that you already have a terrific base on which to build your next degree of improvement;

• Reflective skills can be "taught" and measured; and

• Come to be a reflective practitioner – actively attempt to constantly enhance your exercise.

Postmodern timescales

In HE-level WBL there may be a precise emphasis on searching returned. However, what experienced work-based totally learning tutors try and do, because the center to their interaction with work-based total college students, is well known what has been, is being and could be found out by hired students. This questions the "accurate" order of things, as there may be tons looking back, forth, and throughout, through the work-primarily based learner's experiential learning. This postmodern technique to studying can be visible as simultaneously releasing, because of the opportunities it gives and horrifying because it removes obstacles and the purported "protection", they bring about. Coaching improvements such as huge open online guides and flipping the lecture room similarly play with the order of mastering and prove that the order of studying and the location of expertise are flexible and changeable. WBL programs inevitably contain a non-public and expert "stocktake", an important element of this is "looking returned" to analyze beyond gaining knowledge of experiences. This could experience uncomfortable due to the fact many WBL college students are older than the average student and feel the need to "seize up"; they need or want this qualification (possibly others in their administrative center are graduates, or their profession has changed right into a graduate profession because they joined). No matter a few personnel having vast information and know-how they can start to experience insecure approximately being on a college path however now not being 18, with the same old instructional entry requirements. College students in no way enroll to appearance lower back; they want to transport forwards in the direction of a qualification. Being actually reflective takes time, it may be painful and is perpetually greater tough than college students expect; a few facets in their practice may additionally need to be "un-learned" or as a minimum amended. As Cox (2005, p. 461) states, "encouraging reflective practice in any respect stages is useful for students assignment any sort of work-based activity, even though there may be often resistance to the procedure and trouble in the initial improvement of the reflective and analytical skills required". That is why tutors must turn out to be facilitators and courses, and college students must learn how to consider their tutors, and often their peers inside the course cohort, so that you can be open and sincere with them, "To engage in reflective exercise, people want a feel of protection". It is all too easy for students to feel that tutors and peers are judging them, and possibly seeking to alter and amend their practice for less than altruistic reasons; the spirit of reciprocity ought to be highlighted.

Reflecting "in" and "on" motion

Postmodern concept disputes grand narratives and questions familiar dominant discourses and histories; this shows that time is not strictly linear, and nor do events manifest in any "correct" order or timescale. Reflection is extra all-encompassing than just "looking again". humans instinctively mirror on occasions, possibly to higher apprehend what has taken place and make the experience of it; the concept of getting to know from the beyond, particularly trying no longer to repeat mistakes is nicely set up. Schon noted this technique as, "reflecting on action", but additionally conceded that reflection does no longer need to prevent with looking lower back, useful although it's far to learn from enjoying in this way. It is possible to reflect on what's taking place inside the gift moment, within the context of mind and emotions as they occur. Schon summarizes this as, "reflection in action", and points out its expediency, "mirrored image in motion is wherein we may also reflect inside the midst of movement without interrupting it. Our wondering serves to reshape what we're doing while we are doing it". There are a few overlaps right here with the standards of mindfulness that can be really worth exploring. one of the main motives for polishing reflective abilities is that its miles these skills that enable wise and knowledgeable evaluation of how our different capabilities are doing. Without a few honest mirrored images, how would all and sundry understand that they had to polish, as an instance, their time management or organizational skills? Aside from noticing that things frequently seem to be going badly.

By using consciously focusing automated reflection into a dependent reaction its usefulness is maximized, encouraging the reflector to end up a reflective and self-aware man or woman. This means looking both forwards and backward (and now and then sideways) to make connections with current undertakings. This kind of evaluation can feel fragmented and disjointed, that is every day; the technique is making use of the expertise which lies deep within (tacit know-how) – so deep it's far frequently taken without any consideration and not explicitly stated, but it's miles the data people use to make instinctive selections primarily based upon accrued information from past movements and enjoy. Eraut (1994) discusses the subtle nuances among the tacit, that which is implicitly acknowledged and stated, in place of that is explicitly talked about. Because the mirrored image is a critical part of private development, HE WBL programs encourage freshmen to be actively and analytically reflective.

Lacan and identity approaches

The mirrored image starts to evolve nearly as quickly as we're born and has always, even though subliminally, stimulated how we view ourselves and outline our identities and profile. Lacan's (1977) theories round, "the replicate level" center at the idea that once humans have visible their mirrored image (as a toddler) they increase a superior self-focus and begin to view themselves otherwise. In place of the disjointed arms and legs we look down upon as a small child, we start to consider ourselves as a whole entity. The mirrored image is carefully tied to how we view ourselves both physically and mentally. By using actively considering our thoughts and actions we turn out to be aware of the electricity of reflective wondering as a device for non-stop development and this glaringly has implications beyond the non-public. If used effectively and purposefully, the mirrored image helps ongoing personal and expert learning; developing and developing practitioners capable of demonstrating their development closer to getting to know consequences and required requirements, while also offering a shape wherein to make feel in their gaining knowledge of, so principles and theories grow to be embedded in exercise, even as steady thought and innovation are concurrently fostered for upgrades to take vicinity in a continuous cycle of enhancement.

Mirrored image as an improvement tool

Do this workout – consider a time while an experience and its consequences have had an impact on your moves – this can manifest all the time but we do no longer always well known the process. Learning, especially inside the place of job, does no longer continually arise as a "light bulb second", it could be difficult to pinpoint because of its sluggish and ongoing nature. Because of this, it's far regularly tough to track lower back where that learning came from, and you could even warfare to recall while you did now not understand how to do a positive aspect. In this sluggish studying manner, you do expand abilities – but you do now not continually deliver your self-credit for them or well-known when and where you use them or when they might want to sharpen. Complete the grid below with a state of affairs or happening – it is probably from work, examine or your private existence. What become the final results? Became it deemed a fulfillment? Did you research something? Did you convert your techniques and thoughts because you evaluated your enjoyment? questioning and thinking about our gaining knowledge of reviews is an exceedingly effective way to expand destiny techniques, approaches, and techniques as a way to construct competencies to address future comparable conditions, as well as similarly improving the capabilities which made you successful on this occasion. Exercises like this are designed to make you suspect severely about past actions, in the context of what's occurring within the present and what might also show up within the destiny. Structuring a reflective response to an event embeds the right practice for destiny continuous expert and private development activities. developing an ongoing ethos of reflection way that a man or woman starts evolved to routinely project and query why obligations had been undertaken surely in place of how they have been achieved, and they may turn out to be carried out at recognizing that they are getting to know and constructing skills constantly; it is not a standalone system. Employers have plenty to benefit from an encouraging group of workers to actively mirror their work practices, as Cox (2005, p. 471) claims, "learning through work" is vital to the complete reflective practice manner and can provide precious possibilities for man or woman motion research within the work context". Barnett (1997) describes the traditional view of HE where important questioning and all things cerebral are championed and prioritized. He goes on to signify that the development of accurate reflective practice will assist to disperse this perception of criticality from institution to individual, an action he feels is essential inside the method of helping professional employees to increase themselves, and adopt the perception of getting to know constantly from one's own practice, for continuous self-development. This concept may be applied to all professions and work sports, as it lets in for man or woman complexities and traits.

Whilst reflective practice can be a solitary hobby, peers have a particular role to play in assisting and supporting each other. This might be executed on a one-to-one foundation through "buddying" or in an extra formal mentoring association, in which pairs are determined the usage of appropriate expertise and enjoy as a manual as opposed to seniority or management fame, as an instance ex-WBL college students can be used to mentor new WBL college students. As a substitute, a mentor can be appointed from the scholar's place of job, or zone. this can be a colleague, manager, or line supervisor and does now not want to be a person running at once with the student even though on occasion this might be beneficial; judgments want to be made for individuals' cases but the mentor wishes to be someone the pupil feels they can talk their anxieties honestly and appropriately with. Mentors can end up inspirational position fashions.

Movement mastering sets and groups of practice also are established methods of "learner to learner" aid. Inside such groups and networks college students can discover problems bobbing up from reflective practice with their peers and make use of debate and dialogue in secure and supportive surroundings. this could be helpful when the mirrored image brought on using what is taking place at work is contradictory, or becoming too challenging and as opposed to empowering the work-based learner, it is traumatic them. Having a supportive organization to discuss this with could make all the difference. The ethos of action gaining knowledge of this concept and claims that guide and insightful thinking from peers can help the worker to move past what looks as if a blockage, to constructive and active reflection. This is especially useful if a learner feels they cannot talk about what's bothering them with colleagues at work. They can experience security in a non-judgmental CoP wherein they're all operating confidentially. one of the other main benefits of taking element in such CoP is that a tremendous deal of mastering happens socially with other people and at the same time as a whole lot of reflective practice can be undertaken alone it's miles greater efficient to percentage the getting to know results of it with others – the getting to know might have passed off already – via enjoy at work – but it may come to lifestyles and accept meaning thru sharing it with others who use and adapt it. Such sharing additionally lets in for unique cultural and expert translations to complement and remodel the getting to know, taking it to many different and new ranges.

Chapter Five

Self-Regulated Learning Environment

"Self-regulated studying is - an active, positive procedure wherein inexperienced persons set dreams for his or her learning and then try to monitor, regulate, and manage their cognition, motivation, and behavior, guided and constrained via their desires and the contextual capabilities inside the environment."

Self-regulatory, self-reliant gaining knowledge of as an idea stems from motivational theories of gaining knowledge of. Studying styles, metacognition, and theories relating to the self also are influential in self-sustaining learning. Azevedo (2009) argues that mastering makes use of numerous self-regulatory methods. He talks of planning knowledge activation, metacognitive monitoring, law, and mirrored image. Schunk and Zimmerman (1997) at once connected motivation to the idea of self-regulation. Self-regulated novices are intrinsically encouraged and self-reliant individuals who are proactive in pursuing their own goals for or her getting to know and who take control of the manner in their getting to know.

Self-regulated studying (SRL) is an active, optimistic system and one that requires support, scaffolding, and express coaching as the man or woman's self-regulatory practices broaden. Zimmerman (2002) believes self-regulated freshmen are more likely to be triumphant academically, as well as being extra constructive approximately their future, highlighting SRL's importance for lifelong mastering Dignath (2008) determined that kids and young humans possessing better levels of SRL are more likely to prevail than those with lower stages are, demonstrating the essential function that SRL plays in schooling. Newbies with superior self-regulatory competencies tend to be extra prompted academically and reveal effective studying ability. Winne (1997) sees young rookies as self-regulated when they're able to adapt their techniques to gaining knowledge. Self-law is a skill that can be taught and learned through "aim-directed engagement." newbies who are taught self-regulatory abilities and who are endorsed to evaluate their work via reflection and set studying desires can develop character strategies to be able to prove to be successful in furthering their mastering.

The model and the procedure of growing SRL in faculties is a similar system at university for the scholar instructors, for you to be outlined in a later segment. The manner of helping newbies in developing SRL in faculties entails specific preparation for the student teachers.

The center of the model is worried about the learner information how they examine, the manner they study, and the way they system statistics. The notion of mastering a way to analyze is key in self-regulation. This charts the motion of studying as no longer being as involved with the getting to know of facts as a whole lot approximately studying the capabilities required to learn. The center layer is the law of the learning system. That is the ability of the freshmen to direct their personal studying. For instance, this concerned a category of nine-year-vintage children deciding on their own choice of explorer to analyze for his or her unit on Exploration. The out of doors layer of the model is worried about the law of the self and intention putting. Boekaerts (1999) especially references in my opinion chosen goals. Self-regulated newcomers ought to be able to choose and be dedicated to dreams for his or her mastering. This practice could need careful modeling, scaffolding, and instruction as effective purpose putting is a skill, which could want to be advanced through the scholars. This deposit also includes strategies and reflection as simply self-regulated freshmen will have advanced their very own strategies for mastering independently and will certainly reflect on the system of studying. Self-regulated learning embraces these three areas and links all the circles inside the version. Unlike some fashions, there is not a sense of development thru the layers, more a feeling that a simply independent learner may have developed all three regions. Within the Exploration unit, the youngsters learned the capabilities worried in creating a presentation approximately their selected explorer to proportion with the magnificence on the give up of the unit. The abilities of notice taking had been also explicitly taught and at the fruits of the unit the children gave their personal presentations and the relaxation of the class took notes. The summative evaluation for this unit becomes a quiz on all the explorers in which the kids could confer with their notes to reply to the questions. After the unit, there was a mirrored image finished personally by way of the inexperienced persons who identified skills they excelled at as well as areas they needed to enhance within the next unit. These areas became their mastering goals.

The technique model has been adapted to mirror my doctoral awareness at the number one section of education. I have added the primary emergent SRL region reflecting a stage of explicit training and scaffolding so as for younger newcomers to expand their self-regulatory exercise. Vygotsky (1986) believed that metacognition is not found out in kids until adolescence. He alleged that youngsters may want to master the guidelines for guiding their personal interest, thought, and behavior but that this mastery does no longer become absolutely conscious until the children are capable of reflecting on consideration on the regulations themselves, because of this considering their very own thinking. But, Perry's later studies (1998) examined younger children's self-regulatory practices when writing. She determined that they're indeed capable of handling their personal learning. Perry (1998) mentioned that the seven and eight-year-olds in her examination displayed a focus on their very own questioning strategies and were able to live targeted on the task in hand, therefore more youthful newbies could reply to self-regulatory training.

The adapted Boekaerts' model.
In this phase, reference could be made to the Metacognition and Self-Regulated learning steerage report (2018) from the (training Endowment foundation, 2018). This record presents some of the recommendations for a teaching framework for primary-aged youngsters to analyze metacognitive and SRL competencies, techniques, and practices, a number of these suggestions fit with the areas of the adapted model.
Emergent SRL

In my revised model the new "Emergent Self-regulation mastering" center is in which the skills, techniques, and practices vital to the improvement of self-sufficient learners are initiated, modeled, and explicitly taught by using the teacher. The model is regarded from the middle to the outdoor as growing independence for the learner and diminishing help from the teacher as self-law will increase, this is developmental and now not age-related. The trainer models the procedure of observing taking for instance the use of a mind map, then the kids practice this layout. Over the direction of some weeks, the instructor demonstrates several specific be aware-taking methods and the children practice them. The exercise classes are purposeful and contain gaining research statistics associated with the Explorers subject. Within the summative evaluation, the children might also select the method they found the only. Advice consists of the specific coaching of metacognitive techniques and how the students can plan, display, and evaluate their own getting to know. Reflection with friends or as an entire magnificence can assist the character learner to recollect the purpose of being aware taking and allow them to examine their choice as to the format.

The following layer of the version is worried about the law of processing modes. This pertains to the learner understanding how they examine, they're getting to know styles, and how they procedure statistics. This reflective measurement of self-regulated getting to know relates to the students understanding themselves on the subject of their getting to know and which techniques work high-quality for them, this understanding aids their self-reliant mastering potential. This encourages teachers to increase their pupils' knowledge of themselves as inexperienced persons thru awareness of their strengths and areas for improvement. As noted formerly reflective exercise helps inexperienced persons in identifying their future learning goals.

The function of the teacher is not apparent on this model, however with the focal point of the research being on number one age children, the teacher's function in facilitating and assisting self-regulated mastering exercise is paramount. A part of this would be growing a supportive school room surroundings the use of, for example gaining knowledge of walls to help impartial gaining knowledge of as well as the usage of speaking companions to enable the inexperienced persons to talk about and affirm their know-how. The teacher develops co-built expectations for behavior, noise stage, and classroom routines also support the kid's self-regulatory learning. Even earlier than this stage of mastering the way to analyze, specific coaching might scaffold the development of self-law in more youthful students. The duty for studying shifts to the learner and the function of the trainer is extra supportive becoming less of the conventional "sage on the level," This charts the motion of learning for the scholar as not being as involved with the getting to know of information as tons about getting to know the skills required to learn for themselves. Studying to learn is critical to the development of a self-regulated, self-sufficient learner. Teaching the abilities of learning, growing critical and innovative wondering, communique talents, and social and self-management abilities are prime for newcomers today.

Directing own mastering towards impartial SRL

Moving outward within the model the next layer appears at how guided exercise and scaffold getting to know paves the way for more unbiased gaining knowledge of, leading to greater independent practice. Because the pupil will become greater self-regulated, they'll be able to screen their very own progress, independently reflecting on their work and the strategies they've used, setting dreams for his or her in addition to improvement. The training Endowment basis also highlights the want for timely and powerful comments and techniques for the students for you to decide how successful they may be mastering. Related to the novices in growing rubrics for assessment supports their expertise of the assignment set. In a unit in arithmetic, months-olds worked with trainer steering to put together a rubric for an instructive poster concerning the shape they were to create which was then peer and self-assessed using the agreed rubric.

The NEU (2019) cites interventions within the vicinity of metacognition and self-law as enhancing children's progress with the aid of months thru being taught and modeled with the inexperienced persons.

Teachers in schools

Darby (2005) saw the instructor because of the determining aspect inside the scholars' entertainment of and engagement in their studying. She highlighted the pivotal effect of the teacher concerning the engagement of the inexperienced persons. The autonomy-supportive trainer fashions self-regulatory practices for their elegance. They also can show how failures and mistakes can result in gaining knowledge. The teacher's ardor and excitement for his or her challenge may be infectious increasing the kid's motivation to research. If the kids are excited to research they will strive out new strategies and test with their thoughts extra independently once they have the surest environment created by their teacher. Sierens et al. (2009) determined that autonomy help on the part of the teacher cultivates students' interest and advances their intrinsic motivation. Richardson et al. (2014) explained how an autonomy-supportive teacher should encourage scholars via topic desire and use of era, to growing more self-directed studies initiatives.

The trainer has the capability to create the possibility for self-sustaining studying thru their method to their coaching and the development of a learner-focused schoolroom environment. One such technique is mastering via inquiry. In several primary schools, you'll find inquiry-based totally work in technology and via cross-curricular issues. Emblem and Moore (2011) worked with a trainer professional improvement version in colleges, in which the "instructors as learners" have been supported of their exploration of inquiry coaching in technology by way of a network of peers and research facilitators. The lecturers initiated more inquiry-based totally tactics of their technological know-how coaching and located that this technique elevated hobby and motivation in technology and also had an effect in different areas of the curriculum.

Attractive the students in greater learner-led investigations and collaborative studies inquiries develop autonomy. Kerry (2011) writing approximately pass-curricular coaching discusses how the flow far away from a subject-primarily based approach becomes related to extra focus on capabilities and techniques throughout a variety of disciplines. The teaching emphasis was shifted from didactic teaching to extra self-directed studying on the part of the children. In a unit on Egypt with eight-year-olds, the children decided to position on a play for the fruits of their research on historic Egypt. One boy, who wanted to make a spear for the Pharaoh's guard, researched the sorts of spearheads there were at that time and then performed a survey of the elegance, earlier than making the maximum famous spearhead for the project. That stage of element turned into no longer deliberate for the unit however the youngsters while stimulated and stimulated work very independently, guiding their very own mastering adventure.

Self-regulated learning performs an element in the inquiry technique because the newbies are taught and supported thru the abilities required, moving toward "independently generated inquiry." Banchi and Bell (2008) advocate a continuum of inquiry getting to know, which was especially referencing technological know-how training, however, the 4 levels of the continuum are applicable for different difficulty areas and co-curricular issues. The continuum starts evolved with the greater instructor-supported "confirmation inquiry," reinforcing a formerly introduced concept and specializing in capabilities development. "Established inquiry remains instructor supported initially within the investigation. "Guidedinquiryy" has the research question furnished and the investigation is greater unbiased. The continuum offers improvement of self-regulated mastering transferring from more explicitly scaffold learning to an independently generated inquiry led through the newbies.

SRL in trainer training Programmes

How can providers of instructor training in higher schooling support trainee instructors to be more self-regulated in their studying and encourage them to educate their lessons to be extra self-regulated too?

As my practice as a member of the training college is developing, more periods in my location of curriculum studies and arithmetic training have been designed to include self-regulatory practices, in particular making plans, formative evaluation, and reflective practice. Collectively with a colleague we're inspecting the students' resilience as novices and self-law is covered as one element of this location of studies.

In one module, the scholars write a reflection on two sequences of lesson plans that they've taught. To prepare for this undertaking the periods with the scholar's recognition on reflective exercise for themselves and also where reflection could gain their future coaching in faculties. simply as in the college, the pupil trainer could use children's words to useful resource understanding, we deconstruct the assignment criteria and rewrite them together to help the student's comprehension of what factors of lesson planning, theoretical, and pedagogical techniques require referencing inside the written undertaking.

Formative assessment is an area we explore in evaluation for studying in faculties and as a college school, we additionally use formative evaluation in our modules, searching at examples of lesson plans and assessing them in addition to working within curriculum subject regions developing sequences of instructions and sharing them with friends for remarks. Nicol and Macfarlane-Dick (2006) reference principles of right comments, inclusive of the type of what appropriate performance is in phrases of dreams, standards, and expectations of the assignment or assignment.

The developmental models underneath are shaped busing the ranges mentioned in my tailored model of Boekaerts' (1999) framework and suggest the improvement of inclusion of SRL within the program to aid teaching students in the increase in their personal self-regulatory behavior at college (determine 3) in addition to coaching SRL in their destiny lessons in schools.

We are regularly not aware of the man or woman backgrounds of the students we're teaching as to their independence and skill set concerning learning and reading. Räisänen et al. (2018) note that the transition to college is challenging for many college students. There may be evidence that the primary year is an important time for the students. Brinkworth et al. (2009) located that creating a hit transition isn't simplest related to academic capacity, but additionally depends on the students' capability to make a short change to a new learning sursurroundingat requires greater autonomy and man or woman duty than anticipated.

During their first year, students may be added to the belief of self-law as a key help for their improvement as a pupil in college and as a lifelong learner. Lectures, seminars, workshops, and tutorials define, through specific teaching, the applicable study abilities, supportive techniques, and reflective practices for the students. Reflective practices are especially relevant for instructors. Schön (1983) talks of two kinds of reflective practices for instructors, reflection-on-movement and mirrored image-in-movement. He shows that reflection-in-action is an idea that celebrates the art of coaching, in that it lets in for persistent interpretation, investigation, and reflective conversation with oneself about the coaching state of affairs even as utilizing the records won from past reports to inform and guide new actions.

The student's understanding of themselves as lifelong freshmen pertains to the changing nature of coaching in which there are often new initiatives and changes to the curriculum or new processes to gaining knowledge of. Gaining an intensity of character information of the way that they analyze pleasant helps the scholars in growing the talents and information required to be first-rate practitioners in the future. College and schools may be visible as groups of exercise an idea that becomes developed further by using Wiliam's (2009) "instructor mastering communities." Students may be requested as a collective network of rookies to work together as collaborative learners. Sharing understanding of their reading and discussing ideas concerning teaching can be supportive practices for the students. In the future, I aim to similarly inspire college students to work together in peer aid businesses to aid their learning and improvement.

How Can SRL Practices guide teaching college students in their personal coaching in colleges?
As students start to concerned with school placements they'll interact with planning classes for businesses of kids and are evaluated via self and peer tests. students set goals when on teaching practice and will be encouraged to set

greater preferred desires as properly in terms of their very own studying and precise assignment training. a chain of questions may be provided to manual the students' reflective exercise. Sitzmann and Ely (2010) looked at the impact of self-regulatory question prompts on students over the route of a program These questions brought about mirrored image and assessment of examine abilities and performance. The program leaders also informed the students that their achievement on the direction was underneath their control. That is a thrilling notion and one that is vital to acknowledge in regards to self-law and accepting man or woman duty for one's learning and improvement.

Directing very own mastering

Enabling the students to independently discuss and analyze their personal studies and observations on coaching exercises with their [peers supports their attention to the wide variety of different faculty situations and the individual beginners that exist. the students also can bear in mind how they scaffold SRL practice for the youngsters they educate. putting the context for gaining knowledge in a real existence scenario supported the kid's learning in arithmetic and caused extra significantly, learner initiated work. for example, the trainer of a class of seven 12 months olds mentioned with the kids why they were locating out approximately addition and subtraction. The thoughts raised with the aid of the youngsters caused a unit on money wherein the kids made their own elegance money, keep bank, even requesting credit scorecards. Their final birthday celebration of this unit engaged them in making gadgets for a marketplace stall and then buying them with the magnificence cash that they had earned thru finishing study room "jobs." The kids recorded their transactions using the addition and subtraction techniques they had learned

Self-law

Ultimately, the scholars' self-regulatory practices emerge as embedded of their practice and in their approach to their studying and their teaching with scholars in faculties. What approaches might aid the scholar teachers' development of self-regulated gaining knowledge of strategies?

Techniques for workforce and students

College scaffold practices in their coaching, which college students then adapt for their own self-regulated studying and further utilize of their personal practice after they turn out to be teachers. Cassidy (2011) examined SRL in higher training, especially how aspects of SRL can be stepped forward thru coaching and mastering techniques. Student self-monitoring and self-evaluation have been visible as essential elements in SRL development. Building in opportunities for self-reflection with park-off questions through the modules would aid college students in assessing their learning as well as seeing how reflective exercise helps scholars in faculties. Modeling powerful strategies and using express steering have been additionally emphasized as part of permitting studying surroundings. At university and on placement the pupil instructors will experience sensible sessions wherein they have got top coaching exercise modeled to them. Coaching is considered here, as greater procedure-oriented, and student involvement is paramount within the making plans and shipping of these sessions.

Feedback to the university team of workers offers facts on what turned into success in addition to areas for development. as an instance, the concept of a "one-minute paper" on the consultation written on the cease of a session can provide useful comments for the lecturer. This active studying method is thought to have been initiated using Charles Schwartz, a physics professor at the college of California within the early 1980s. The capacity for this brief piece of writing is for college kids to reply to two questions: first of all regarding what they have learned and secondly outlining any unanswered questions. This allows the university faculty to quickly determine their taught sessions and informs them of any misunderstandings as well as any required gaining knowledge of needs. Nicol (2006) mentioned how improving assessment and comments ought to beautify the mastering revel in particular for first-year college students thru SRL. If students experience control in their mastering on the path they are greater stimulated academically and are more likely to experience the achievement of their study and assignments.

Self-law is visible as vital inside the improvement of lifelong learning abilities for all, motivation toward learning, and reflective practices. Self-regulated learning has been advanced from my doctoral look at searching at learners' SRL and their teachers' support to student instructors' SRL and the methods that instructor training programs can broaden extra self-regulatory competencies and techniques for the student instructors to make use of themselves, in addition, to take into their exercise in their very own classrooms inside the destiny.

Expectations, the specific teaching, and modeling of self-regulatory practices will expand college students' motivation toward their own studying. Cautioned that college school wants to consciously promote wonderful learning surroundings and SRL for their college students.

The adverb right here is essential, as often our intentions do now not match our movements. If we consciously construct the gaining knowledge of surroundings thru collaborative work, expand self-regulatory practices, have interaction in interventions, and help whilst required, we can sell ma meaningful engagement and a hit gaining knowledge of for our student instructors in university, in addition to thru self-regulated coaching for kids in faculties.

In end, as Karamarski et al. (2013) stated our goal must be the empowerment of teachers to broaden SRL newbies. Introducing extra specific teaching of self-regulatory practices, techniques, and capabilities would gain our scholar instructors in their very own improvement each as self-regulated lifelong novices and as practitioners in schools wherein SRL competencies and techniques support their teaching and expand self-sustaining, self-regulated rookies of their classrooms.

Self-regulated studying is critical for absolutely everyone. In teacher schooling, the college wants to explicitly train, version, and exercise the applicable skills and techniques so all novices in primary colleges are set onto their successful route of lifelong studying with the aid of a self-regulated and autonomy-supportive trainer. Self-regulated learning refers to our capacity to apprehend and manipulate our getting to know environments. To do so, we have to set dreams, choose strategies that help us acquire those dreams, enforce those techniques, and screen our progress towards our goals. Few college students are completely

Self-regulated gaining knowledge refers to the methods through which man or woman learners try to reveal and manage their very own gaining knowledge. There are numerous extraordinary fashions of self-regulated gaining knowledge that suggest one-of-a-kind constructs and approaches, but they do proportion some primary assumptions approximately learning and regulation.

Assumptions

One commonplace assumption might be called the lively, optimistic assumption that follows from a well-known cognitive attitude. This is, all of the fashions view rookies as active optimistic participants within the gaining knowledge of the process. A second, but related, assumption is the ability to manage assumption. All the models count on that beginners can potentially screen, control, and regulate sure factors of their personal cognition, motivation, and conduct in addition to some capabilities in their environments. This assumption does no longer mean that people will or can reveal and control their cognition, motivation, or conduct at all times or in all contexts, instead just that a few tracks, manipulation, and regulation are viable. All of the fashions apprehend that there are biological, developmental, contextual, and man or woman difference constraints that could impede or intervene with person efforts at law.

A third widespread assumption that is made in those models of self-regulated studying is the aim, criterion, or general assumption. All models of law anticipate that there's some form of criterion or widespread (also called dreams) towards which comparisons are made on the way to verify whether the process has to preserve as is or if a few sorts of trade are important. The common-sense example is the thermostat operation for the heating and cooling of a residence. As soon as the desired temperature is set (the aim, criterion, or preferred), the thermostat monitors the temperature of the residence (monitoring process) and then activates or off the heating or air conditioning devices (manage and law methods) to be able to reach and keep the same old. In a parallel way, the general instance for getting to know assumes that individuals can set requirements or dreams to try for of their gaining knowledge of, display their development closer to these desires, and then adapt and modify their cognition, motivation, and conduct as a way to reach their desires.

A fourth standard assumption of a maximum of the fashions of self-regulated learning is that self-regulatory activities are mediators among private and contextual characteristics and actual achievement or performance. that is, it isn't simply people' cultural, demographic, or persona characteristics that impact fulfillment and studying directly, nor simply the contextual traits of the study room surroundings that form fulfillment, however the people' self-regulation methods that mediate the family members among the man or woman, context, and eventual fulfillment. Most fashions of self-law anticipate that self-regulatory sports are directly linked to effects such as success and overall performance, even though a lot of the studies examine self-regulatory tactics as effects in their personal right.

Given these assumptions, a widespread operating definition of self-regulated gaining knowledge of is that it is an energetic, constructive manner wherein newcomers set desires for their getting to know and then try to monitor, alter, and manage their cognition, motivation, and conduct, guided and restricted via their dreams and the contextual capabilities inside the environment. Following this widespread definition, research on models of self-regulated studying have delineated 4 popular domain names that learners can try and self-modify: (1) cognition, (2) motivation, (three) behavior, and (four) the environment.

The cognitive domain includes the various cognitive techniques that learners can use to help them recall, recognize, purpose, and hassle clear up. plenty of the work on this domain has targeted at the studying strategies that students can use in academic contexts to recognize text, to analyze from lectures, to take notes, to solve math issues, to write papers, (e.g., checking out their comprehension as they read a textual content). Similarly, studies have targeted meta-cognitive techniques that beginners can use to plot, monitor, and manipulate their own cognition. In lots of approaches, metacognition is now visible as one a part of the more preferred assemble of self-regulated mastering. In trendy, appropriate self-regulating newbies use some of the exclusive strategies to govern their cognition in methods that help them reach their dreams.

The incentive and affective areas consist of the diverse techniques that individuals can use to try to manage and modify their personal motivation and emotions. this may consist of strategies for enhancing their self-belief or self-efficacy consisting of effective self-speak ("I know I will do this mission") as well as strategies to try to manage their hobby (e.g., making the mission greater thrilling by making a sport out of it). Other techniques can be aimed at controlling poor feelings inclusive of anxiety that can intrude with studying. In some studies, these motivational and emotional manipulate techniques are known as volitional control strategies, but they can also be visible as part of the bigger assemble of self-regulated learning. As with cognition, true self-regulating novices do attempt to manipulate their motivation and feelings to be able to facilitate the attainment of their desires.

The 0.33 domain includes actual attempts to control overt conduct, now not simply inner cognitions or motivational beliefs and emotions. This will involve growing or lowering effort on an assignment, as well as persisting on an undertaking or giving up. Help-in search of conduct is every other critical self-regulatory conduct. Precise self-regulators could alter their effort ranges to the assignment and their desires; they know whilst to persist, whilst to invite for assist, and whilst to forestall doing the project.

Finally, self-regulated novices can attempt to display and manipulate the surroundings. Of path, they'll now not have as a good deal manages over the general lecture room context or instructional obligations as they do over their very own cognition, motivation, and conduct, but there are a few components of the context that may be managed. For instance, exact self-regulated freshmen will try to manipulate distractions by asking others to be quiet or busingmoving to every other location. Suitable self-regulators also attempt to understand the undertaking needs and the schoolroom norms after which try to regulate their mastering to match these needs. In different words, they're sensitive to the contextual demands and constraints which are operating within the study room and try to deal with them adaptively.

The development of Self-regulation

There are a bunch of things that can affect the improvement of self-regulation; 3 are stated here: cognitive development, motivation, and lecture room contexts. Given the complexity of self-regulated mastering, it's far a phenomenon that emerges later in a child's lifestyle. There are clear developmental and maturational constraints on self-regulated gaining knowledge. even though there are manifestly components of self-law in place by the point a younger baby reaches school, the improvement of self-regulation for educational tasks takes vicinity over the direction of ok–12 training. There isn't as lots research on the improvement of self-regulated learning as there may be on how it operates, but it might be not until the middle to past due standard school grades (third grade to sixth grade) that scholars start to broaden a number of the crucial self-regulation techniques. In reality, it is probably that an awful lot of the development of self-regulated studying takes area in youth, given general cognitive-developmental adjustments as well as the changes in the classroom context in middle schools and excessive schools. At the identical time, numerous students do no longer develop self-regulated strategies at all, even a number of those greater a success ones who go on to college. As a consequence, there's a need to expand specific instructional strategies and applications to help students study self-law and develop expertise in regulating their learning.

Self-regulated learning is likewise time-consuming and quite difficult for some students, even if supplied with express training in self-regulation. as a consequence, it's miles important that scholars are inspired to be self-regulating. Research of Paul R. Pintrich (1999) on the role of motivation in self-regulated learning has cautioned vital generalizations approximately the family members among motivation and self-regulated studying. First, students ought to feel self-efficacious or assured that they can do the tasks. if they experience they can accomplish the academic tasks, then they're much more likely to use diverse self-law strategies. Second, students ought to be inquisitive about and price the schoolroom tasks. college students who are bored or do no longer find the tasks useful or worthwhile are tons less probably to be self-regulating than folks who are interested and find the responsibilities vital. ultimately, college students who are centered on goals of getting to know, know-how, and self-improvement are much more likely to be self-regulating than college students who are pursuing different dreams such as trying to appear smarter than others or trying now not to appearance silly. Those generalizations were determined in a large number of research and appear to be pretty sturdy, however,r of the route,e there is a want for more research on the role of motivation in self-regulated getting to know.

Finally, except developmental and motivational factors, there are contextual factors that play a function in the improvement of self-regulation. One of the maximum vital is that individuals clearly have the possibility to try to take manage their personal learning and are given the danger to attempt tasks on their very own. Of direction, responsibilities mustn't be too difficult or too clean, however in the students' range of competence. Further, the modeling and demonstration of diverse self-regulatory strategies by way of mother and father, instructors, and friends can assist college students' research these strategies. Students additionally want the opportunity to have guided exercise with the use of these techniques, with guide and steering from knowledgeable others, whether or not they be mother and father, instructors, or friends. Sooner or later, there must be incentives in the context for the usage of those techniques, such that students who are successful in using the techniques are rewarded in terms of reward or extra tangible rewards inclusive of higher mastering and fulfillment.

Significance of Self-Regulated learning

Self-regulated mastering is an important component of learning and fulfillment in educational contexts. Self-regulating college students are much more likely to be successful in faculty, to study greater, and to gain at better levels. Thus, its miles important for schools and lecture rooms to try and foster the development of information in self-regulated getting to know. Of course, there are developmental, motivational, and contextual elements that can facilitate or constrain self-regulated studying, however, there are implicit and expressexpresswaysp foster self-regulated learning. inside the twenty-first century and because the explosion of statistics and more than one way of mastering increase, it turns even more crucial that individuals realize the way to self-modify tthey'regetting to know and that fostering self-regulated getting to know turns into the crucial intention for all educational structures.

Chapter Six

Learning Styles Dimensions

Studying fashion plays an active role in engineering education that portrays the strategies in which inexperienced persons generally acquire, maintain, and get lower back records. It facilitates students to boom their cognitive capability and to deal with the gaining knowledge of difficulties which successively improves their instructional performance. Each scholar has exceptional mastering fashion preference depends on their likings and disliking. They collect understanding first-rate via auditory, listening, watching, and doing. Sure outside environmental inputs like seeing, hearing, reflecting, and appearing enables college students in learning. These inputs support college students as mastering method is a way of reflecting and appearing, reasoning logically and intuitively, memorizing and visualizing. College students gain expertise well in a class while teaching patterns to fit their desired mastering styles. Along with, the studying styles are the choices and traits through which a person receives and manner records. As an example, a schoolroom is constructed from dissimilarities in terms of instructional historical past, desired to learn fashion, cultural impact, and cognitive capacity from a social attitude. Furthermore, mismatches among coaching techniques with students desired studying patterns can also lead them towards poor educational overall performance. Therefore, to recognize college students mastering choices that accomplish their desires and enhance their instructional achievements requires determining the pleasant feasible learning style. In better schooling, third and fourth yr students are speculated to be matured sufficiently to cope with their capacity of expertise assignments and topics by personal. But, the majority of college students who fail examinations generally blame their failure on outside stimulus together with mismatch coaching strategies or loss of instructional requirements [eight]. instructors are essential in facilitating and guiding assets in the lecture room for this reason they should possess the capacity to remember that how properly college students accumulate facts and in what ways. Therefore, it's far necessary that educators ought to regulate their coaching strategies according to college students learning styles alternatives as discrepancies in teaching and gaining knowledge of patterns can create problems to recognize subjects and assignments in elegance. subsequently, there is a need to deliver powerful coaching that needs to be comprised of teaching fashion and preferred gaining knowledge of the style of their coaching sports, in particular, considering cognitive and intellectual sports. Moreover, a non-stop system of learning styles may lead to college students' better overall performance [eleven]. Felder reviews that the robust choice of any student for a particular studying style can also trouble if teaching fashion does not match with pupils getting to know fashion. Every student has one-of-a-kind mental technique, studying styles, the pace of pickup any records, ardor, and motivation to research but teaching methods and educational activities are one-of-a-kinds. So, the mastering patterns attempt to discover man or woman wondering skills, motivation, and preferred methods of acquiring understanding to enhance college students' overall performance. For that reason, by offering academic centers in a schoolroom; educators need to understand categories of college students to enhance the gaining knowledge of competencies so one can meet predicted academic dreams. Dunn (1993) described studying style as the approach in which each learner initiates to concentrate on, technique, and keep new records. Felder (1996) describes mastering styles are individuals absorb statistics via preferences and strengths in their preferred approaches of getting to know. Vermunt (1996) expresses gaining knowledge of fashion as a logical interest of gaining knowledge of activities that scholars typically hire of their educational orientation and intellectual studying activities. Keefe (1985) defines learning fashion as the mixed characteristic cognitive, affective, and physiological behaviors that assist as especially steady signs and symptoms of how college students have a look at, interrelate with and react to the academic surroundings. Felder-Silverman getting to know style version (FSLSM) The Felder-Silverman gaining knowledge of styles model (FSLSM) become evolved by way of Richard Felder and Linda Silverman and was first posted in 1988. The model became originally developed to deal with studying variations amongst engineering training. The version categorizes students into 4 dimensions. The first-measurement technique statistics distinguish freshmen into active novices and reflective freshmen. Lively novices study satisfactory by using applying, and trying matters out, and working with gaining knowledge of materials. Also, they tend to be extra interested in communication with others and prefer to analyze through working in businesses in which college students can discuss the discovered material. Whilst reflective newcomers like higher to consider materials and replicate on the substances. The second measurement of the FSLSM version is perceived records that consisted of sensing and intuitive learners. Sensing newbies opt to analyze information and concrete material also they're taken into consideration extra realistic and practical. Moreover, they like to relate the learned fabric with actual international. at the same time as intuitive beginners like better summary getting to know assets as an example theories and their essential meanings. Intuitive learners want to discover relationships and opportunities and that they will be predisposed to be greater revolutionary and creative than sensing rookies. The 1/3 dimension is input records that differentiate beginners into visual learners or verbal learners. Visual freshmen research first-rate by photos, diagrams, flowcharts, or by demonstrations while verbal inexperienced persons analyze satisfactorily through written and spoken substances. The dimension of the FSLSM model is to understand information that classifies newcomers into two styles sequential and worldwide beginners. Sequential rookies learn nice with the aid of small incremental steps, grade by grade paths in finding solutions, and from small components to whole. Whereas, global learners analyze pleasant using a holistic thinking process and study in large leaps. Similarly, the main awareness of Felder's work is studying the fashion possibilities of students. To degree the mastering style alternatives based totally on FSLSM version, Index of gaining knowledge of patterns (ILS) questionnaire was designed via Felder and Soloman. Index of gaining knowledge of style questionnaire is primarily based on Felder Silverman's learning style model that consisted of forty-four items. ILS items are divided in keeping with FSLSM version dimensions, every measurement consists of eleven objects with two solutions "a" and "b". Wherein "a" denotes subscales energetic, sensing, visible, and sequential respectively and "b" denotes reflective, intuitive, verbal, and worldwide respectively. Concerning the psychometric features of instrument ILS, various studies illustrated that the ILS offers predictive value and more consistency than different generally used studies. The index of mastering gadgets became grouped based totally on semantic similarities as defined in the FSLSM version. Gaining knowledge of procedure is a way of verbal exchange among students, teachers, and teaching sources. For better results, students learning manner have to continually be given importance. Preferably, trainer's coaching methods have to be matched with freshmen' preferred mastering fashion. Mismatches in practice and the preferred learning fashion of students often lead them towards decrease instructional grades. For example, in training mastering fashion is gambling the first-rate function, teachers ought to not forget college students gaining knowledge of options in classes to decorate their cognitive and academic performance. The objective of look at:

• To perceive the styles of studying patterns among engineering college students.

• To become aware of the mastering style differences

among engineering guides.

Technique gift examine followed quantitative survey research as this approach offers higher accuracy and consistency of study's findings. The survey technique can provide feasible facts regarding the populace and statistics collection from respondents approximately their educational, economic, and social backgrounds. The reason for this study is to explore the styles of getting to know the kinds of engineering students constitute.

To perceive the kinds of mastering patterns amongst engineering students Index of gaining knowledge of patterns by way of Felder and Solomon turned into used to categorize students based totally on their options. The subsequent is the scoring method of index of learning fashion questionnaire became defined by way of Felder and Spurlin. Students getting to know style ratings had been calculated with the aid of allocating a cost of one to each of the questions inside the gaining knowledge of fashion dimensions.

The learner has a moderate choice for one dimension of the dimensions and could research greater without difficulty in teaching surroundings that favors that size. If the rating on a scale is 9/11 then the pupil has a robust preference for one dimension of the scale and might have a problem studying in an environment that does now not assist that preference. The mastering style rankings had been transferred to an Excel spreadsheet to analyze the information.

Dialogue and conclusion understanding the learner's desired mastering patterns may assist to increase the quality of learning and teaching. As Sabine Graf noted that identifying desired gaining knowledge of fashion of beginners is street to enhance studying and coaching in the classroom.

The majority of college students have a sturdy desired learning style observed to be visible getting to know. Besides, engineering courses are mostly primarily based on design diagrams however a few topics are based totally on theories. Educators want to reform their teaching fashion based on students' options so that higher academic performance may be obtained. As on this have a look at engineering students showed their strong preference on visual studying. This means that institutes need to consciousness extra of the visual learning environment so that newcomers can without difficulty decorate their academic success. This suggests an extreme issue that mismatching coaching and studying can motive problems to students' instructional performance. Moreover, getting to know styles and coaching styles are carefully connected to every different. Several studies determined that when educators teach publications in keeping with 'students' desired to study styles, college students carry out properly and that they enhance their instructional achievements. Via this suit among studying styles and teaching styles will supply a great effect on newbies' instructional achievements. The objective of this take a look at revealed that there's no difference exists between the engineering courses. This implies that engineering guides are one of a kind by nature but students' options for mastering are equal. Consequently, coaching techniques need to be made bendy so that better outputs may be won. It argues that curriculum and coaching strategies need to be made according to guides. based totally on observe findings, the researcher indicates that lectures, teaching substances need to exercise greater visual graphical gear which includes demonstration, presentation using software program PowerPoint, and many others in classroom teachings. So that it will fit in step with visual gaining knowledge of style choices. Moreover, educators should additionally generate a mix of coaching surroundings to aid energetic studying between the newbies. Sports doings like discussion, cooperative mastering, demonstration, brainstorming, trouble primarily-based learning, and assignment-based mastering are strongly advised. By nature, by and large, engineering topics are concerned with processes. Due to this purpose educators ought to supply commands systematically like from clean steps to tough steps. Finally, educators can begin a lecture by using highlighting on information then observe by fingers on doings to aid the learner's view on new information. At the time, handing over examples will assist the rookies to relate magnificence work with actual work circumstances outside the academic room.

Individuals getting to know styles are various in keeping with the tendency of every person. The precise studying fashion ought to help students to reap good educational record in any situation they learned. Consequently, this study aimed to determine the relationship between scholar achievement and getting to know style for a technical and non-technical challenge. Solomon Felder mastering style Index changed into dispensed to the participants and the Felder and Silverman model was used to interpret the facts. result confirmed that the electrical engineering students have an energetic form of learning style for the primary dimension, the sensing for the second size, visual for the 1/3 dimension, and series for the fourth size. The result showed that there is no good-sized relationship between the dimensions of learning styles and educational success for electrical technology challenge and simplest the second dimension has a significant relationship with instructional fulfillment of the Polibriged difficulty. In end, mastering fashion isn't the main factor to beautify students' success, however, it could be used to perceive the tendency of getting to know styles possessed by using students.

Creation scholar overall performance in learning can be stimulated with the aid of several factors. The fundamental issues of pupils gaining knowledge of as explored by institutions of researchers were which includes home history, learning surroundings, and government rules. In different studies, the finding syndicated that own family background factors and gaining knowledge of styles determined instructional performance. Francis and Segun (2008) concluded that the faculty surroundings and trainer-associated factors have been the dominant factors influencing achievements, specifically if the student became extraordinarily self-influenced. Freshmen have to take a look at and revel in the required cognitive strategies to learn them and recognize how, where, and while to use them. Proponents of getting to know styles maintain that adapting study room coaching methods to suit students' favored varieties of gaining knowledge of improves the educative method. However, fighters of learning style theories hold that little empirical proof ought to assist this proposition. As an alternative, the fighters agree that mastering patterns contain strategies that students are likely to apply to a given coaching state of affairs. Every character can fit extraordinary patterns which result in college students adopting attitudes and behaviors that are repeated in unique situations. There are numerous instructional packages offered at the university and university level in Malaysia along with Technical and vocational education (TVE). Polytechnic is one of the technical establishments which supply human capital to meet the wishes of the nearby industries. Most of the people of the program offered on the polytechnics are engineering applications. college students are anticipated to develop abilities in two exceptional areas which include technical (center and non-obligatory subjects related to engineering) and non-technical subjects (co-curriculum, languages, and Islamic or moral topics). Technical-based subjects that are electric technology (ET101) are evaluated via numerous levels of assessment inclusive of formative assessment within the form of assignments, quizzes, exams, and organization discussion sports in addition to summative evaluation through examinations. Non-technical topics based at the technical curriculum particularly Polibriged (AR101) also assessed through examinations basic assessment entails numerous stages which includes a continuous assessment which includes sensible, quizzes, written tests, displays, tutorials, and problem-based totally getting to know. This takes a look at was carried out to perceive any variations within the learning forms of engineering students for both, technical and non-technical subjects, based totally on Felder and Silverman gaining knowledge of style model (FLSM) (Felder & Silverman, 1988). This takes a look at applying the FLSM model as a way to see the pattern of getting to know styles for the electric engineering college students at the polytechnic. This study also investigated the relationships between the scholar's getting to know patterns and academic success in a technical and non-technical problem. in step with the teachers, low overall performance in any of the technical and non-technical subjects can be one of the reasoning for the students to drop out from the engineering software in their first twelve months of look at.

This has a look indicates that the mixture of energetic, sensing, visual and sequential are getting to know styles that electrical engineering college students choose to study. This locating supported with the aid of other researchers take a look at. The visual style is the most dominant fashion possessed by the scholars and that they were likely to analyze with pictures, charts, and writing to get better expertise and memorizing what they'd learned. The observe additionally indicates the electric engineering students on the polytechnic tend to be socially gaining knowledge of, cozy operating in agencies and prefer to offer data for their friends and be able to recall things easily. This case is supported using Mior Ismail (2003) in which the curriculum at polytechnic gives priority to sensible work and concept. Engineering students are required to go into the engineering workshop to do the practical workshops. The lively pattern being chosen through respondents as maximum engineering college students have innovative questioning. Kamaruddin and Mohamad (2011), concluded based totally on studies for the Kolb model, the man or woman who adopts imaginative and creative mastering style will continually consciousness on to be had information and system the facts in a response to the others. The findings showed that students who've innovative minds tend to take part in social activities, interaction, and sharing of ideas. This is many of the fundamental motives for the energetic sample has grown to be one of the studying patterns which can be frequently used in electrical engineering scholar at the polytechnic. This has a look also display the sensing sample had been selected by way of respondents due to the fact engineering college students worried with reasonable accuracy in work. Each laboratory or workshop emphasized protection components in herbal sciences or engineering discipline. By Jamaludin (2001), protection engineering also consists of tools, equipment, devices, surroundings, and the safety of other folks that have to be obeyed by students at the same time as they're within the workshop. The relationship between learning style and academic fulfillment for the subject ET101 drastically above the level selected. This locating suggests that there may be no substantial courting between students' studying styles and educational fulfillment for technical subjects. These findings show that studying style does not affect instructional achievement. Yusof, Othman, and Karim (2005) stated that studying fashion cannot be used as a basis to evaluate the overall performance of a scholar however motivation, academic capability, and technique whilst analyzing are the factors that affect student fulfillment. Those findings also are supported using studies by Num (1999) at the student college technology Malaysia (UTM) which suggests that the mastering fashion of college students with low, mild, and extraordinary achievement does not have extensive distinction. analysis for the four dimensions getting to know patterns and academic fulfillment of non-technical subjects indicates that active-reflective size, visible-verbal dimension, and sequential-global dimension does not have a good-sized courting with the fulfillment of Polibriged (non-technical challenge) besides for the sensing-intuitive measurement. Seven factors of soft competencies were carried out in higher training establishments namely communique skills, essential wondering and trouble-fixing competencies, teamwork capabilities, non-stop learning and statistics management, entrepreneurial abilities, professional ethics, and management abilities. Sensing-intuitive measurement confirmed abnormalities relationship with AR101 concern due to the fact the concern has applied to gain knowledge of smooth competencies. Smooth abilities concerned are teamwork skills, vital wondering, and professional ethics. Smooth talents that inherent in the take a look at of this subject parallel with functions sensing-intuitive patterns. In end, although the visual pattern is the maximum dominant pattern, it's miles important for college students to have various styles to make getting to know each other more powerful. Besides the visual pattern, active, sequential, and sensing, international patterns are additionally required in the technology of technological advancement. Instructors and the Ministry of Training (MOE) need to attempt to make certain that coaching for college students extra holistically and feature the ability to generate greater progressive engineering. Further, the principal component that wishes to be applied with the aid of institutions and instructors is incorporating a variety of getting to know styles with suitable coaching strategies. No longer only that, the achievement of non-technical subjects (AR101) may be enhanced by way of combining sensing intuitive patterns to fulfill the getting-to-know curriculum for sports that require soft abilities. This combination can improve the academic success of curricular subjects. Average, getting to know patterns aren't have a critical relationship with academic achievement however it can be used to become aware of the fashion of getting to know patterns which can be owned with the aid of students or even can be utilized by instructors to improve coaching strategies.

Mastering styles

Special learners have extraordinary alternatives about how they apprehend, organize, and remember new facts. Some favor to examine in corporations, even as others favor to have a look at by myself. A few humans opt to assume matters through, even as others choose to be more energetic. Some research quality by using listening, whilst others find it less complicated to remember information if they could see it. These variations inside the way we like to examine are called studying styles. Know-how your own preferences can be a crucial first step in improving the way you examine.

There are many distinct theories approximately how beginners prefer to look at, and therefore many exclusive types of 'mastering styles'. A few studies suggest there are over 70 special fashions. Some of the most important ones are mentioned below.

Kolb learning patterns

Educators first have become inquisitive about learning

patterns following Kolb's description of them in the mid-Seventies. He's getting to know styles are linked with the Kolb learning cycle. He counseled that even though inexperienced persons want to go through the equal stages as they progress via gaining knowledge of the cycle, they regularly prefer some aspects of the cycle to others. This led Kolb to perceive four learning styles, which he called accommodative, divergent, assimilative, and convergent. Each of those, and its connection to the studying cycle, is proven beneath. Ingenious, true at generating ideas, see things from specific perspectives, interested by human beings and cultures.

Honey & Mumford learning styles

Another wonderful version is the Honey and Mumford version, which's extensively used inside the UK. This version adapts Kolb getting to know patterns. In this version, which becomes developed by way of Honey and Mumford following widespread studies, the patterns are without delay aligned to the ranges in the learning cycle (this contrasts with the Kolb studying styles, in which the styles are from overlapping stages). The patterns are activist, reflector, theorist, and pragmatist, which relate to the do, replicate, conclude, and plan levels of the cycle. Each of those is defined in more detail inside the desk beneath.

Getting to know fashion
Relation to Kolb studying cycle
Traits

Abilities

Activist

Prefers to do

Wishes to be involved in new and tough tasks doesn't want to forestall and reflect whilst a project is finished.

True at speaking, solving troubles, taking action.

Reflector

Prefers to mirror

Desires time to assume things via and put Together for responsibilities, would not like closing dates.

Accurate at staring at, listening, visualizing, brainstorming.

Theorist

Prefers to make conclusions

Desires to impeach and explore the good judgment in the back of ideas like the highbrow project.

Good at setting up, classifying, evaluating, contrasting, ordering.

Pragmatist

Prefers to plot wishes to peer a direct link among the gaining knowledge of and the actual world.

Proper at solving troubles, experimenting, predicting, exploring.

VAK version

Perhaps the most well-known model of mastering styles (and the only one used on this website) is the VAK version. VAK is short for visible, auditory, and kinesthetic, which are the three learning patterns. Their meanings, and the variations among them, are shown underneath.

Visual

Visual newbies learn first-class by seeing. The subsequent will all resource visible novices in their look at:

- Photographs
- Handouts
- Charts, graphs, maps, time traces
- Visual aids (e.g. PowerPoint, whiteboard)
- Colour-coding (like this)
- Studying

Auditory

Auditory freshmen study excellent by way of listening. The following will aid this kind of learner:

- Lectures
- Recordings (e.g. mp3, podcasts)
- Discussions
- Debates
- Repeating phrases

Kinaesthetic

Kinaesthetic novices study first-rate by using moving and touching. Examples of activities to assist this sort of learner are:

- Bodily movement
- Tasks
- Experiments
- Discipline journeys
- Common breaks

Dunn & Dunn version

The Dunn & Dunn version is one of the most popular and extensively used fashions inside the US It describes individuals' reactions to twenty-one exclusive elements, such as sound, mild, motivation, individual work. Each of those factors is grouped under five dimensions: environmental, emotional, sociological, physiological, and psychological. A few other getting-to-know patterns, e.g. the VAK gaining knowledge of patterns, are protected within these headings.

The five dimensions and the twenty-one factors are shown below, collectively with a few key questions for college students and instructors to do not forget.

Measurement   - elements -   Key questions
Environment   - Sound, mild, temperature, design
• Does the student prefer a noisy or quiet environment?
• Does the type of lights make a difference?
• Does the scholar like to look at it in a cool or warm environment?
• What kind of room design works pleasant? Formal surroundings with rows of desks? A casual one with sofas and pillows?
Emotional   -   Motivation, staying power, responsibility, structure
• Does the scholar need numerous emotional assist and encouragement?
• Will the student persists in learning obligations or give up without problems?
• Can the scholar anticipate duty for their getting to know?
• Does the pupil want step-by means of step instructions, or do they choose more open-ended responsibilities?
Sociological   man or woman, pair, friends, group, person, various

• Does the scholar opt to work alone or with others?
• Does the scholar prefer pair work or group work?
• Does he/she opt for a peer or the authority of an adult?
Physiological   Perceptual, consumption, time, mobility
• Is the student a visual, auditory, or kinaesthetic learner?
• Does the pupil like to snack whilst studying?
• When is the satisfactory time of day for learning? Morning? Midday? Nighttime?
• Does the scholar opt to take a seat nevertheless or flow round while getting to know?
Mental   international/   analytic,   hemisphericity, impulsive/ reflective
• Does the scholar favor to begin on a problem immediately, or take time to reflect on it first?

Other types of getting to know fashion
As stated above, there are over seventy different fashions of gaining knowledge of styles, too many to list here. other fashions consist of variations of the VAK version, e.g. by way of dividing the kinaesthetic style into 'tactile' newbies (who experience touching and manipulating) and natural 'kinaesthetic' freshmen (who definitely experience transferring even as studying), or using including every other measurement, 'analyzing', wherein case the version is referred to as the VARK version. some fashions combine or adapt elements of both the VAK and Dunn & Dunn models, e.g. via do not forget visual as well as social newcomers, or by way of including an 'olfactory' style for novices who locate that smells and taste can add to gaining knowledge of.

How to use getting to know styles to enhance your look at

With so many patterns, it may be puzzling to pick out your very own favored fashion, let alone recall how to utilize this information. A vital first step is to be aware of the specific getting to know patterns that every folk has. Just due to the fact everybody else within the lecture room prefers to work in companies in loud, shiny surroundings, would not mean you do too. think about the fashions above and determine which one you discover most convincing, and try some online questionnaires to help you to perceive your personal fashion (even though you probably recognize yourself well sufficient to know what your choices are). Try and adapt what you have a look at to take your chosen styles under consideration, e.g. through using extra pictures and snapshots in case you are a visual learner, or via analyzing outdoor if you opt for natural to artificial light. There's no proper or incorrect mastering style. Apprehend yours, and use it that will help you study.

Chapter Seven

Visual and Verbal Learners

Visible and verbal beginners

Visual inexperienced persons don't forget pleasant what they see—snapshots, diagrams, drift charts, time strains, films, and demonstrations. Verbal beginners get extra out of words—written and spoken factors. Each person learns extra when statistics are offered each visually and verbally.

In maximum university training, very little visual information is offered: college students particularly pay attention to lectures and study cloth written on chalkboards and in textbooks and handouts. Alas, most of the people are visible learners, which imply that most college students do no longer get nearly as a lot as they could if the more visible presentation were used in class. Accurate freshmen can process data provided either visually or verbally.

Characteristics

•   Relate to such words as see, appearance, examine, study.

•   Like to study books and magazines for both records and pride.

•   Revel in watching TV documentaries and movies in which both visible and verbal statistics are supplied concurrently.

- Study a newspaper or mag often as a supply of news.
- Choose to read what an expert has written on a topic than to pay attention to a lecture or discussion.
- Favour to look over written direction and diagrams to gather or use something as opposed to listening to a person explain a way to do it.
- Feel pissed off whilst instructors really provide oral commands for assignments and tests as opposed to additionally writing the commands at the board or on a handout.
- Take good-sized notes for the duration of elegant lectures and discussions to check later.
- Make lists often of each day's dreams and activities.

Teaching strategies to assist learning

- Written instructions for all assignments and tests.
- Visible / Verbal aids: handouts, outlines or summary notes of lectures, written definitions of latest phrases, written oral explanations for charts, graphs, and diagrams.
- Comply with-up analysis for any elegant lectures and discussions.

Verbal newcomers

Verbal inexperienced persons also are referred to as auditory rookies and prefer a route that is provided in the shape of a lecture or magnificence discussion. Verbal inexperienced persons tend to study out loud, repeat records and ask a diffusion of questions for rationalization. They research high-quality thru online boards, verbal instructions, and webinar lectures, and email.

Characteristics

- Learns from oral rationalization/direction and blessings from auditory repetition.
- Is aware of the sector via speaking about it.

- Faucets a pencil, hums or sings if matters are too quiet.
- Likes track, rhythm, and exciting sounds.
- Enjoys listening to himself/herself and others speak.
- Loves to recite information or examine orally.
- Whilst studying silently, they movements' lips, say phrases to themself, and frequently read slowly.
- Desirable at remembering and telling jokes.
- Might as an alternative pay attention to a tale; enjoys speaking approximately stories.
- Effortlessly distracted with the aid of sounds and noises.
- Spoken language is easy, written expression greater hard.
- Counts to self; talks to self-whilst solving problems.
- Discusses issues and talks via the steps whilst solving a tough problem.
- Demonstrates appropriate oral spelling.
- Can remedy math issues in the head.
- Plans for destiny by using speaking about it.
- Has trouble with maps, diagrams, and visuals.
- Learns by way of oral clarification.
- Studies through analyzing notes to friends; likes "talking thru" data.
- Offers ten reasons for everything can be verbose.
- Can keep in mind names higher than faces

Teaching techniques to help to get to know

- Read causes out loud. Make sure to move over all vital information out loud.
- Make up songs to go with situations be counted. The crazier the higher.
- Say phrases in syllables.
- Makeup and repeat rhymes to recollect facts, dates,

names, and so on.

- Create a observe group to help the verbal rookies.
- Use mnemonics and phrase links

Visible novices

Visible beginners tend to examine higher by way of seeing what they need to, a good way to see

The whole idea of what they need to understand. This will be carried out in terms of photos (diagrams), go with the flow charts, and timelines and sometimes consists of watching demonstrations. Visual novices don't generally tend to study a whole lot they would prefer to pay attention to instructions that might be being taught.

Visible beginners can help themselves inside the destiny via looking to locate diagrams which include drawings, snapshots, and drift charts to represent matters visibly. Helping yourself within the destiny in case you are a visible learner might be accomplished by making a map so that it will list all of the crucial elements of what you are reading. Color-coding your notes is always useful for a visible learner and this will help them inside the future as they may have the ability to inform work apart.

Verbal inexperienced persons

Verbal inexperienced persons analyze greater with the aid of listening to phrases which means they could interpret greater knowledge of what they're desiring to do. It doesn't remember if their phrases are spoken or provided verbally. Verbal rookies can get information entry this is presented to them formally or casually.

Verbal novices can help themselves in the future by outlining a course's wishes in their personal phrases, this may assist them to benefit a higher understanding and help them examine more rather than nevertheless, and hearing a rationalization.

Visual/verbal learners' traits

• Like to read books and magazines for each information and delight

• Read a newspaper as a supply of information

• Favour to read what a professional has written on a subject, in place of pay attention to a lecture

• Favour to appearance over written directions to collect or use something, instead of pay attention someone explains a way to do it

• Sense annoyed whilst instructors actually deliver oral commands on the board

• Take vast notes in class

• Make lists frequently of the day by day desires and sports approaches

You analyze quality

• Having written instructions for all assignments and tests

• Using aids: handouts, summary notes of lecture, written definitions of recent terms, written and oral explanations for charts, graphs, and diagrams

• Observe-up studying for any class lectures and discussion a successful look at strategies

• Take cautious notes to pay attention at some stage in elegance lectures

• Write summaries of notes for your very own phrases

• Write down any oral instructions for assignments to

have a visible resource to refer to later
• Spotlight vital ideas for your assigned reading with colored markers
• Make flashcards with definitions
Make lists and different written reminders of something you want to take into account to do

Visual/nonverbal beginners' traits
• Understand and preserve statistics nicely by using looking at pix, diagrams, and charts
• Who leaf through books and magazines and cognizance in particular on pictures?
• Discover ways to do matters by way of gazing, in preference to verbal instructions
• Choose established responsibilities to oral and written instructions
• Decide on the TV as a source of news rather than a newspaper
• Have a robust visible reminiscence (recall faces, locations, in which they positioned matters) methods you learn excellently
• Whilst assigned duties are confirmed
• Seeing samples of correctly finished assignments
• The usage of visible aids: diagrams, charts, pics, films
• Having the opportunity to attract pictures or diagrams of ideas and ideas
• Whilst you are introduced to new standards, having a photograph or example to which you may relate a success observe techniques
• Draw photographs, charts, diagrams or vocabulary, standards, or troubles

• Use a spread of shiny hues to focus on essential facts for your lecture notes and textbook
• Try to get a mental picture of what you are reading or listening to approximately in a lecture (this can assist keep you alert and centered)
• Summarize the main factors of what you have studied in a chart
• Ask for examples or memories to help you recognize new or difficult standards
• Ask for efficaciously finished assignments or issues

Information and your studying style

The idea of mastering styles began in the Seventies, in which a growing literature and enterprise posited that novices have specific, individualized ways of getting to know that work great for them. This coaching Tip discusses the difference between gaining knowledge of styles and learning preferences and summarizes the Solomon-Felder index of gaining knowledge of styles.

The studies on mastering patterns

There are many exceptional theories of getting to know styles, including ones that classify humans as visual, auditory, or tactile newcomers, or ones that outline unique cognitive approaches people absorb their learning.

However, there is definitely no evidence that helps that people have mastering patterns, nor that when taught in a way that "meshes" with their learning fashion that there is extra gaining knowledge of. A set of psychologists reviewed the literature and in their file (gaining knowledge of styles: standards and evidence). The nation that at the same time as there were studies performed on how people can have alternatives for mastering, almost none of the studies hired rigorous research designs that would exhibit that humans gain if they're told in a way that fits their learning fashion.

In a latest have a look at, Matching studying fashion to training technique: consequences on Comprehension, Rogowsky, and associates (2015) performed an experimental check of the meshing hypothesis and determined that matching the sort of preparation to learning fashion did no longer make a distinction on students' comprehension of the material. Furthermore, certain teaching strategies are best acceptable for all newcomers depending on the material that is being taught—gaining knowledge of a way to make dilutions in a chemistry path, for example, calls for a fingers-on experiential approach, even if you have a preference to learn from the mirrored image!

Studying preferences

Learning fashion alternatives talk to the "feature strengths and preferences inside the approaches [humans] absorb and method information". The Soloman-Felder model of studying patterns consists of a maximum of the main approaches to knowledge studying alternatives and is designed for use with university and university students to self-check their mastering preferences. Every one of the 4 scales of the Soloman-Felder index of getting to know styles has two contrary options. Each person uses all choices at specific times, but now not normally with equal ranges of self-belief.

The energetic/reflective scale: How do you opt to manner facts?

Lively   Reflective

Lively rookies learn with the aid of doing something with

records. They prefer to technique statistics by using speaking approximating it and trying it out. Reflective freshmen research by way of considering facts. They opt to assume matters via and recognize matters earlier than appearing.

The sensing/intuitive scale: How do you opt to take in information?

Sensing   -   Intuitive

Sensing novices opt to take in statistics this is concrete and sensible. They are oriented towards details, records, and figures and prefer to use demonstrated approaches. They may be sensible and prefer practical packages. Intuitive beginners choose to soak up facts this is abstract, authentic, and orientated towards the concept. They take a look at the large picture and attempt to hold close overall styles. They prefer coming across opportunities and relationships and operating with ideas.

The visible/verbal scale: How do you prefer data to be presented?

Visual   -   Verbal

Visible beginners pick visual presentations of cloth – diagrams, charts, graphs, images. Verbal learners opt for motives with phrases – each written and spoken.

The sequential/international scale: How do you opt to prepare facts?

Sequential   -   Global

Sequential rookies favor preparing data in a linear, orderly style. The research is logically sequenced steps and works with records in an organized and systematic manner. Worldwide freshmen prefer to organize data greater holistically and in an apparently random way without seeing connections. They regularly appear scattered and disorganized in their thinking but often arrive at an innovative or accurate cease product.

How can unbiased inexperienced persons assist themselves?

Active

• Atone for lack of debate using scheduling regular conferences with advising faculty member or are seeking for out other students interested in same or comparable subjects and organize dialogue corporations

• Whilst growing your work to assess, find innovative approaches to apply the cloth found out

• communicate approximately fabric discovered with a circle of relatives and pals

Reflective

• Agenda time to mirror on cloth

• Don't simply read – stop periodically to review the material and consider feasible questions or programs

• Write short summaries of materials study

• Use reflective writing responsibilities (i.e., journals)

Sensing

• Make connections to the real international

• searching for out precise examples of principles and techniques

• Brainstorm about real global connections along with your advising faculty member, other college students, family, or buddies

Intuitive

• Are looking for out interpretation and principle to hyperlink together records

• Attempt to find theoretical connections to a fabric found out

• Talk theories and interpretations with your advising

school member

•   Take care now not to miss the details when producing work to evaluate

Visible

•   Are seeking for out diagrams, graphs, sketches, schematics, pics, glide charts, or other visual representations of cloth

•   Are looking for out the video, CD-ROM, or internet animations of material

•   Organize material right into an idea map (or drift chart)

•   Coloration code your notes

Verbal

•   Write summaries and outlines of cloth learned

•   Convert diagrams, graphs, and so forth, into written descriptions

•   Meet with advising faculty member often to talk about material

•   Organize dialogue companies with different college students

• Explain cloth to the circle of relatives and friend

Sequential

•   Research material in steps

•   Ask advising college member to fill in any skipped steps while explaining data

•   Take time to organize fabric in a logical order

•   try and strengthen global skills via relating new subjects to cloth already found out

International

•   Generate the large picture before seeking to grasp information

•   Are trying to find out widespread overview articles that summarize literature earlier than analyzing individual

studies papers
- Skim thru readings earlier than you examine material carefully
- Instead of spending a bit of time on a subject day by day, try and schedule large blocks of timeless frequently to immerse yourself inside the subject
- Discover connections to material already found out

The consequences of novices' Verbal and visual Cognitive patterns on instruction choice

Abstract. In designing studying commands there may be often the idea that person newbies have extraordinary fashion alternatives. Cognitive fashion may be defined as the individual version in ways of interacting with gaining knowledge of the environment and perceiving statistics. However, special sorts of learning instructions may additionally affect a learner's selection of coaching, their appreciation of those instructions, and learning results. we have carried out an observation to analyze how beginners' verbal and visual cognitive fashion affected the choice of guidance for getting to know Sudoku, their appreciation of the selected education, and the time they spent fixing a Sudoku. Five exceptional Sudoku instructions have been used which vary in the media used. Fundamental cognitive pattern dimensions (Verbal-visual) were assessed using the verbalizer and visualizer questionnaire (VVQ). This paper aims to take into account the relationship among mastering selection, mastering appreciation, and cognitive fashion and to indicate ways wherein gaining knowledge of commands may accommodate a learner's cognitive fashion so that you can offer effective learning surroundings.

Key phrases:
- Cognitive style
- Studying hobby choice
- Variation

A good deal of study investigates adaptive learning systems which use man or woman learner traits to confirm studying content material to improve learner motivation and studying results. Additionally from an academic technological know-how point of view, consistent with, there's a developing frame of gaining knowledge of theories, but these stay unrealistic if they do no longer include statistics approximately man or woman newcomers, and successful educational programs rely on expertise the individuals' mastering needs. In addition, it is stated that educators must renowned mastering differences and use generation to enhance the getting to know the technique. at the same time as conventional eLearning has contributed to the flexibility in learning and reduced schooling cost, for the new generation of e-studying the concept of variation has acquired growing interest several studies have proven that the primary problem with e-mastering is the dearth of personalization. The significance of the edition has been recognized in each conventional and pc-based guidance. Making use of an adaptive medium will help character mastering, leading to stepped forward enjoyment of mastering and aim success. Further, the effect two M. Alhathli et al. on character differences, which include getting to know performance, getting to know fashion, and ability has been extensively investigated. Several personalization strategies had been proposed for developing adaptive studying systems, e.g... It is critical to analyze whether newcomers' cognitive style (focusing on the verbal-visible dimensions) affects their instructional alternatives and influences their learning cloth appreciation. We can use the theoretical framework of the twin Coding concept to interpret inexperienced persons' picks and endorse avenues for destiny research. Also, we should look at the impact of the learner's verbal and visual cognitive style on the choice of gaining knowledge of coaching using thinking about dual coding concepts. associated Work maximum personalization research relies upon the expertise of psychological phenomena, inclusive of cognitive topics consisting of getting to know the structure, cognitive fashion, problem-solving, and knowledge acquisition, as well as much less cognitive topics, along with persona, learner hobby, motivation, and anxiety. This has a look that applies dimensions of cognitive fashion (Verbal - visual) and dual coding theory (DCT), a concept of cognition that indicates that each verbal and non-verbal processing is important for studying. Dual Coding theory. Cognition in line with the twin coding concept involves mental subsystems, a verbal machine that deals with language objects, and an imagery gadget that offers nonlinguistic objects. These subsystems are thought to be separate but interconnected additives of human cognition. Numerous research has been performed using the dual coding principle in teaching and mastering methods. As an instance, Purnell et al. investigated the outcomes of the use of texts and pics on inexperienced persons' comprehension. Combining Visualization-Verbalization has been used successfully to help learners who had skilled difficulty studying mathematics. Different studies have shown that the usage of a visible-verbal aggregate can enhance analyzing-writing ratings, and the teaching of numbers and mathematical operations. Cognitive fashion. Cognitive fashion has generally been used to distinguish character behavior of wondering, interacting, and perceiving facts. Frequently, it's far taken into consideration as a way to gain highbrow goals. Kogan defined cognitive style as "individual variant in modes of perceiving, remembering and questioning, or as distinct methods of apprehending, sorting, transforming and utilizing records". Grabowski and Jonassen maintain the view that "we all differ in how we engage with our environment, extract and perceive data from it, and reflect and prepare the know-how that we've received". Even as diffusion of definitions of cognitive style had been counseled, Messick defined cognitive fashion as a character manner in the manner of organizing and Investigating the outcomes of newbies' Verbal and visual Cognitive styles 3 processing statistics. A sizable effect of character and cognitive style has been proven in learning environments. Cognitive fashion works as a bridge between cognition and character. In our previous work, the effect of persona and mastering fashion on mastering pastime appreciation became investigated. We found little effect of gaining knowledge of fashion. In this examine we will check out the verbal-visible cognitive fashion. The visible-verbal size has appeared in exclusive contexts; occasionally its miles are described as a cognitive style, other instances as a mastering style, or getting to know choice. But, this size has been worried in many studies as a cognitive style. The authentic concept changed into driven from the twin-coding idea. In step with, perceiving and processing records may be through two mental representations: verbally and visually, and the aggregate of these can increase by getting to know effects. Studies on this dimension have, on the whole, agreed that some people tend to think in phrases and others in the picture. College students who desired visual modes of presentation tended to pick pictorial help displays, whereas students who preferred verbal models of presentation tended to choose verbal assist displays. No matter this, the effect of being visual or verbal has been a controversial and a miles disputed challenge inside the subject of schooling and personal conduct. Several issues approximately studying patterns had been pronounced which includes the uncorrelated findings to mastering outcomes, and the dearth of a relation between visualizer/verbalizer and visual/verbal materials. It has even been counseled that supplying substances for a non-desired getting to know style could be greater relevant than offering those for a preferred style. Numerous measures were advanced for the verbal-visual fashion. three take a look at design First, an online survey became conducted to determine the perceived suitability of different learning activities for a verbal-visual learner, and to what volume those getting to know pastime sorts make contributions to acquiring a learner's appreciation in phrases of enjoyability, increasing abilities and confidence. subsequent, an examination became performed in which inexperienced persons found out to clear up Sudoku puzzles and attempted to solve one, and we investigated the effect in their cognitive style (verbal-visual) on training selection, appreciation, and the time they took to remedy the puzzle. They have a look at is worried about the twin coding principle of getting to know and its application to the design of getting to know commands. The goals of the present have a look at had been to: Look at if newbies' cognitive patterns (Verbal-visible) have power on their selection of learning commands. Inspect to which extent novices appreciate their choice in terms of entertainment, growing skills, and self-belief. Discover whether or not beginners' preparation selection and cognitive fashion impacted the time they took to clear up the Sudoko. Offer insight for future research into the validity of matching gaining knowledge of instructions to beginners' verbal-visible cognitive patterns thinking of studying idea along with twin coding principle. four M. Alhathli et al. (a) Listening (b) analyzing (c) visible

Without a doubt for the visual learners, it is indicated that to a certain volume they will feel the furnished gaining knowledge of commands proper a learner's cognitive patterns, in particular verbal-visual. Right here we looked at the getting to know activities that might be most relevant to the second part of the look at, particularly: (1.) Which cognitive fashion is better desirable to listening activities (e.g. audio recorded lectures), (2.) Which cognitive style is higher suited to analyzing activities (e.g. hand-outs, books), (three.) Which cognitive style is better suited to visible activities (e.g. photos, diagrams). Subsequent, contributors rated sports on how fun they think they're, and to what extent they may boom the learner's abilities and self-assurance. Sudoku learning commands - a person takes a look at individuals who have been recruited through an online platform. Five versions of studying commands were created with equal statistics about gambling Sudoku: (1.) A consisted of an audio file simplest, (2.) ATL consisted of an audit report and a long textual content containing the same records as the audio (no figures), (3.) FTS consisted of figures and short textual content, (four.) FA consisted of figures and an audio document, and (five.) FTL consisted of figures and long textual content. This involves dealing with the dual coding concept of getting to know and its utility to the layout of mastering commands. Some hypothesize that newcomers will decide upon and respect mastering instructions that can be aligned with the usage of their two subsystems (verbal-nonverbal), in particular: 1. Verbal beginners will select AO, ATL, and FA. AO because it's far a verbal pastime that fits their cognitive fashion, and ATL and FA because they integrate Audio (a verbal activity) with visible information (text or figures) taking into consideration twin processing. Investigating the results of novices' Verbal and visual Cognitive styles. Visible newbies will pick out FTs, ATL, and FA. FTs due to the fact it's far a visual hobby (with predominate figures) which matches their cognitive fashion, and ATL and FA because they integrate Audio (a verbal activity) with visible records (textual content or figures) making an allowance for dual processing. We accept as true that inexperienced persons will avoid choosing to gain knowledge of instructions that may purpose cut up interest effects. In particular, they believe that rookies will now not choose FTL because reading the lengthy text might use a lot of visible processing (further to verbal processing) which might intrude with searching on the figures. Measures. Cognitive patterns had been identified by the Verbalizer-Visualizer Questionnaire (VVQ) which turned into devised via. This includes a self-record of genuine-false gadgets, decided on from a longer eighty-six gadgets methods of thinking questionnaire, proposed through. The gadgets of the VVQ have coded in one of this manner that higher ratings suggest a visual fashion and lower rankings a verbal style.

Sudoku studying instructions - person study rookies' verbal-visual cognitive styles. On the mirrored image, we trust that that is because they avoided facts overload, as each audio and the lengthy textual content require a whole lot of processing. Maximum visible freshmen selected FTs and FA which in step with our hypothesis, but the wide variety of visible novices is too small to draw any conclusions from this. Inexperienced persons who were slight in their cognitive fashion most customarily decided on FTs, which may be because this would require the least processing or because it maximum suits the everyday way instructions tend to be furnished. Relation between cognitive style and appreciation for the selected coaching. Novices should rate their selection of coaching before and after the Sudoku game. Verbal inexperienced persons should also rate the verbal AO practice higher than mild beginners in phrases of enjoyment and growing capabilities, however no longer in terms of growing confidence. In popular, learners' ratings should then be investigated to understand the effects of newcomers' Verbal and visual Cognitive styles for the AO coaching after the game than before the sport. Mild rookies tend to price FTs barely higher after the game in terms of leisure, increasing skills, and confidence. In contrast, ratings for ATL will remain approximately the same after the game. We additionally investigated the Pearson correlation among the freshmen' degree of verbalness and their rankings for his or her decided-on commands. In designing mastering instructions there's frequently the belief that a few commands are greater effective than others. This study investigated the effect of learner's cognitive patterns (verbal-visual) on the choice of getting to know commands, mastering appreciation, and time finishing touch. We agree that thinking about DCT when adapting studying contents will beautify the learning procedure and improve the choice of substances for individuals. Normal, we discovered that cognitive styles affect learner's choices. Newbies with a selected fashion are more likely to choose to gain knowledge of commands that matched their fashion or require less processing. A challenge of the study is the low range of members, especially of visible inexperienced persons. also, appreciation becomes best measured for the guidance decided on; some other observe needs to analyze whether cognitive style impacts the appreciation of instructions that had been not decided on. This examination also focused on amateur novices, and the impact of rookies' revel in needs analyzing as nicely.

Chapter Eight

Sequential and Global Learners

What's international mastering?
Global gaining knowledge may be defined as an approach to getting to know approximately worldwide improvement through recognizing the importance of linking humans' lives in the course of the arena. There are several definitions of the term 'international studying' and 'development education. Within the context of the worldwide getting to know Programme, global mastering encourages critical examination of global troubles and a cognizance of the effect that people can have on them.

Colleges taking part in global studying understand the effect that expertise and information of improvement can bring to scholars' gaining knowledge throughout the curriculum.

Global studying helps the long-time period development and success of students, by improving their essential wondering abilities and boosting their relationships with peers.

Incorporating a global element into teaching throughout the curriculum can help schools to:
- Broaden a richer, extra exciting curriculum
- Use actual-global contexts to enthuse, encourage and

have interaction students
- Guide raising requirements
- Deliver SMSC and respond positively to the current attention on British values
- Assist scholars make sense of the world wherein they stay and to understand their position within a global society
- Expand an ethos encouraging empathy, fairness, and recognition.

Global gaining knowledge of can help students advantages extra knowledge approximately the developing international, the causes of poverty and what can be done to reduce it. It could additionally assist them to develop the competencies to interpret that know-how so that it will make decisions approximately worldwide poverty. Through this, younger humans can:
- Higher apprehend their position in a globally-interdependent international and to discover strategies by which they could make it greater simply and sustainable;
- Become more familiar with the concepts of interdependence, improvement, globalization, and sustainability;
- Pass from a charity mentality to a social justice mentality;
- Gain extra cognizance of poverty and sustainability
- Think severely about worldwide problems
- Explore opportunity models of development and sustainability
- Take into account the relative merits of various approaches to reducing worldwide poverty and conclude approximately the causes of global poverty and the way it can be addressed.

Characteristics of global learning

College students of contemporary time have to emerge as skillful both at taking part and interacting and concerned with humans from distinct qualifications and backgrounds and at contending efficiently with the styles of unplanned encounters that painting lifestyles and work within the complex world they will flow into commencement. For that reason, worldwide studying is broadly recounted as an essential part of liberal training.

Worldwide gaining knowledge of is a method of education that makes college students ready to analytically compare and participate in complicated global structures, their pointers for the lives of humans, and sustainability of the earth. it could be possible thru these days' civic engagement at domestic and abroad, examine overseas, collaborating video conferencing, and other practices. Worldwide learning is also an effective pedagogy and detail of liberal mastering that desires students to participate across disciplines to resolve multifaceted and actual global problems. There are numerous traits of worldwide mastering; right here we talk about some of them:

1. Local to international pattern

To begin with, mastering is at its private or nearby, it has the capability for authenticity, proximity, and awareness then it looks for being international. newbies joining with an international peer set in face-to-face collaboration or accomplishing out to help in solving time-honored troubles must first have self-information and notice themselves as beginners and thinkers of each the exchange and the collaboration, and this self-know-how attention is continually local.

2. Learner-focused lecture room

As students have access to all information viable, there sincerely is no need to 'spoon-feed' the awareness or provide a grounding in 'one-size fits all content material. Today's global getting to know provides college students exceptional gaining knowledge of surroundings in line with extraordinary personalities, needs, and desires via presenting personalized commands. While learners are accredited to make their very own picks, they own their studying, upsurge inherent thought, and installed extra effort.

Productivity

Students of the contemporary have the modern and utmost equipment and strategies; till now, the usage in lots of cases only is going far from interconnecting with buddies and circle of relatives via textual content, or calls. Although college students have become digital natives and plenty are far far away from developing any virtual content material. They personal multi-featured gadgets to produce infographics, blogs, blogs, tutorials, and the way-to motion pictures. With that equipment and technologies, college students can produce virtual testimonies, innovative blogs, and brief films that they experience happy with a proportion with others.

New technologies

For you to provide picks, having one's own realistic experience and expertise with students will be useful. State-of-the-art technology is rising day by day, getting to know a device or generation as soon as and for all is not an option. Contemporary technologies are new for amateur and experienced trainers similarly, so anybody can adopt them at any time.

Collaborative

The use of tools and era permits collaboration between college students and teachers. Producing presentations, projects, virtual resources, collectively with other teachers and college students will make the schoolroom similar to the world. Group attempts ought to go similarly to sharing documents via electronic mail or making displays. a lot of exceptional minds by no means move past a discussion that's a large loss. Collaboration at the global stage can alternate our whole revel in.

Consequences of the world gaining knowledge of can be advanced through numerous activities, containing engagement with foreign places inexperienced persons and scholars, the world over focused capstones, frequent taking part videoconferences, and internships.

Sequential and international novices

Someone who's a sequential learner approaches studying and problem-solving in a "systematic" manner. Systematic means that their technique is to use a chain of logical steps. It miles analogous to writing a program for a computer— first, try this then do that, and so forth. Sequential novices can help themselves analyze by asking the instructor to fill in any missing steps and reorganize their class notes right into a logical order. Some other manner they can help themselves is to attempt to narrate the issue fabric to a topic they already realize. International inexperienced persons will soak up statistics at random and then all at once understand. They do no longer necessarily need all the man or woman steps laid out and they will have a problem explaining their technique from beginning to finish. This form of learner desires the big photograph explained which will apprehend. Global learns can help themselves analyze through usually asking the instructor to offer and define the massive picture and trying to narrate the difficulty to something they already recognize. Another method is to skim the chapter ahead of time to get an idea approximately the large image.

A key distinction among the two patterns is that the sequential research will recognize and be able to complete the person steps but won't absolutely recognize the big picture. In comparison, an international learner will understand the massive picture, but may not be able to explain the way to get from the beginning to complete.

Designing a class around Sequential and worldwide novices

The magnificence subject matter is manufacturer surplus. I would begin the elegance with a discussion masking how the subject suits the field of economics. The dialogue will begin with a broad generalization and cease with how the subject suits our story (i.e. the way it links to destiny and former instructions). As an example, I'd begin with an announcement like "Economics is set how society offers with the allocation of scarce assets" and end with discussing how manufacturer surplus alongside patron surplus can be used to calculate society's overall welfare.

After the huge dialogue, I'd offer and define the elegance. The general define I'd follow might be (1) review of subject matter, (2) producer surplus definition, (three) graphical illustration, (4) graphing strains/finding area, (five) finding producer surplus, (6) examples, (7) finding adjustments in customer surplus, (8) examples, and (nine) end.

For components (four), (5), and (7) step-by means of-step instructions may be given to help sequential learning. The examples will follow these steps. The belief provides the possibility to recap what we have executed within the class and provide any other huge image explanation a good way to assist college students to analyze.

A sequential learner learns exceptional when they're taught in levels with linear steps in which every step follows the remaining logically. They may locate the most logical way to get to an answer through the usage of step-by-step paths to discover solutions. Sequential freshmen may not understand the whole photograph till they understand and understand all of the steps and a way to get to the final solution, because they'll logically be able to place all the material together.

Sequential learners need to use the cloth they had been taught and order it in a logical way that makes in view that to them. They'll be able to follow those steps to find answers in other locations and to different troubles.

International inexperienced persons lean in huge jumps, taking in material and records randomly without making links between the statistics and then expertise it. A worldwide learner may not understand the work till they realize everything after which they may abruptly just recognize what they were taught.

Sequential vs worldwide inexperienced persons

Every one in every of our college students is precise, and so is how they learn. Some specific fashions were proposed to explain those varying learning styles. Within the model proposed through Dr. Richard Felder and Barbara Soloman, they discuss one getting to know fashion recognized as sequential or global. They endorse that students lean in the direction of a choice for both a sequential or a worldwide presentation of facts.

Keep in mind that international and sequential learning patterns exist on a continuum, with a few human beings heavily favoring one or the alternative, and others the usage of a touch little bit of both. As a result, methods for helping worldwide novices and sequential newbies aren't mutually distinct. An aggregate of those techniques can help all your students.

Assisting Sequential novices

Sequential newbies study quality with the aid of knowing the details of a topic and slowly constructing a photograph of the larger photo. Sequential rookies work very well with details however regularly have hassle knowledge large principles and ideas. You may assist sequential rookies by:

• Displaying an outline or prepared shape for the presentation of the latest fabric

• Constructing your presentation of recent fabric in steps that result in the principle concept or concept

• Starting with less difficult standards and constructing as much as more complex ideas supporting global rookies

Global newcomers need to peer the bigger image and how the brand new cloth connects to records they've already found out. Worldwide inexperienced persons work properly with large standards or thoughts however warfare with the info. You can assist international freshmen via:

• Giving a quick overview of the topic before jumping into the information

• Drawing connections from precise details or statistics to the larger principles

• Having them work on issues or issues that inspire innovative methods in preference to the utility of a chain of steps

I've read one or two matters recently about possibilities for sequential getting to know vs. international gaining knowledge of i.e. learning matters in a step-via-step manner vs. expertise how distinctive portions suit together. This reminds me of my expertise in new mathematical proofs while I used to be at college. In books, proofs are usually written out as a series of logical steps. Evidence not written out in logical steps isn't always taken into consideration evidence. However, expertise a proof is much extra than being able to reproduce the logical steps of the proof. I'm no longer sure that I should say exactly what it way to apprehend evidence, but just knowing how one line follows from the preceding one sincerely is not information proof.

One of the first 'real' theorems you encounter when you study arithmetic at college is called Lagrange's Theorem. It says that 'the size of any subgroup of a finite organization divides the size of the institution'. That glaringly might not make any sense at all if you haven't had the pride of university-degree mathematics and do not know what a collection is, however, try to endure with me and get the gist of what I'm saying if not the info.

If I would in no way seen the proof of Lagrange's

Theorem earlier than and changed into seeking to apprehend its evidence, what I might do is first try to determine out the overall shape of the evidence e.g.

First, we prove that the costs of the subgroup are equivalence lessons, then we display that every cost is the equal length. It follows that the scale of the group is the number of costs times the dimensions of a cost, so the dimensions of the subgroup divide the order of the group.

Then I'd cross down a stage and examine how every one of those bits is proved. So for example I would make certain I understood why every cost must be the same length. Maybe at this sort of point, I'd get stuck - something that was apparent to the person who wrote the proof wasn't apparent to me in which case I might just leave and figure out why it turned into actual.

From time to time, with greater complex proofs, I might pass down greater tiers. This is a piece like if you're looking to figure out the path from A to B with something like Google maps. You would begin with a massive scale view in which you could see the start and give up of your adventure. For a few bits like a long stretch on a motorway you would not zoom into very a whole lot while other bits in which you were going through a town, you may need to zoom into with a variety of elements.

When I used to be reading the proof, I'd be skipping back and forth plenty even as I went via this process, operating the general image after which zooming in on specific bits. Just to make things more complex, even as I was doing all this, I might probably have a selected instance of a set in my head and be concurrently strolling through whatever a part of the evidence I used to be on with that example. I would not believe a part of the evidence as it is manifestly actual for the example, but it'd probably assist me to visualize and remember what changed into happening. on occasion, with a new roof, I wouldn't even do any of this at all - I would pretty a lot ignore the proof inside the book and just take the declaration of the theory and try and prove it from scratch for myself. Once I was given caught sneak a study of the evidence for a touch. But in exercise, there simply wasn't time to try this for each evidence which you came across.

What I without a doubt did not do become read via a proof in a step-by means of-step manner. But regardless of this, I would really have hated it if the evidence became not been written out sequentially. I did not need the evidence to be written out in the equal manner that I understood it. I assume it'd have made it an awful lot harder to apprehend. Why is that this? I am now not certain. Perhaps, it is as it became the real technique of understanding the evidence that became vital, and to have it written down would have made it too easy to bypass this manner. Perhaps due to the fact it would be difficult to get it right - something I would have struggled on, someone else would possibly have visible immediately and vice versa. Maybe it is due to the fact when you're caught on a sequential proof, it is simpler to pinpoint in which you are caught. Perhaps, it is because, once I understood a proof, I honestly did think about it sequentially so having it written down sequentially made it a more useful reminder afterward.

Very every so often, you'll find an eBook that did try to explain the evidence in a forward and backward kind way, however, I never truly preferred that until it becomes honestly demarcated with a separate 'right' proof. With one semi-exception, the teachers I favored at university had been the step-through-step ones who also gave overviews rather than the hand-wavy ones. I wager what I preferred maximum becomes a preferred proof with either an outline of how the evidence labored on the beginning with more lines thrown in like 'Now we show that all the costs are the equal size'.

Is that how different mathematicians apprehend proofs? I am not certain, though it labored for me. it would be thrilling to recognize what correlation there may be between ability at arithmetic and the way people pass about knowledge proofs. What seems a getting-to-know preference could just be a case of not knowing better. As a substitute, it could turn out that maybe it simply is a persona factor. Or it can be greater complex nonetheless - the Fields medalists of this global may approach things differently from human beings like me as I maybe did from the many people who struggled with mathematics at college. the one element I'm positive of is that it's a piece more diffused than being both a sequential learner or a worldwide learner.

Collection studying

In cognitive psychology, series studying is inherent to human capacity because it's far an integrated part of conscious and non-conscious learning in addition to activities. Sequences of information or sequences of actions are used in numerous regular tasks: "from sequencing sounds in a speech to sequencing movements in typing or gambling instruments to sequencing actions in driving a vehicle." Series getting to know may be used to examine ability acquisition and in research of various businesses ranging from neuropsychological patients to babies. Consistent with Ritter and Nerb, "The order wherein material is offered can strongly affect what's discovered, how speedy overall performance increases, and once in a while even whether the fabric is found out at all." Collection gaining knowledge of, extra known and understood as a form of explicit getting to know, is now additionally being studied as a shape of implicit studying as well as different forms of studying. sequence studying can also be called sequential conduct, behavior sequencing, and serial order in conduct.

Inside the first half of the twentieth century, Margaret Floy Washburn, John B. Watson, and different behaviorists believed behavioral sequencing to be governed using the reflex chain, which states that stimulation due to a preliminary movement triggers an extra movement, which triggers any other additional motion, and so forth. In 1951, Karl Lashley, a neurophysiologist at Harvard University, posted "The problem of Serial Order in behavior," addressing the cutting-edge ideas about sequence getting to know and introducing his speculation. He criticized the preceding view based on six lines of proof:

The primary line is that actions can arise even when sensory comments are interrupted. The second is that a few motion sequences arise too quickly for factors of the sequences to be induced with the aid of comments from the preceding factors. Next is that the mistakes in conduct propose inner plans for what is going to be carried out later. Additionally, the time to provoke a motion series can grow with the length or complexity of the collection. The following line is the properties of movements happening early in a sequence that can anticipate later capabilities. Then lastly the neural interest can imply education of upcoming behavior occasions, which include upcoming behavior events inside the fairly lengthy-term destiny.

Lashley argued that sequence gaining knowledge of, or behavioral sequencing or serial order in conduct, isn't always a consequence of sensory comments. As an alternative, he proposed that there are plans for conduct because the anxious machine prepares for a few behaviors however no longer others. He said that there has been a hierarchical enterprise of plans. He got here up with numerous strains of proof. The first of those is that the context adjustments useful interpretations of the equal behaviors, including the way "right, right, proper, rite, and write" are interpreted based totally on the context of the sentence. "Right" may be interpreted as a route or as something exact depending on the context. The second line of proof says that errors are concerned with human conduct as a hierarchical company. in addition, "hierarchical company of plans comes from the timing of behavioral sequences." the larger the word, the longer the reaction time, which factors into "interpreting" or "unpacking" hierarchical plans. Extra evidence is how smooth or difficult it is to research a sequence. The mind can create a "reminiscence for what is set to show up" in addition to a "memory for what has befallen." The final evidence for the hierarchical business enterprise of plans is characterized through "chunking". This talent combines more than one unit into large units.

Forms of collection learning

There are two broad classes of collection studying—

explicit and implicit—with subcategories. Express series getting to know has been regarded and studied for the reason that discovery of series getting to know. However, currently, implicit series gaining knowledge of has received more attention and research. A form of implicit getting to know, implicit series gaining knowledge of refers to the underlying strategies of learning that human beings are ignorant of—in other words, studying without knowing. The exact homes and quantity of mechanisms of implicit studying are debated. Other sorts of implicit collection mastering encompass motor sequence getting to know, temporal collection learning, and associative series learning.

Sequence learning problems

Collection mastering issues are used to better recognize the exclusive types of series mastering. There are four basic sequence studying troubles: sequence prediction, sequence era, sequence reputation, and sequential decision making. These "problems" display how sequences are formulated. They display the styles sequences observe and the way these different series gaining knowledge of troubles are associated with each other.

Sequence prediction attempts to expect the subsequent instant detail of a sequence-based totally on all the preceding elements. Collection era is basically the same as a series prediction: an attempt to piece collectively a series separately the manner it clearly takes place. Sequence reputation takes sure standards and determines whether or not the series is valid. Sequential choice making or sequence era through actions breaks down into 3 variations: aim-orientated, trajectory-orientated, and reinforcement-maximizing. These three versions all need to pick the action(s) or step(s) that will cause the goal inside the future.

Those collection mastering troubles mirror the hierarchical organization of plans due to the fact each detail within the sequences builds on the previous elements.

In a traditional test published in 1967, Alfred L. Yarbus verified that though topics viewing pictures pronounced apprehending the portrait as an entire, their eye actions successively fixated on the maximum informative elements of the picture. Those observations suggest that underlying an apparently parallel process of face perception, a serial oculomotor procedure is concealed. It's far a not unusual commentary that when talent is being received, we are extra attentive within the initial segment, however, after repeated exercise, the talent will become almost automatic; that is additionally referred to as subconscious competence. we can then concentrate on getting to know a new motion even as acting formerly found out actions skillfully. hence, it appears that a neural code or illustration for the found out talent is created in our mind, which is commonly referred to as procedural reminiscence. The procedural reminiscence encodes tactics or algorithms as opposed to data.

In this chapter, the author briefly reviewed the literature related to this examination. The belief of studying patterns along with a definition of the key phrases, categories of mastering styles, and Oxford's concept on language gaining knowledge of styles had been first reviewed. Then the writer tested the gender and overseas language mastering theories associated with learning patterns.

Sooner or later, the writer reviewed preceding studies that have been made on the connection between getting to know styles and second or overseas language mastering each abroad and home.

Theories associated with getting to know styles

This segment includes definitions of different phrases of studying patterns, categories of learning styles, and Oxford's principle of language learning styles.

Extraordinary terms concerning gaining knowledge of patterns

The definitions of styles and mastering styles are first reviewed, and then cognitive patterns and gaining knowledge of patterns are differentiated in this component.

Definitions of styles and learning styles

• Styles

Before reviewing the literature of getting to know styles, it is essential to recognize the definition of "patterns". The concept of "styles" changed into first recommend with the aid of cognitive psychologists. Brown (2002: 104) defines fashion as "a term that refers to consistent and alternatively enduring inclinations or options inside a character." consequently, styles are those fashionable characteristics of intellectual functioning (and persona kind, as properly) that particularly pertain to one as a character, which differentiates one from someone else.

• Getting to know styles

Concerning studies of getting to know styles, the maximum critical problem is the confusion of its definitions. in the past many years, learning patterns have been used in various and occasionally difficult methods inside the literature. It is very common to pay attention to special opinions on its definitions based totally on specific findings on this comparatively new research subject of learning patterns, for each study defines it from a particular perspective. However, there isn't an agreed-upon definition of studying patterns. Getting to know styles can be described within the following approaches.

Keefe defines learning styles as "the characteristic cognitive, affective and physiological behaviors that function especially solid signs of how freshmen perceive, engage with and respond to the gaining knowledge of the environment. Dunn et al. (1978:11) define learning styles as "how all and sundry absorbs and keeps statistics and/or capabilities; no matter how that procedure is defined, it's far dramatically different for each person".

In case you need help with writing your essay, our professional essay writing carrier is here to Sims & Sims recommend that studying styles are typical methods a person behaves, feels, and procedures facts in getting to know conditions. Therefore, mastering style is verified in that pattern of conduct and performance by which a man or woman's tactics instructional revel in. Oxford et al. (1991) briefly define the mastering style as the general strategies college students used to learn a brand new subject or address a brand new problem.

Claxton and Murrell (1987, cited in Eliason, 2002: 19-20) use an onion metaphor wherein the layers of the onion constitute "layers" of learning patterns: fundamental character characteristics shape the middle; information-processing traits shape the second layer; social interaction traits form the third layer; educational options shape the fourth and outermost layer. Claxton and Murrell postulate that the center of the onion represents the most solid characteristics, with each successive layer being steadily extra amenable to alternate.

Tan Dingliang (1995: 12) defines mastering patterns as: "the way that a learner often adopts in the studying procedure, which incorporates the getting to know techniques which have been stabilized within a learner, the desire of a few coaching stimuli and getting to know tendency."

Reid (1995) summarizes definitions of studying patterns as internally primarily based characteristics of people for the intake or information of new facts. Basically studying styles are primarily based upon how a person perceives and processes records to facilitate getting to know. Amongst these definitions, Kinsella' definition of gaining knowledge of patterns is extensively conventional concludes that gaining knowledge of fashion is a character's natural, habitual, and desired way(s) of absorbing, processing, and keeping new data and skills which persist no matter teaching strategies or content material area. Kinsella also emphasizes that "anybody has a mastering style, however, anybody's is as particular as a signature. Every signature appears to be prompted by each nature and nurture; its miles a biological and developmental set of traits."

Cognitive styles and mastering styles

The second problem about the observation on mastering patterns is the confusion of the meanings of the terms of learning styles and cognitive styles as they may be frequently used interchangeably in research. The explanation of the phrases might be helpful to higher apprehend gaining knowledge of patterns.

Messick's (1984) definition of cognitive patterns has been

broadly cited. He defines cognitive patterns as "regular person differences in preferred methods of organizing and processing statistics and enjoy." Cognitive patterns are "characteristic self-regular mode of functioning which character shows of their perceptual and highbrow sports". In line with Tan Dingliang, cognitive styles especially seek advice from the methods of statistics processing, this is, character's regular methods of processing perception, memory, and wondering.

Brown (2002: 104) shows that "the manner we analyze matters in widespread and the particular assault we make on a trouble appear to hinge on an alternatively amorphous link among character and cognition; this link is referred to as cognitive style". According to Brown (2002), whilst cognitive patterns are especially associated with an academic context, wherein affective and physiological elements are intermingled, they are normally extra commonly referred to as studying styles. Hence from this attitude, gaining knowledge of styles is seemed to a subset of cognitive patterns. Meanwhile, cognitive styles can once in a while be seen as a subset of learning patterns. Keefe (1986) reviews that studying styles encompass no longer only cognitive methods, but also integrate affective and physiological behaviors that assist freshmen to perceive, have interaction with, and reply to the learning surroundings.

Renzulli & David Yun Dai (2001) differentiate the phrases in element: cognitive styles are mainly concerned in the psychological domain, whilst mastering patterns are specially proposed by researchers of educational discipline; researchers of cognitive styles adopt an extra nice technique, whereas researchers of mastering patterns cognizance on a more phenomenological attitude. Regarding the technique, overall performance-primarily based degree is generally utilized by cognitive patterns researchers, while self-record is the degree that learning styles researchers generally use.

Classes of getting to know styles

Confusion additionally exists inside the literature on classes of gaining knowledge of styles for lots same or similar elements researched underneath the identical name. Reid (1995) divides studying-style studies into three important classes: cognitive patterns, sensory getting to know patterns, and character mastering patterns.

Cognitive gaining knowledge of patterns

Cognitive studying styles consist of area-independent/subject-structured, analytic/global, reflective/impulsive mastering patterns, and Kolb's experiential mastering model, belonging to the aspects of psychology. Among them, researches on the field - impartial/discipline-structured (FI/FD) appeal to the maximum attention of the SLA domain.

In line with Reid (1995), subject-unbiased beginners analyze greater efficaciously step by step, or sequentially, beginning with studying facts and proceeding to ideas. They see the bushes instead of the woodland; whereas area-based (field-sensitive) newcomers analyze greater efficiently in contexts, holistically, intuitively, and are especially sensitive to human relationships and interactions. They see the wooded area in preference to the bushes. Chapelle (1995) explains that FI/FD refers to how humans perceive and memorize statistics. Reid (1995) defines that analytic newbies analyze greater efficiently personally; pick placing personal dreams, and reply to a sequential, linear, step-through-step presentation of materials; while worldwide (relational) freshmen research extra successfully thru concrete experience, and via interactions with others.

According to Reid (1995), if learners can learn more efficaciously given time to don't forget alternatives earlier than responding, they're reflective newbies; and they're often greater correct language beginners; while if novices can examine greater efficaciously being able to respond immediately and to take risks, they may be impulsive freshmen; and they may be often more fluent language rookies.

Kolb (1984) categorizes his experiential gaining knowledge of the model of perception (concrete stories and abstract conceptualization) and technique (reflective observation and active experimentation) into four learner types which can be converger, diverger, assimilator, and accommodator. Converger (not unusual sense learner) learns extra correctly while he or she can perceive abstractly and to manner actively. Diverger (innovative learner) learns greater successfully while she or he can perceive concretely and to technique reflectively. Assimilator (analytic learner) learns extra efficaciously when he or she can understand abstractly and to technique reflectively. Accommodator (dynamic learner) learns extra efficaciously whilst he or she is capable of understanding concretely and to manner actively.

Sensory gaining knowledge of styles

In step with Reid (1995), sensory learning patterns include dimensions

Perceptual studying patterns and environmental gaining knowledge of patterns. Perceptual gaining knowledge of patterns comprises 4 varieties of mastering patterns that are auditory, visual, tactile, and kinesthetic patterns. Auditory learners examine more correctly thru the ears; visible newcomers research greater correctly via the eyes (seeing); tactile novices analyze more correctly thru contact (fingers-on); kinesthetic inexperienced persons examine greater effectiveness through concrete whole frame studies (entire-frame motion). Physical and sociological patterns belong to the environmental mastering patterns. Physical freshmen examine extra efficiently while such variables as temperature, sound, light, food, mobility, time, and school room/observe association is considered. Sociological beginners learn more effectively while such variables as an institution, person, pair and group work, or tiers of instructor authority are considered.

Affective/Temperament gaining knowledge of patterns

Gaining knowledge of varieties of this type is based on having an effect on, personality, tolerance of ambiguity, and brain hemisphere. Myer and Briggs record that affective and persona elements have an impact on newcomers' getting to know patterns an awesome deal. Mayer-Briggs team examined dichotomous styles of functioning of their Mayer and Briggs Temperament patterns (MBTI) which consist of extraversion-introversion, sensing-perception, thinking-feeling, and judging-perceiving. in step with Reid (1995), extroverted and introverted styles belong to extraversion-introversion. The extroverted learner learns greater correctly through concrete enjoy, settlement with the outside international, and relationships with others; whereas introverted learner learns greater efficiently in person, impartial situations which might be extra worried about ideas and ideas. Sensing-notion carries sensing and notion styles. Sensing learner learns extra successfully from reviews of observable statistics and happenings; prefers bodily, experience-based enter. Conversely, notion learner learns greater efficaciously from significant stories and forms relationships with others. In questioning-feeling styles, the thinking learner learns extra effectively from impersonal situations and logical results; whereas the feeling learner learns extra efficaciously from personalized circumstances and social values. And in judging-perceiving patterns, judging learner learns greater correctly by mirrored image, and analysis, and methods that contain closure; conversely, perceiving learner learns greater efficaciously through negotiation, feeling, and inductive methods that postpone closure.

Reid (1995) indicates that tolerance of ambiguity patterns additionally belong to the affective/temperament studying patterns. The ambiguity-tolerant learner learns more effectively whilst possibilities for experiment and hazard, in addition to interaction, are present; whereas ambiguity-illiberal beginners learn extra correctly when in less bendy, much less unstable, extra based situations.

Reid (1995) additionally claims that whether or not the learner is left-brained or proper-brained will have an impact on the learner's learning patterns. Left-brained rookies tend in the direction of visible, analytic, reflective, self-reliant mastering; conversely, right-brained novices generally tend toward auditory, worldwide/relational, impulsive, interactive studying.

Oxford's Language studying patterns principle

Oxford and Burry-inventory (1995) put forward the maximum sizeable styles for ESL/EFL getting to know which include global/analytic, discipline-unbiased/field-dependent, feeling/questioning, impulsive/reflective, intuitive-random/concrete-sequential, closure-oriented/open, extroverted/introverted, and visible/auditory/palms-on styles. They advocate that every fashion desire offers vast advantages for learning and that the critical thing for rookies is to pick out the fashion alternatives and to use them every time viable.

Oxford (1991, mentioned in Kang Shumin, 2003) businesses all of the above getting to know styles into three classes: sensory gaining knowledge of styles (visual, auditory, and arms-on), cognitive learning patterns (intuitive-random and concrete-sequential, closure-oriented/open and worldwide/analytic), and personality gaining knowledge of styles (extroverted and introverted).

Sensory gaining knowledge of patterns

• Visual patterns

• Visible students experience studying and that they select material in a schoolroom environment to be offered in a visible format including books, board work, and handouts.

• Auditory styles

• Auditory students enjoy lectures, conversations, and oral instructions. They decide on the material in a classroom environment that is presented as auditory enter such as radio, oral preparation, oral verbal exchange, and audiotape.

• Hands-on patterns

• Arms-on college students like plenty of movement and

enjoy working with collages, flashcards, and tangible items. They opt to be bodily worried about obligations, tending to prefer activities inclusive of total physical reaction (TPR) and position-play.

Oxford et al (1992) discover that sensory alternatives (visual, auditory, and palms-on) are very important in the multicultural ESL/EFL lecture room. Reid (1987) additionally argues that ESL/EFL students from exclusive cultures vary appreciably in their sensory choices. People with Asian cultural backgrounds, as an example, are frequently tremendously visible, even as Hispanics tend to be auditory. Students from non-Western cultures in which fingers-on reviews are valued often decide on a corresponding getting to know style.

Cognitive gaining knowledge of patterns

- Intuitive-random/concrete-sequential patterns
- Intuitive-random ESL/EFL students choose to increase a mental photograph of the second language in a summary, random manner in search of the underlying language gadget. Within the absence of complete expertise of the target language, intuitive-random style novices usually rent speculative and predictive strategies.

Concrete-sequential ESL/EFL students choose rigidly done, strictly planned, and adhered to sequential instructions. They like language mastering substances and techniques that involve combos of sound, motion, sight, and touch, and that may be applied in concrete, sequential, linear ways.

- Closure-orientated/Open-oriented styles
- Closure-orientated ESL/EFL students carry out extra successfully if provided with established sports and greater time. Normally, they desire carefully deliberate and

completed duties, rather than ambiguity and uncertainty in a classroom environment.

Open-oriented ESL/EFL students desire an extra open and flexible schedule, demonstrating a high diploma of tolerance towards ambiguity in the schoolroom. generally, they approach a language challenge or a category interest as even though it were an entertaining recreation, and they don't worry approximately any longer comprehending everything and do no sense the want to come back to speedy conclusions approximately the subject.

• Worldwide/Analytic styles

• The global style ESL/EFL students normally hire a holistic view early inside the studying manner, into which they suit greater particular facts as learning progresses. They usually have a look at several elements of the subject in an equal time, constantly making corrections among the theoretical elements and realistic applications as they learn, and make tremendous use of analogies. Moreover, this sort of learner employs holistic techniques to remedy issues which includes guessing and paraphrasing, favoring a look for the general idea rather than for accuracy. Ellis (1989) argues that "global inexperienced persons" opt for experiential getting to know and getting to know through communication.

The analytic fashion ESL/EFL college students don't have any trouble selecting out considerable info from a welter of background gadgets. They typically attention to their interest greater narrowly on portions of records, how within the hierarchical shape, preferring element in preference to the general picture. They're oriented in the direction of rules tending to consciousness on step-with the aid of step presentation of cloth. Commonly, theoretical and sensible components are discovered separately. Moreover, this sort of learner employs language techniques that prefer precise wording instead of guessing or paraphrasing in their aim of attaining accuracy. Ellis (1989) suggests that "analytic newcomers" select formal, person getting to know in a lecture room surroundings.

Character mastering patterns

- Extroversion/Introversion
- The size of patterns particularly affects school room control, mainly the grouping of students. Extroverted students carry out most productively in a group environment, enjoying sports that involve different college students, along with function-play, communication, and other interplay favoring social dreams instead of impersonal rewards. Conversely, introverted college students are inspired most via their personal inner global of ideas and emotions. They prefer working alone in any other case in a pair with a person they realize properly. They dislike plenty of non-stop institution work in the ESL/EFL schoolroom. This contrast is really much like the categories of institution/individual fashion made by way of Reid (1987).

Gender variations in Language gaining knowledge of patterns

Many investigations display that men and women examine differently. in which do the gender variations come from? Numerous sources may be postulated for gender differences in language gaining knowledge of styles. Among these are mind hemispheric and socialization.

our instructional experts are prepared and waiting to help with any writing assignment you could have. From easy essay plans, to complete dissertations, you could assure us we've got a provider perfectly matched to your desires.

Gender differences in mind Hemisphericity

In keeping with Oxford (2002), brain hemispheric or lateralization (right, left, and included) is a feature of many learning style surveys. Studies on the 2 cerebral hemispheres show that every hemisphere can be answerable for a specific mode of thinking. The left hemisphere is associated with logical, analytical thought, with mathematical and linear processing of statistics. The right hemisphere perceives and recalls visual, tactile, and auditory pix, and its miles greater green in processing holistic, integrative, and emotional statistics. Each hemisphere offers language in another way. According to inclined (1988, noted in Oxford, 2002), right-hemisphere-dominant individuals–those whose proper side of the mind typically dominates their questioning procedures–have a tendency to be extra field structured (less able to separate the details from a complicated historical past), worldwide, and emotion-oriented. Willing (1988) and Leaver claim that left-hemisphere-dominant people–those whose dominant brain hemisphere is the left–are extra field-unbiased, analytic, and logical-oriented.

A few researchers inclusive of Spring & Deutsch (1989) and Elias (1992) (referred to in Oxford, 2002) discover numerous sources of gender differences in brain dominance:

•   In men, the left hemisphere might be extra lateralized (specialized) for verbal activity and the proper hemisphere may be extra lateralized for abstract or spatial processing.

•   Girls would possibly use each the left and the right hemispheres for both verbal and spatial pastime, as a result displaying greater integrated brain functioning and much less hemispheric differentiation.

• In ladies in comparison to men, a part of the corpus callosum (the bundle of brain fibers linking the left and proper hemispheres) is bigger on the subject of standard mind weight, allowing greater records to be exchanged among the two hemispheres.

• Primarily based on such research findings, Oxford (2002) postulates that men might typically procedure language learning facts greater with ease through the left-hemispheric, analytic model, but ladies might extra frequently method language gaining knowledge of statistics thru the integration of left-and right-hemispheric modes. However, other researchers oppose the idea that brain hemispheres are more included in ladies than in adult males or that brain hemispheric differences could make a giant difference. The prevailing opinion seems to be that there are indeed gender differences in mind hemispheric that deserve consideration and in addition exploration. And our information of language studying fashion–for each ESL and foreign languages could benefit if those variations have been explored.

Gender variations in Socialization

In keeping with Tan (1995), the difference between women and men is a result of each nature and nurture. The rationale of gender variations that forget about sociological elements is incomplete. Oxford (2002) claims that socialization which is the way we deliver up our young and combine them into society thru a widespread network of social roles may additionally be a tremendous influence on gender differences in language mastering styles. Through gender socialization, special behaviors and attitudes are advocated and discouraged in women and men. Parents reply in a different way to boy babies and lady babies from the first hour of life and after that train their kids "intercourse-appropriate" behaviors. Socialization technique takes region not most effective inside own family, but additionally within the college. Faculty sporting events a good deal of influence on the advent of gendered attitudes and behaviors. In school, teachers help the preceding socialization styles, paying greater interest to competitive, disruptive boys than to women with the same behavior, and responding to passive and dependent girls—even though instructors decide on the behavior of ladies. In school, curriculum materials, instructors' expectations, academic monitoring, and peer relations encourage women and boys to research gender-associated capabilities and self-standards.

Dating between mastering styles and overseas Language getting to know

Ellis (1994) factors out that each one freshman analyze input and store data approximately the L2 in a great deal the identical way. However, he also admits that it's far real that novices range enormously in each way they set approximately leaning an L2 and additionally in what they simply achieve studying. Therefore, he regards the look at individual learner differences (IDs) as a crucial location of labor in second language acquisition (SLA) research. He sets up a primary framework for investigating individual learner variations to guide the examinations of IDs.

Framework for investigating individual Learner differences

In his framework for investigating person learner variations, Ellis (1994: 473) identifies three units of interrelating variables. The primary set includes IDs that are of three most important kinds: beliefs approximately language mastering, affective states, and fashionable factors. general factors encompass age, language aptitude, studying style, motivation, and character. the second set of variables consists of the exclusive strategies that a learner employs to examine and use the L2. The learner strategies embody studying techniques and use strategies. The 0.33 set concerns language learning effects which can be taken into consideration in phrases of usual L2 proficiency, achievement concerning L2 performance on a selected mission, and a fee of acquisition. The inner part of the triangle is gaining knowledge of strategies and mechanisms, so placed for they are in large part hidden.

Those three sets of variables are interrelated. ID research till now has focused on investigating the effects of different identity variables on learner talent, achievement, or charge of progress, measured in phrases of performance on some sort of language test (Ellis, 1994). "The overall factors constitute major areas of impacts on getting to know and can be ranged alongside a continuum in line with how mutable they are". In keeping with Liu Runqing (1995) and Ellis (1994), the principal standard factors which have received the most interest in SLA research are age, language aptitude, getting to know fashion, motivation, and character. newcomers' beliefs and affective states are likely to have a right away impact on L2 studying, but they themselves may be motivated by way of several preferred factors relating to beginners' potential and choice to research and the manner they select to head about studying.

Man or woman learner differences-beliefs approximately language gaining knowledge of-affective states -popular factors studying techniques N and mechanisms(2)(three) Learner strategies, Language learning outcomes-on scalability-on fulfillment-on fee of acquisition

The position of mastering patterns in foreign Language mastering

Reid (1995) presents a few fundamentals of learning patterns. She claims that mastering patterns inside the ESL/EFL lecture rooms is primarily based on six hypotheses: (1) anybody, college students and teachers alike, has a learning style and getting to know strengths and weaknesses; (2) mastering styles are often defined as opposite, however without a doubt, they exist on a huge continuum; (3) studying styles are fee-impartial; this is, no person fashion is better than others (however it's miles actual that there are college students with some getting to know patterns work higher than people with some other learning styles); (4) students should be advocated to "stretch" their gaining knowledge of patterns so that they'll be more empowered in a ramification of gaining knowledge of conditions; (5) students' strategies are regularly connected to their gaining knowledge of styles; (6) instructors have to allow their college students to turn out to be privy to their mastering strengths and weaknesses.

McCarthy (1980) claims that the learning patterns principle affects training in the following three aspects: practice, curriculum, and evaluation.

(1) Instruction—teachers have to lay out their practice techniques to hook up with college students' gaining knowledge of styles, the usage of diverse combinations of revel in, mirrored image, conceptualization, and

experimentation. instructors can introduce a huge variety of experiential factors into the schoolroom, including sound, song, visuals, movement, enjoyment, and even talking.

(2) Curriculum–Educators should area emphasis on instinct, feeling, sensing, and creativeness, similarly to the traditional competencies of evaluation, motive, and sequential trouble solving.

(3) assessment–instructors must hire a selection of assessment techniques, focusing on the improvement of "whole brain" potential and each of the distinctive learning styles.

Ellis (1994) concludes that newbies virtually fluctuate especially in their preferred method to L2 studying, however, it's miles impossible to mention which learning style works high-quality. And quite possibly it's miles newbies who show flexibility who's maximum successful, however, there may be no actual evidence yet for the sort of end.

Preceding Researches on getting to know patterns and foreign Language getting to know abroad and domestic.

Previous Researches executed within the West

While getting to know patterns were to start with delivered, the difference between field independence (FI) and field dependence (FD) has attracted the most interest in SLA studies (Ellis, 1994). The results of many research display that human beings tend to be dominant in a single mode of Fl/FD or the other. Consistent with Ellis (1989), each FI/FD rookie can benefit from language success in SLA and the embedded-figures exams have very little relationship with language achievement. Brown (2002) provides evidence that FI can be critical to both classroom learning and performance on paper-and-pencil checks and he believes that FI/FD is taken into consideration to be contextualized and variable within one individual. In different words, the utilization of FI or FD of character beginners depends on the context of getting to know them. However, no evidence has been discovered to show such attention.

In the meantime, many researchers look at man or woman' mastering style options from different dimensions. the following are a number of the most consultant ones.

Dunn develops the learning style inventory. The studying style elements identified inside the SLI are: 1) Environmental stimulus which incorporates the man or woman learner's preference closer to quiet or noisy surroundings, a proper or casual seating layout, and the desire for light and temperature. 2) Emotional stimulus. This area mainly concerns whether or not an individual learner possesses a high diploma of motivation, staying power, and duty in addition to whether or not he prefers fantastically dependent learning substances. Sociological stimulus. This category consists of elements that include whether a person learner prefers to observe as a member of a team and whether he depends on authority to verify his judgment and whether he likes to observe in routines. 4) Physiological stimulus. This kind incorporates the perceptual preferences of a person learner, i.e., his tendency to auditory, visible, tactile, or kinesthetic styles and his mobility while getting to know and his tendency to the time of mastering along with morning and afternoon. in keeping with Kinsella, Dunn, and Dunn upload the mental stimulus in 1979. This category incorporates the man or woman learner's preference toward proper or left hemisphere mastering fashion which incorporates elements including analytical/global, reflective/impulsive learning patterns, etc. Dunn's version is very important for it representing the complexity of variables that potentially impact college students' wonderful processes to mastering comprehensively. Many researchers advanced their research primarily based on Dunn's model.

Reid (1987) classifies freshmen into six different types by their fashion differences, namely, visual, auditory, kinesthetic, tactile, organization, and man or woman types. Based on her very own concept, Reid conducts a look at in 1987 to analyze the preferred learning types of students with extraordinary language backgrounds. The studies report that freshmen' options frequently differ extensively from those of local speakers folks. They show a preferred desire for kinesthetic and tactile gaining knowledge of styles and that they view institutions studying fashion as a terrible one. A Skillability degree is irrelevant to getting to know fashion choices. However, regardless of which heritage a learner comes from, the longer he remains in the US, the more his studying patterns resemble the local audio system. Melton (1990) makes use of Reid's Perceptual mastering style preference Questionnaire to look at the six mastering sorts of three hundred and thirty-one Chines.

There are many variations of opinion when it comes to cognitive styles. Some researchers aid the notion of sorts of processing techniques for brains which are called holistic and analytic beginners.

What are the characteristics of a Holistic philosopher?

We on occasion discuss with holistic inexperienced

persons as the pupil type who is deep and contemplative. This type of pupil—the clever over-achiever who every so often comes across as scatterbrained and disorganized—can occasionally turn out to be aggravated via his or her own brain.

Holistic brains need to take their time while encountering a new concept or a new chew of statistics. It takes a while for a holistic wondering person to allow new ideas to "sink in," so it could emerge as irritating to someone who doesn't understand that that is natural and flawlessly satisfactory.

when you have ever read a web page and felt like it becomes all fuzzy for your head after the first read, it simplest to discover that the data slowly starts to evolve to come back collectively and make feel, you may be a holistic philosopher. Right here are a few more traits.

• They reside on statistics and make steady intellectual comparisons when they encounter new fabric.

• They like to evaluate new concepts to ideas they already understand, whilst they read, the use of mental pics, similes, or analogies.

• Because of the constant "thinking about questioning," holistic brain kinds seem to be frustratingly gradual on the subject of answering questions. This is the trait that makes college students reluctant to elevate their arms in magnificence.

However holistic learners should not get too frustrated with the reputedly sluggish process of learning. This form of the learner is especially appropriate for evaluating and breaking down records. This is so essential whilst carrying out research and writing technical papers just like the procedure essay.

Once making a decision you're a holistic learner, you can use your strengths to improve your take look at abilities. By using zeroing in for your strengths, you could get greater out of observing time.

Are You a Holistic or a worldwide Learner?

A holistic (large picture) individual likes initially a big concept or concept, then passes on to take a look at and apprehend the components.

• As an international learner, you may be more likely to respond to a problem with emotion first, in place of logic.

• You may accept an algebra equation without expertise in the way it works.

• You'll be past due for faculty lots because you reflect on consideration on everything. And you believe you studied even as you do the whole lot.

• You tend to bear in mind faces, however, forget names. You can act on impulse. You are probably simply first-class with gambling track whilst you take a look at. (Some students cannot concentrate even as the track plays.)

• You may not enhance your hand a good deal to answer questions as it takes you a while to find out your solution.

• Whilst you ultimately do come up with a solution, it's miles tons more thorough than the quick answer you heard five minutes in the past.

• You are likely to study and study and turn out to be frustrated, after which all of sudden "get it."

A few holistic freshmen generally tend to glaze over material to pursue the huge idea. That may be pricey. Regularly, the one's small details display up on tests!

Holistic or global rookies can spend a lot of time questioning they react too past due.

Holistic philosopher's take a look at pointers

A holistic learner may benefit from the following.

•   Take note of outlines. If your instructor gives a define at the beginning of a new time period, always reproduce it down. Outlines will assist you to establish a framework for "storing" new records.

•   Make your very own definition. This is a great way to don't forget essential info you would otherwise leave out. The visible device allows your mind to arrange greater fast.

•   Don't skip advent or precise. You'll gain from studying these before you read the actual e-Book. Once more, holistic beginners need to set up a framework early for storing and applying standards.

•   Look for boundaries. Holistic learners can also have problems discerning in which one idea or event ends and another starts to evolve. It is probably useful for you to set up the concrete starting and finishing points.

•   Ask for examples. Your mind likes to make comparisons, so the greater examples, the higher. Write down the examples, however, label them as examples so that you're no longer stressed later. (Your notes tend to be disorganized.)

•   Use pictures. Use pics and charts if they're offered. When analyzing an extended passage or clarification, make your personal charts and photos.

•   Draw timelines. This is another way of making obstacles. Your mind likes them.

•   study pattern assignments. Your mind likes to apply examples as a frame of reference. without them, it's sometimes tough with a view to understanding where to begin.

•   Make drawings of principles. The extra you could sketch out and signify principles, the higher. the usage of political events, for example, you can draw circles and label them. Then, fill in sub-circles of beliefs and set up ideologies.

• Make summaries as you develop. There is a difference between passive and lively studying. You need to end up an energetic reader to recollect your material. One tactic is to forestall after every phase to put in writing a summary.

• Use a time-keeper device. Holistic rookies can get over-excited taking into consideration possibilities and lose the tune of time.

• Avoid deliberating all of the opportunities. Holistic beginners like to make comparisons and locate relationships. Don't get distracted from the venture handy.

Chapter Nine

Learning Styles and Academic Achievement

Gaining knowledge of styles are the person procedures used for knowledge and preserving information, thereby gaining knowledge or competencies. While a few proofs have indicated that mastering patterns fluctuate between undergraduate scientific college students and postgraduate residents, restrained statistics exist concerning whether or not learning patterns differ among undergraduate college students, even though different teaching methods are hired in numerous tiers of the curriculum. Inside the faculty of medicine, Chiang Mai University, Chiang Mai, Thailand, medical college students normally examine within the lecture room during the preclinical years, at the same time as inside the scientific years of this system, the principal teaching technique is gaining knowledge of in clinical conditions. College students develop medical and expert competencies with the aid of running as part of a multidisciplinary healthcare group inside the hospital. If coaching strategies range among the preclinical and medical stages, the associations among studying patterns and excessive success can also range relying on the year of examination. College students who fail to adapt to a brand new instructional context can also face educational problems. therefore, this examination aimed to examine whether studying styles differed among preclinical and clinical students, to explore correlations among studying patterns and excessive academic fulfillment, and to decide whether such correlations differed between preclinical and clinical students. Our effects can also assist scientific instructors to supervise scientific college students who revel in difficulties associated with instructional fulfillment.

Getting to know style refers to the particular ways a person tactics and keeps new data and abilities. on this have a look at, we aimed to discover the gaining knowledge of sorts of Turkish physiotherapy college students and look at the relationship among instructional performance and gaining knowledge of style subscale rankings to determine whether or not the getting to know forms of physiotherapy students should affect instructional performance.

Techniques

The studying kinds of one hundred and eighty-four physiotherapy students have been determined using the Grasha-Ricchmann pupil getting to know style Scales. Cumulative grade factor common became familiar as a measure of academic performance. The Kruskal-Wallis check changed into performed to compare instructional overall performance among the six learning style groups (unbiased, dependent, aggressive, Collaborative, Avoidant, and player).

The most common gaining knowledge of fashion was Collaborative. Academic performance becomes negatively correlated with Avoidant rating and undoubtedly correlated with player rating the instructional performance of the participant learning style institution changed into notably higher than that of all of the other organizations.

Even though Turkish physiotherapy college students' maximum typically exhibited a Collaborative getting to know the style, the player getting to know fashion became associated with substantially better academic overall performance. Teaching strategies that encourage greater participant-style studying may be effective in increasing instructional overall performance amongst Turkish physiotherapy students.

Studying can be described as everlasting modifications in conduct induced using existence. Consistent with experiential getting to know the concept, gaining knowledge of is "the manner wherein knowledge is created via the transformation of experience".

Facilitating the mastering system is the number one goal of teaching. Expertise in the learning conduct of students is considered to be a part of this process. Consequently, the idea of studying patterns has become a popular subject matter in recent literature, with many theories approximately getting to know patterns recommend to better recognize the dynamic technique of mastering.

Studying fashion refers to an individual's desired manner of processing new statistics for efficient studying. Rita Dunn defined the idea of mastering fashion as "a unique way advanced by way of students whilst he/she became studying new and hard knowledge". Studying style is about how college students learn instead of what they analyze. The learning system is special for every character; even within the identical educational surroundings, gaining knowledge does no longer arise in all college students on the same level and great. Studies have proven that individuals showcase distinctive approaches within the getting to know the manner and an unmarried method or approach becomes unable to provide the most useful mastering situations for all individuals. This could be related to students' distinct backgrounds, strengths, weaknesses, pursuits, pursuits, degrees of motivation, and techniques to reading. To improve undergraduate training, educators should emerge as more privy to these numerous procedures. Gaining knowledge of patterns may be beneficial to assist students and educators understand how to improve the way they learn and train, respectively.

Determining college students' mastering styles offers facts approximately their particular possibilities. Expertise gaining knowledge of patterns can make it simpler to create, regulate, and expend extra efficient curriculum and academic programs. It may additionally inspire college students' participation in these programs and motivate them to benefit from expert know-how. Consequently, figuring out gaining knowledge of style is quite precious with a purpose to acquire extra effective learning. Discovering studying patterns affords records on how college students study and discover solutions to questions.

Considering the ability problems encountered in the undergraduate schooling of physiotherapists, figuring out the studying style of physiotherapy college students can also permit the improvement of techniques to enhance the getting to know manner. Studies on gaining knowledge of styles within the field of physiotherapy have often been performed in developed international locations which include Canada and Australia. An observation conducted in Australia examined the studying forms of physiotherapy, occupational therapy, and speech pathology students. The results of this have a look at recommending that most fulfilling mastering surroundings have to additionally be considered even as getting to know how students examine. The authors additionally said that destiny studies changed into needed to investigate correlations among gaining knowledge of patterns, instructional strategies, and the educational performance of college students in the fitness professions.

To the best of our knowledge, there are no earlier guides within the literature that file Turkish physiotherapy students' gaining knowledge of patterns. Moreover, previous studies, on the whole, used Kolb's getting to know style inventory (LSI), Marshall & Merritts' LSI, or Honey & Mumford's gaining knowledge of style Questionnaire (LSQ) to evaluate getting to know patterns. A number of these research also advised that gaining knowledge of conduct and patterns must be investigated the usage of unique inventories. Furthermore, a scale that turned into indicated as valid and reliable for Turkish populace become had to appropriately determine the gaining knowledge of kinds of Turkish physiotherapy college students. Consequently, we opted to use the Grascha-Riechmann learning fashion Scales (GRLSS) to evaluate the studying varieties of physiotherapy college students, as a way to be a primary within the literature.

Mastering style possibilities are influential in getting to know and educational achievement and might explain how college students research. Preceding research has confirmed a close affiliation between learning fashion and educational performance. Learning styles were diagnosed as predictors of educational performance and guides for curriculum layout. The aim of this study changed into to determine whether studying style choices of physiotherapy college students could affect instructional performance through figuring out the learning kinds of Turkish physiotherapy students and assessing the connection between these getting to know patterns and the students' educational performance. because physiotherapy training specifically includes exercise instructions and medical practice and by and large requires active student participation, we hypothesized that physiotherapy students with a Collaborative learning fashion in step with the GRLSS might have higher educational overall performance

Gaining knowledge of styles are various procedures or methods of gaining knowledge. They involve teaching methods, particular to a person which are presumed to permit that character to research best. Most people select an identifiable approach of interacting with, taking in, and processing stimuli or records. Based totally on this idea, the idea of individualized "getting to know patterns" originated within the 1970s, and acquired considerable recognition. These days that way of life notion, the studying variations are arising of intelligence variations and exceptional cognitive capabilities have been changed and it's miles tested that mastering differences are arises of intelligence variations and other elements consisting of persona traits, task trouble, and studying patterns. According to James and Gardner (1995) getting to know styles is the situation that enables newbies to percept, process, storage, and don't forget the learning contents. Peirce (2000) believes that getting to know fashion is the method that people choose over the ones different strategies in learning which include gaining knowledge of in school. Its miles important that teachers, faculty managers, and other members of the educational crew take into account variations of studying types of students. Research consequences found out that take note of character variations and mastering traits of newcomers via teachers and others of the instructional team had an important role in enhancing nice of getting to know and increase the instructional achievement of students. Felder and Silverman (1988) used a five-dimension scale to categorize learning patterns. Percept size (sensing-intuitive) and procedure measurement.

Lively- reflective are dimensions that borrowed from Brigs and Kolb's version of mastering patterns. Sensing newbies generally tend to like studying facts; intuitive novices often prefer discovering possibilities and relationships. Active beginners tend to hold and apprehend records nice using doing something active with it-- discussing or making use of it or explaining it to others. Reflective novices favor thinking about it quietly first. other dimensions of Felder and Silverman's model of gaining knowledge of patterns are enter (visible-verbal), organized (inductive-deductive), and understand (sequential-worldwide) dimensions. Visual newbies do not forget first-rate what they see--images, diagrams, waft charts, time traces, films, and demonstrations. Verbal rookies get extra out of phrases--written and spoken factors. Sequential inexperienced persons generally tend to gain understanding in linear steps, with each step following logically from the previous one. International freshmen tend to research in huge jumps, absorbing cloth nearly randomly without seeing connections, and then all at once "getting it." The major aim of this study became to research the connection between mastering sorts of excessive school women students and their academic fulfillment. Homayoni and Abdolahi (2003) in their research, "the connection among studying patterns and academic success of high faculty ladies" showed an immediate correlation between the abstractive conceptualization of getting to know the style and educational achievement in arithmetic and overseas language (English). getting to know patterns in college students whose speech-language turned into each Persian and Turkish compared with whose changed into handiest Persian with the aid of Emamepur and Shams (2003) and revealed that, gaining knowledge of sorts of binary language (Persian and Turkish) students have been sensing and verbal, while students with handiest Persian speech-language (single speech-language) had intuitive and visible patterns. In some other study (2004) they discovered that students of the university whose fundamental have been the architect in examining with other college students, had been an extra visible and sequential learner, and there was a significant relationship among gaining knowledge of styles and educational fulfillment so that sequential and intuition learning styles expected higher instructional success. Rahmanpur, Palezeyan, and Zamane (2008) showed that gaining knowledge of sorts of students whose majors became engineering is exceptional from students whose majors had been speculative. Felder and Silverman (1988) in comparison to getting to know varieties of chemistry students with architect students and finish that chemistry student is greater energetic, sensing, verbal and sequential in phrases of getting to know styles. Felder (1993) additionally in his have a look at showed that scholars whose studying patterns had been coordinate with their educational patterns had better overall performance in getting to know. According to the result of Dunn's and his colleague's (2000) study, studying sorts of boys are differing from ladies. They conclude that boys tend to be touching or kinaesthetic greater than girls and feature visible studying fashion, while women tend to learn thru the auditory route. Cassidy (2004) showed that context unbiased inexperienced persons had the inner motivation and that they have been impartial in studying, in assessment context structured beginners had outside motivation. In keeping with Pashler, Daniel, Rohrer, and Bejork (2008) there is no report supporting this concept that which of patterns is useful of some other, however in fact when learning forms of students are accordant with their character traits, they study higher. Hargadon (2010) found that teaches ought to be aware of learning variations of college students and because of these variations, instructors must use specific strategies of coaching so as their students profits better performances. The fundamental intention of this have a look at became whether or not there is any courting among learning types of girls' students and their educational achievements based totally on their essential in high faculty (named in Iran route of taking a look at)?

It's far usually believed that mastering styles are not truly involved with "what" freshmen research, but instead "how" they prefer to research and it is also an essential aspect for college kids' educational fulfillment and attitudes. Students have exclusive strengths and preferences inside the methods how they absorb and technique information which is to mention, they have different gaining knowledge of styles. Some favor working with concrete records (experimental records, facts) even as others are greater cozy with abstractions (symbolic statistics, theories Mathematical fashions). Its miles common to explain and classify precise styles in many domain names. For example, various architectural patterns can be categorized via factors of shape, cloth, term, and indigenous geographic location. In addition, there are many awesome literary styles, labeled with the aid of shape, genre, and technique. But, style isn't always a time period that is in particular nicely related to the tactics that incorporate the complex mechanism of personalized learning. However, recent research suggests that the style through which one learns and applies information is a crucial feature to don't forget within the mixture instructional techniques. Acknowledgment of specific studying patterns is a try to characterize the complicated tactics by which one acquires expertise. Getting to know fashion may be thought of as a formula of preconceptions via a character engaged in the interest of mastering. The Dual Coding theory for example states that records are processed thru one of commonly unbiased channels. A learning fashion is defined as the traits, strengths, and alternatives within the way how people acquire and technique data. It refers back to the truth that anyone has his or her personal approach or set of techniques while mastering. Studying patterns aren't dichotomous (black or white, present or absent). Mastering patterns commonly operate on a continuum or more than one, intersecting continua. There are numerous debates in the better education community on how teaching or coaching effectiveness can be defined, as an example, defining powerful teaching as "that which produces beneficial and functional student learning through the usage of suitable techniques such as each teaching and studying of their definition", and defining effective coaching because the "introduction of conditions in which appropriate mastering happens; shaping the one's conditions is what successful teachers have discovered to do efficaciously". Learning patterns are generally considered as a feature, cognitive, affective, and mental behaviors that serve as extraordinarily strong indicators of how beginners perceive, have interaction with, and reply to mastering surroundings. Even though there are various definitions of mastering patterns that are unique and steady, techniques of effective learning and data processing are extensively familiar. A good strategic learner ought to recognize the way to become aware of their learning purpose, combine the studying fashion, follow the right talents, and be self-regulated to attain the excellent consequences from studying.

Teaching strategies additionally range
Teaching and getting to know are the two aspects of a coin. The most common criterion for measuring true teaching is the number of scholars gaining knowledge of that course. There are continually high correlations between college students' ratings of the "amount discovered" inside the route and their average rankings of the instructor and the course. Individuals who learned more gave their instructors better scores. Some instruct lecture, others demonstrate or discuss; a few focus on concepts and others on packages; some emphasize reminiscence and others on knowledge. In literature there

exist several getting to know styles and studying fashion models. The variations among definitions and fashions result from the reality that mastering is done at extraordinary dimensions and that theorists outline mastering styles by specializing in one-of-a-kind components. Explaining that "different ways utilized by people to system and organize statistics or to respond to environmental stimuli seek advice from their gaining knowledge of patterns", defines learning style as a sort of way of wondering, comprehending, and processing records. To Kolb (1984), studying style is a technique of private desire to understand and process information. On this feel, getting to know fashion is, on one hand, sensory and, alternatively, intellectual. in the Nineteen Forties, Isabel Briggs Myers evolved the Myers-Briggs Type Indicator (MBTI), an instrument that measures, among different things, the diploma to which a character prefers sensing or intuition. In the succeeding decades, the MBTI has been given to masses of thousands of humans and the resulting profiles had been corrclatcd with career possibilities and aptitudes, control patterns, learning styles, and diverse behavioral dispositions. Complicated mental techniques with the aid of which perceived data are transformed into know-how can be without problems grouped into categories: active experimentation and reflective observation. energetic experimentation Kolb confirmed that mastering styles will be visible on a continuum strolling from 1) concrete enjoy: being worried in a brand new revel in, 2) reflective statement: looking others or growing observations approximately very own enjoy 3) abstract idea of visualization: growing theories to explain observations, 4) lively experimentation: the usage of theories to remedy troubles and make selections. Kolb's studying patterns gave examples of how one may educate them: 1) for the concrete experiencer: offer labs, subject work, observations or films, 2) for the reflective observer: use logs, journals or brainstorming, 3) for the summary conceptualizer: lectures, papers, and analogies work well, 4) for the energetic experimenter: offer simulations, case research, and homework. It includes doing something in the external global with the information to talk about it or explain or check it in a few ways and reflective commentary entails inspecting and manipulating the statistics introspectively. Induction is a reasoning progression that proceeds from particulars (observations, measurements, and information) to generalities (governing regulations, laws, and theories). Deduction proceeds in the opposite direction. In induction one infers ideas; in deduction one deduces effects. Lively experimentation includes doing something within the outside international with the records to talk about it or explain or take a look at it in a few ways and reflective remark includes examining and manipulating the information introspectively. The handiest and most commonplace form of which entails presenting the records each textually and visually. "The whole mind" studying is understood to be a far more effective manner to examine. The higher connected the two halves of the mind are, the greater the capability of the brain for mastering and creativity is. Sequential inexperienced persons comply with linear reasoning strategies when fixing issues; international beginners make intuitive leaps and can be not able to explain how they came up with answers. Sequential freshmen can work with fabric when they understand it partially or superficially, even as international learners might also have extraordinary trouble accomplishing that. Visible freshmen recall pleasant what they see: pictures, diagrams, waft charts, time strains, movies, and demonstrations. Verbal newbies get extra out of phrases: written and spoken explanations. Each person learns more whilst data is offered each visually and verbally. Visible newcomers most successfully technique visual statistics; auditory newbies apprehend high-quality through hearing, and kinesthetic/tactile beginners research via touch and motion. A study conducted via specific Diagnostic research found that twenty-nine percent of all students in primary and secondary faculties are visual learners, thirty-four percent study through auditory way, and thirty-seven percentage analyze high-quality through kinesthetic/tactile modes. Know-how, attitudes, and competencies are the content regions had to produce a properly-trained expert. In quick, learning fashion preferences of students cannot be the only foundation for designing practice, and prescription-based totally on prognosis need to be tentative, various, monitored, and validated. Undertaking tasks that allow college students to use their man or woman studying styles is not an immediate path to better-order thinking. But, it's far viable to create products that mirror shallow and superficial thought. Within the mid-the the to late 1970s, paradigms began to be evolved to identify the greater outside, applied modes of gaining knowledge of styles. Fashion refers to a pervasive best within the getting to know techniques or the mastering conduct of an individual, "a pleasant that persists though the content material may trade". One of the additives within the Dunn and Dunn version of mastering patterns which in all likelihood has a few organic foundations is a time-of-day choice. Certainly, the latest research points to a genetic effect, or "clock gene", that is connected to peak alert time. Expertise college students' gaining knowledge of styles has been diagnosed as an essential element for re-mastering improvement, shipping, and guidance, which can cause improved student performance. An easy cognizance of variations in scholar mastering patterns is crucial for educators so that it will useful resource the getting to know the procedure. Powerful coaching reaches out to all students, no longer just those with one particular gaining knowledge of style. College students taught completely with techniques antithetical to their getting to know fashion may be made too uncomfortable to study effectively, however they should have at least some publicity to those strategies to increase a full range of gaining knowledge of talents and strategies. The general public extracts and retains extra information from visible shows than from written or spoken prose. Normally, wealthy statistics have been acquired via research on learning styles; however, the statistics have hardly ever been exploited by designers of tutorial programs thereby a greater knowledge of newbies' strategies to getting to know can be received. All information will become the subjective lifestyles of a man or woman after giving which means technique may additionally have character-unique differences in ensuring the permanence of gaining knowledge of and remembering. to explain studying styles and to analyze which elements affect getting to know styles, many studies had been conducted for years. Newcomers have unique methods of getting to know, which can also greatly affect the gaining knowledge of the system and therefore their instructional success and its outcomes. newcomers examine many methods via seeing and hearing; reflecting and acting; reasoning logically and intuitively; memorizing and visualizing. Researchers drew a difference between learning styles and strategies focusing on the methods they fluctuate from each different. To teach and analyze extra correctly, teachers and beginners want to higher understand and recognize those person variations and the way they affect the mastering technique. Mastering styles had been considerably discussed in the instructional psychology literature students will study content material higher via their favored getting to know fashion. We understand that instructors generally tend to educate in their personal favored learning fashion. Gaining knowledge of fashion includes how they technique learning, revel in learning, and utilize statistics. Filling in questionnaires and quizzes to determine desired mastering styles can be amusing however will no longer be effective until they turn out to be a part of an ongoing program of learning the way to examine for college kids. Learning patterns refer to the variations in your ability to accumulate in addition to assimilate information. it's far pretty easy to determine and you can have already had an idea that you would possibly have a selected learning style. In other cases, it could not be quite clean to identify.

The impact of college students' studying patterns on their educational fulfillment
What does studying style imply in well-known? Getting to know style is virtually the distinctive methods someone perceives and technique facts. Knowing your learning style helps you to understand why you examine certain matters

in the manner you do. It also lets you determine out whilst and how to use your studying fashion efficaciously as well as incorporating other gaining knowledge of patterns as properly. The way humans perceive information generally variety from a concrete experience to a summary revel. people who perceive concrete information is greater hands-on versus the folks who understand summary records who're more of the folks who take time to investigate and spoil down the situation.

It additionally allows me to write down cloth that has been taught orally on paper because it is less difficult for me to method what I have heard properly if I see it on paper. I benefit from special handouts as well as illustrations as it facilitates me to clearly see a clean photograph. I choose to study on my own, take notes and do fingers-on sports in magnificence to help me higher recognize the fabric. I had located some getting to know guidelines which have been useful to boom my learning revel in other training as properly. In math, I find it useful to take quite a few notes, in addition, to writing down many examples. This helps me due to the fact I can take the trouble and discover an example similar to the hassle and discern out how to work it out due to the fact I have something guiding me inside the proper course. I also discover that pictures may be helpful as well due to the fact now I have a visual idea of how to better work trouble. In reading, I discover it less difficult to document my lectures. I need to hear the topic time and again as see it to get clean expertise of what it's asking me to do. Additionally, snapshots are very helpful properly due to the fact I am capable of seeing precisely what is going on. in view that I have been in university I've needed to alternate a number of my personal take a look at behavior to preserve appropriate grades in college. I've learned to absolutely schedule look at time as opposed to just choosing a random time to take a look at.

The development of a rustic is depending on the capability of its human resources. The expertise and technological advancement of society rely upon the satisfaction and practice of manpower who have sound technical understanding, personal and interpersonal abilities as scientists and technologists. As such, it's miles of extreme importance that the highest requirements are set in defining the goals, components, strategies for information generation, and business era programs of higher schooling establishments. Expertise and schooling are commonplace goods. The purchase and alertness of know-how is part of the collective societal endeavor. They want to produce able graduates of their unique area who possessed the competencies and attributes to deal with the ever-converting work surroundings in the 21st century is a herculean challenge assigned to HEIs in the Philippines. One of the critical steps to undertake to make certain high-quality and most appropriate studying enjoy amongst college students is to consider their different gaining knowledge of patterns and options. Learning style refers to how college students learn and technique records in their own approaches. Some of the preceding studies have investigated the connection between college students' learning styles and educational performance, In fact, Moeinikia and Zahed-Babelan (2010) and Williams,

Brown, and Etherington (2013) confirm that there's a high-quality link between mastering patterns and academic performance inside the university settings. Gaining knowledge of fashion is described because of the characteristics, strengths, and possibilities inside the way how humans receive and process statistics. It also refers to the reality that all people have his or her very own technique or set of techniques while studying. Likewise, James and Gardner (1995) as mentioned by Dung and Florea (2012) described gaining knowledge of styles as a complex technique for a person learner to successfully gather data. Consequently, Reid (1987) as mentioned through Ghaedi and Jam (2014) defines studying patterns as the changes amongst newcomers in using one or extra senses to apprehend, organize, and, preserve reports. As the idea of the existing observation, Threeton and Walter (2009) confirms that there is a dearth of mastering style studies of college students in the alternate, generation and industry region of career and technical training. Kolb and Kolb (2009) affirm that studying patterns differ significantly from distinct professional and technical fields of specialization. A person tends to select diploma courses in which gaining knowledge of surroundings nurtures their learning styles. This gift observation focused on the assessment of the getting to know style choices of students enrolled in applied science guides with the quit intention of contributing to the prevailing frame of knowledge about the distinct mastering varieties of college students in those disciplines. Awareness of the special gaining knowledge of style alternatives of college students enrolled in carried out sciences publications will ultimately result in greater powerful getting to know stories. In reality, Alavi and

Toozandehjani (2017) concluded that having a background of the mastering types of students can beautify what they're getting to know and at the same time help college students give a boost to self-actualization. Teevan, Michael, and Schlesselman (2011) additionally emphasize that know-how of the getting to know patterns can help facilitate teachers to hire suitable teaching strategies and strategies to nurture students' instructional performance. This could additionally offer both teachers and students tremendous feedback on their strengths and weaknesses within the coaching and mastering state of affairs. Likewise, the know-how of the mastering styles can offer implications to curriculum design allowing teachers to put in force a learner-centered curriculum version within the schoolroom. Dalmolin, Mackeivicz, Pochapski, Pilatti, and Santos (2018) propose that determining the learning types of college students will in the end improve their instructional experience. Preceding exiting literature confirms that mastering styles predict students' academic performance. Jiraporncharoen, Angkurawaranon, Chockjamsai, Deesomchok, and Euathrongchit (2015) studied getting to know styles and educational fulfillment of undergraduate college students in Thailand observed a superb affiliation among the two. Barman, Aziz, and Yusoff (2014) also studied the getting to know style consciousness and academic performance of students concluded that students 'cognizance in their strengths which includes studying fashion and how to make use of their strengths may additionally enhance their instructional overall performance. Some other variable being investigated is the take a look at behavior and competencies of college students enrolled in carried out science publications. The literature similarly suggests that study behavior is a predictive element of academic overall performance. Ebele and Olofu (2017) found out that there may be an extensive relationship between observing the conduct and college students' educational overall performance. Looyeh, Fazelpour, Masoule, Chehrzad, and Leili (2017) investigated the relationship between the have a look at habits and the academic overall performance of medical Sciences college students discovered the enormous relationship among the examine conduct of college students and their educational performance. In addition, out that a wonderful relationship of zero.66 among observing habits and academic success. The outcomes implied that the take a look at behavior needs a giant interest if we are to enhance performance. Moreover, Chilca (2017) studied the study of behavior and academic performance among college students in Peru concluded that look at conduct does affect academic overall performance. For this reason, in every college placing particularly in higher education institutions, the educational performance of college students is a trademark of a satisfactory studying experience. Educational success is measured within the shape of college students' tremendous rankings across their situation courses and the display of studying results which may be assessed via overall performance, classroom checks, assignments, outputs, and foremost examinations. Previous studies gift that there are intellective and non-intellective factors affecting the instructional success of students throughout stages. Students' mastering fashion choice and look at behavior ought to be understood. The interaction of mastering fashion options, observe behavior and educational success of college students enrolled in applied technology courses at Cagayan state college precipitated the researcher to research the relationship existing amongst those variables. Likewise, figuring out the substantial differences of these variables while grouped in keeping with their socio-financial profile will offer a better image of what precise non-public mastering interventions can be implemented. Furthermore, to stand the challenges of advancement, the improvement of talented IT professionals and particularly skilled business technologists will ultimately spur the development of the Philippine society. For this reason, spotting their innate learning tendencies and their mindset toward their studies may be a basis for the college to design and enforce instructional interventions to enhance their educational overall performance and the satisfaction in their learning reports. This examination turned into achieved a few of the students of Cagayan Nation University at Lasam, the Philippines enrolled within the carried out science guides namely Bachelor in records era and Bachelor in business technology programs. Those implemented science publications are instructional fields rather appeared as applying scientific know-how to expand packages like generation and innovations for fixing sensible demanding situations. Therefore, their conceptual abilities, vital wondering, and creative abilities are required to be developed by using the students as their graduate attributes. The development of their top have a look at habits will make them better newcomers in their own methods through manner of presenting powerful instructional techniques and provision of different instructional interventions to enhance their instructional performance is vital. As a result, this takes a look at correlated the getting to know styles preferences, observe habits and educational performance of students enrolled in carried out technology publications. The look at normally endeavored to assess the perceptual learning varieties of undergraduate college students enrolled in era-related guides of Cagayan kingdom university at Lasam. therefore, the study sought to cope with the subsequent research goals: first of all, identify the getting to know style options of students; secondly, examine the observe conduct of the respondents; thirdly, describe the level of the instructional overall performance of respondents; fourthly, check the significant differences on the perceptual studying styles, take a look at the conduct and academic performance while grouped in keeping with their profile variables, and finally, determine the relationship a number of the gaining knowledge of patterns, observe behavior and academic overall performance of the respondents. Further, this has a look at examined the studies hypotheses in null shape at 0.05 alpha stage: 1) if there are no massive differences inside the perceptual studying styles, study habits, and educational performance while grouped according to their profile variables, (2) there is no huge courting between learning patterns, observe habits and academic overall performance of the respondents

Every twelve months, the Malaysian authorities spend an exquisite deal of cash on the improvement of the quality of schooling. Schooling is an expensive investment in the future of college students, and much emphasis is located on the curriculum and values of training to allow the students to fulfill the needs of the enterprise. Coaching and mastering is the foundation of all development in all levels of training, particularly, number one, secondary, university, and college. The distinction among the degrees is the level of difficulty that students face. The Taxonomy of instructional goals with the aid of Bloom (1956) categorized getting to know into three fundamental areas; cognitive, affective, and psychomotor. The cognitive area and level said in academic settings help teachers understand and implement what they want to obtain of their teaching objectives. The structure of Bloom" s Taxonomy consists of information, comprehension, application, analysis, synthesis, and assessment. Anderson and Karthwolh (2001) revised Bloom" s Taxonomy and changed the authentic variety of classes with the aid of introducing the FourKnowledge size of Taxonomy: factual know-how, conceptual expertise, procedural information, and metacognitive understanding. Splitter (1995), Caviglioli et al. (2004), and Tee et al. (2009) advised that all educators ought to offer college students multiple abilities and for teachers to cater their mastering abilities with various teaching strategies. Teachers, however, cannot expect that scholars will easily apprehend the getting to know content material when they best sit down in class and comply with instructions. A recognition of the interplay among college students, teachers, and coaching materials has to also be a gift. Scholar learning is frequently taken for granted. Students are assumed academically able to knowledge instructions and assignments. The majority of them do bypass, however for people who fail, the blame falls on the instructional standards or coaching strategies. Little attention is given to the approaches that scholars study and the scholars" learning styles. Ideally, the manner teachers teach must suit the way college students study, as well as how they favor studying. Teachers have to adapt their coaching tactics to shape the approaches students analyze and their learning patterns. The elements of gaining knowledge of styles (LS) were regarded in the studies literature as early as 1892. The time period "learning patterns" changed into probably first utilized by Thelen who located institution dynamics at work. LS will also be defined because of the tendency to adopt a specific method of studying. Instructors, then, should have the capability to recognize how college students learn. According to Felder (1993), students and teachers may also decide on one getting to know the style in a single problem but normally decide upon one fashion for maximum topics that they study or train. Therefore, instructors may additionally use this data from Felder (1993) to make certain they make use of all different gaining knowledge of styles, and students can use this information through knowing how they prefer to receive information. Faculties, institutions, faculties, and universities have to undertake an idea of gaining knowledge based totally on the lecture room method. Diverse gaining knowledge of theories exists, and caution needs to be exercised in the course of selection. The mastering theories have to match the subjects" needs, inclusive of cognitivism, behaviorism, and constructivism theories. The fine of teaching is measured using how correctly the getting to know technique the instructor decided on functions to attain the getting to know goals in a specific situation. However, thinking about teachers who normally do now not know which technique may be the handiest, the measurement of a teacher's fulfillment is left to the scholars. The connection between the coaching method used and what the scholars found out, can be visible as a system in which a teacher's beliefs will have an impact on their teaching techniques, so one can in turn impact scholar learning styles. A student's mastering fashion represents the form of learner they end up with. Several inventories could three identify what form of learner a scholar maybe have been published. In a study room where the simplest method to learning is endorsed with the aid of an instructor, a few college students can also in all likelihood work and study much less efficaciously than others. For that reason, recognition of gaining knowledge of styles is critical for teachers. College students in vocational education (VE) are exposed to an academic system that is oriented greater toward getting a task, and their gaining knowledge of styles are one of a kind from college students in educational fields. Accordingly, VE is in all likelihood an academic pursuit orientated to provide the necessary understanding and talents to carry out a particular process, profession, or expert interest inside the exertions market (international Labour corporation, 1995). VE is also connected to technology switch, innovation, and development. In vocational teaching, as in lots of understanding regions, figuring out and know-how learner variations to adopt the institute's desires to exceptional fit the learning conditions and aptitudes of the students are essential. The need to evolve coaching techniques to pupil studying patterns and choices is a fact in the classroom, which can be found in real situations or digital strategies. However, those findings do now not suggest that character techniques need to be created for each student in a study room. The best shape of interaction for each of them needs to be recognized through constructing businesses of learners with commonplace traits. Historical past of the trouble the cognitive tactics that contribute to pupil mastering require that the scholar have the potential to govern statistics and thoughts to clear up problems and convey new information. Many features of modern cognitive theories on coaching and mastering reflect earlier fashions of teaching which include Bruner's, Taba's, and various institution-based and student-focused coaching models. In VE, the significance of the cognitive procedure is based totally on some factors, specifically, the cognitive skills wished inside the contemporary work environment, the ability to conform to changing VE necessities in a global context, and the demands of cognitive development. In their cognitive studies, Johnson and Thomas (1992) summarized that 4 getting to know does not robotically trade and that expertise the studying content is hard. Cognitive approaches aren't recommended through passive getting to know. VE college students have their own studying options, thinking about they rely less on their cognitive abilities and more on their psychomotor abilities, together with bodily motion, coordination, and use of motor abilities. They need to boom their cognitive competencies with an appropriate technique so that they may be creative and revolutionary employees to be able to do nicely in their work scenario. The correct approach in this situation is perhaps the identification of the scholars" gaining knowledge of styles that identical to VE traits to produce hints on overcoming the issues. Bloom (1989) additionally states that the potential of students to examine primary concepts and their ability to apply know-how or defined what they discovered. A scholar's mastering is encouraged by way of some factors. The fundamental issues of pupil mastering as explored by Muhammed et al. (2008) include home history, mastering environment, and government policies. Martins et al. (2007) said that family heritage factors decided educational performance, and Azizi et al. (2003) claimed that getting to know styles prompted a student's academic performance. Francis and Segun (2008) concluded that the faculty environment and instructor-related factors had been the dominant elements influencing achievements, particularly if the scholar becomes tremendously self-inspired. Mastering in VE is defined as the transition from the use of fundamental problem-solving techniques towards the usage of professional problem-solving strategies. Inexperienced persons in VE should look at and revel in the desired cognitive approaches to study them and recognize how, wherein, and whilst to apply them. One of the factors debated over the previous few years became the connection between scholar success and mastering patterns. Proponents of getting to know styles hold that adapting classroom coaching strategies to match college students" favored forms of gaining knowledge of improves the educative method. However, warring parties of gaining knowledge of fashion theories preserve that little empirical evidence is to be had to aid this proposition LS worried techniques that scholars generally tend to apply to a given teaching state of affairs. Every person can fit into special patterns which could bring about students adopting attitudes and behaviors which can be repeated in distinctive conditions. Figuring out getting to know styles mastering patterns can be categorized into various classes, for example, sensory, auditory, visual, and tactile. Dunn and Dunn (1992) reported that getting to know patterns is a person's reaction to several environmental, emotional, psychological, and sociological factors. In vocational schools, the VE college students have their personal traits, in keeping with Brennan (2003). They're verbal novices who watch and see in place of study and concentrate. The arms-on and learn by doing and training. They analyze in organizations and are established learners who want teacher steerage for clean understanding. Considering that the characteristics of college students in VE are more palms-on, and they analyze using doing, a knowledge of this form of LS will assist instructors to provide a coaching shipping technique that matches their college students" needs. "College student's" need" is a time period defined through Posner et.al (1992) as a description of ways students cope with curricular obligations by employing relevant studying systems. The purpose of teaching VE students is to advantage revel in and to use existing expertise in new situations. The function of the instructor is to create learning environments for students handling the supplied tasks. It is important to shows how a VE scholar's learning ability is motivated via various factors. Adapting to college students gaining knowledge of VE contains a wide variety of courses or talents that assist college students to prepare to go into an occupational-primarily based employment or workplace. The concept behind VE is to bridge theory and realistic components, consisting of lab- and workshop-oriented understanding to place of work expertise, with unique abilities. As a result, vocational students have their very own LS. In here studies on studying strategies among vocational students, Briggs (2000) concluded that vocational college students benefited from three sorts of guides, particularly, "fingers-on courses," "combined guides," and "paper-based totally publications." She also labeled the analysis of LS into visible, auditory, and kinesthetic (VAK) to create a basis for innovation in coaching and learning techniques. a visual style is predicated on seeing and reading, auditory relies upon listening and speaking and a kinesthetic fashion focuses on touching and doing. It also indicates the usage of LS in hands-on courses. Hands-on guides check with hairdressing, plumbing, expert craft catering, and painting. This group showed that their choice becomes for visible strategies. The discern illustrated three classes of students" rating as teacher behavior study room environment pupil capability and characteristics scholar activity pupil behavioral pastime (performance venture) indicating robust, medium, and weak use of visible, auditory, and kinesthetic mastering fashion techniques. The consequences display that the student's maximum favored visible mastering strategies the effects display that the best variety of college students scored invisible techniques. This means the scholars scored strongly in several visible strategies. In the meantime, students strongly used auditory getting to know strategies, and most effective 18 college students strongly carried out the kinesthetic method to getting to know. College students" gaining knowledge of patterns in fingers-on guides Briggs (2000) used the same method of the use of studying strategies for "blended" guides. Mixed courses confer with courses that involve an aggregate of paper-based and arms on materials. Blended courses constitute the route related to engineering education and acting arts. The result confirmed that this organization preferred visible strategies the maximum and kinesthetic techniques the least. Students" learning patterns in blended publications suggests the profiles of LS for college students in a paper-based path. The scholars investigated had been involved in the enterprise, public provider, and fitness technological know-how courses. One way of enhancing studying performance is to evolve the model of each pupil's style. Research is needed to locate the maximum efficient methods of doing this. Student gaining knowledge of assembly the students" wishes calls for the teacher to identify numerous components approximately the students" mastering, consisting of the person learner traits, learner traits in the wider network, learning procedures in the getting to know the environment, and gaining knowledge of technique inside the curriculum. In Malaysia, the focal point is the learning technique in the curriculum. The college curriculum includes core subjects and elective subjects based totally on the students" achievements and alternatives. The secondary faculty device consists of educational, technical, vocational, Islamic, and private faculties. Each school in Malaysia has an extraordinary curriculum. Instructors agree that one of the elements that affect students" gaining knowledge of is teaching fashion. Various inventories, questionnaires, and indexes had been produced to perceive the scholar's gaining knowledge of patterns. One of the mastering style models is the Felder and Silverman studying styles version (FSLSM), which is designed to identify college students" getting to know styles primarily based on the data processing and dimensions that scholars acquire of their mastering. The unique FSLSM turned into evolved through Richard Felder and Linda Silverman to address the scholar studying engineering schooling. However, studies display that the usefulness of FSLSM has on account that extended to numerous difficult disciplines, which include language, medical, technology, and engineering-associated disciplines. The up-to-date FSLSM reduced the five dimensions of getting to know styles into four because of pedagogical motives associated with the teaching requirements. The variety of dimensions became modified due to pedagogical motives related to coaching desires. The four dimensions are, particularly, processing, perception, enter, and information. FSLSM is the precise gaining knowledge of fashion version with which to observe and interpret students" mastering in vocational education. The Index of learning fashion (ILS) become developed with the aid of Felder and Soloman (1997) to measure the dimension of FSLSM. The ILS can help identify the scale of mastering and the fourteen types of learner primarily based on a forty-four-item questionnaire. Every size is associated with eleven compelled-preference gadgets, every both with an option (a) or (b) to fit up to 1 or every other class of the measurement. The information of ILS is in addition defined inside the chapter on literature and study methods. FSLSM is a studying style version regularly used in other difficulty disciplines that may offer a more distinct description of LS. No unique model of is LS proposed to degree LS for vocational students, however, FSLSM traits can be used. The size of FSLSM and the items within the Felder–Soloman studying patterns Index are suitable for identifying college students'" mastering patterns in the BC route (BCC). In related research, Muhammad et al. (2011) classified sixty-eight vocational college students into four getting to know kinds in step with the Index of getting to know patterns (ILS). The dimension of innovative thinking in hassle fixing amongst students changed into additionally investigated. The outcomes confirmed that the dominant kind of freshmen was the visual learner. In addition, they observed a huge distinction among visible newcomers who used creative questioning in hassle fixing

Chapter Ten

Learning and Diversity

Learning is a journey far away from the learner's comfort quarter, leaving the relative narrowness and obstacles of the existing world. As tons as mastering needs to verify identification and create a sense of belonging, it's also a process of journeying away from the acquainted, everyday international of revel in. This adventure is one of personal and cultural transformation.

Those, then, are the two conditions of learning in a context of deep and multifaceted range:

• Situation 1: powerful learning engages the learner's identity. It builds on the learner's understanding, experiences, hobbies, and motivation. In any gaining knowledge of the community, there may be an extraordinary deal of range, and that is due to the fact the ordinary life worlds from which college students come are usually various. A pedagogy of BELONGING brings this diversity into the lecture room, values it, and makes use of it as an aid for mastering.

• Condition 2: powerful studying takes the learner on an adventure into new and unusual terrains. However, for mastering to occur the adventure into the unexpected wishes to live with a sector of intelligibility and protection. At each step, it desires to journey just the right distance from the learner's lifeworld start line. A pedagogy of TRANSFORMATION takes beginners out of their consolation zones, as a result of which they form new frames of information, ways of meaning, capacities to act, and expressions of identity.

How the studying using design technique Addresses Learner range

The learning via design project addresses learner variety in several methods, including:

•   The Learner aid side of the getting to know element is designed for self-paced character mastering or self-managed group learning. All novices do no longer have to be on the identical page at the same time.

•   Entry points: The studying element asks the question of earlier mastering on the assumption that the answer will no longer be identical for all.

•   The understanding tactics deliver diversity into the getting to know revel in:

- Experiencing the regarded: bringing in college students' numerous stories.

- Experiencing the new: always at a cautiously measured distance from what college students already realize (intelligibility).

- Analyzing significantly: measuring human pastimes is constantly towards your own attitude.

- making use of appropriately: taking what you have got learned again on your very own global of regular revel in.

- Applying creatively: deliver a couple of views and reports of your life collectively in a creative way.

•   The combination of information techniques lets in specific emphases and interest types as appropriate to students' specific 'gaining knowledge of orientations'.

•	All of the expertise procedures additionally the alternate course of the understanding flows and the balance of duty for studying toward a more active view of mastering-as-engagement—in this context, learner identities, and subjectivities emerge as greater take place.

•	Gaining knowledge is conceived as an adventure, in a transformational (rather than static) view of variety. The learner, for example, may tour from everyday Experiencing the recognized, to depth and breadth views (Conceptualizing, Analyzing), and lower back to the everyday international through applying appropriately or Creatively—by which period neither the arena nor the learner are quite similar to they had been whilst the adventure started.

•	Learning results: evaluation isn't of the right/identical solutions or one correct manner to do matters, however similar performance with regards to standards. You shouldn't do the identical work to be doing equivalent work.

•	Go out factors: The studying Pathways query at the top of the studying detail assumes that this will be answered in different ways for special newbies.

Diversity and inclusion inside the schoolroom – creation
•	Advent
•	Start here
•	Inclusive school rooms
•	GenEd Requirement
•	Resources on Campus

Diversity, inclusion, and cultural competency
The University of Rhode Island is dedicated to promoting inclusion and cognizance of various problems to our college students and school.
Whether or not you educate a class in biology, engineering, writing, or sociology, there are modifications you could make to your study room and your approach to coaching that create an extra inclusive and alluring environment for all your students. In this phase, we provide the basics for mastering approximately and taking the primary steps in designing an inclusive classroom and/or teaching multicultural consciousness for your students.
What is diversity?
Range may be conceptualized in one-of-a-kind approaches relying on the context. on the subject of our school rooms, we conceptualize diversity as information every scholar brings specific studies, strengths, and thoughts to our schoolroom. Those differences can be alongside dimensions of race, ethnicity, sexual orientation, gender, socio-economic repute, age, capacity, religious or political beliefs, or different extraordinary ideologies. Diversity is the exploration and incorporation of those variations to enhance getting to know and in our classrooms.
Why does variety be counted in my schoolroom?
Our students come to URI with an extensive variety of reports and academic backgrounds. As educators, we have a responsibility to ensure our college students are organized to work in various environments and collaborate with others who carry new views. When we incorporate a diffusion of views into our very own coaching and provide college students new approaches of searching at their field we prepare our college students for the diverse workforce.

See how range makes us smarter from the medical American for extra information.

How do I include diversity in my lecture room?

There are a variety of ways you can contain variety into your study room and it relies upon the desires you've got in your students. This isn't always a one-step technique, however, whether or not you are incorporating numerous views into your course content material or teaching college students about cultural differences, you want to make sure your study room is welcoming and you've created a deferential, safe environment. Our inclusive school room section gives a few sources on which to start.

What is an inclusive study room?

In an inclusive lecture room, instructors are aware of the range of college students and work with students to create safe and collaborative getting to know their surroundings. Instructors use more than one strategies to deliver direction content and provide college students with diffusion of possibilities to share what they recognize. Inclusive lecture rooms understand college students learn in one-of-a-kind methods and have treasured perspectives to bring to the content being learned.

Diverse coaching strategies for various newbies

That minority and coffee-earnings children frequently perform poorly on checks is widely recognized. However, the fact that they do so because we systematically expect much less from them is not. Maximum Americans count on that the low success of terrible and minority youngsters is certain up in the children themselves or their families. "The children don't attempt." "They have no location to examine." "Their parents don't care." "Their lifestyle does no longer price training." those and other excuses are often provided up to explain the fulfillment hole that separates terrible and minority students from other young Americans.

The truth is that we know a way to teach negative and minority children of all kinds—racial, ethnic, and language—to excessive ranges. Some instructors and some entire schools do it every day, months in and year out, with incredible consequences. But the nation as an entire has now not but acted on that knowledge. ...

Diverse scholar learners consist of college students from racially, ethnically, culturally, and linguistically various households and groups of lower socioeconomic fame. If educators act at the understanding research offers, we can recognize the academic excellence we choose for all children.

In keeping with Diplomas count: A critical manual to commencement coverage and quotes, the national commencement rate is 69.6%. This record estimates that in 2006 greater than 1.2 million students—most of them members of minority companies—will no longer graduate from high school in four years with a regular degree. Nationally, whilst close to 30% of college students do not graduate, best "51% of Black college students, 47.4% of Yankee Indian and Alaskan local college students, and 55.6% of Hispanic students graduated from high school on time with a general degree," compared with greater than three-quarters of non-Hispanic whites and Asians.

Furthermore, the Diplomas count number tells us that the average commencement rate in city districts is 60%, in comparison to a 75% commencement fee in suburban groups. Faculty structures with excessive degrees of racial segregation have a commencement charge of most effective 56.2%, compared to 75.1% in school structures with low degrees of racial segregation. Nationally, a couple of third of college students fail to make the transition from ninth to tenth grade. In precise, the patterns in terrible school districts mirror the ones found in racially segregated districts.

Demographer Harold Hodgkinson, who advocates common preschool education as a way of offering real same educational possibility, reflects on the variety in U.S. schools (2003):

The maximum numerous group in the US is our youngest kids, and they will make the country more varied as they age. Nearly nine million younger people ages five to seventeen talk a language apart from English in their home and a pair of.6 million of them have issues speaking English. For our children's magnificence of 2000, we ought to estimate that almost one-1/2 million are being raised in families that communicate no English at home and that at the least one hundred twenty-five thousand will need a unique interest in preschool and kindergarten to learn to talk and study English.

About one-third of our black and Hispanic children are being raised in poverty whilst 10% of non-Hispanic whites stay in poverty. But, the largest variety of terrible youngsters are white while the very best percentage of terrible kids are black and Hispanic. Of the fourteen million youngsters ages start to 18 residing in poverty in 2000, nine million had been white and four million were black. Four million Hispanics have been residing in poverty, but had been included in both white and black totals, as Hispanics aren't a "race."

irrespective of race, the kids in married-couple households are much less likely to be terrible (about 8%) at the same time as 29% of white children and fifty-two% of black and Hispanic children who live with a single mother are in all likelihood to be poor. nearly half of these single mothers are working, commonly at very low-salary jobs.

Hodgkinson advocates academic applications that, like Head begin, recollect not only instructional desires but conceive of youngsters as whole people with social, emotional, and physical wishes and strengths, in a circle of relatives context (2003).

Overall, the proof that brilliant schooling before the kid's 5th birthday can yield lifetime benefits is undebatable. We know the way to do it. Why do not we make such applications to be had to all? There are few federal packages in any corporation which could assist effects like these, but Head begin enrollment has normally hovered below 50% of these eligible.

However, many schools do not have the possibility to work with children at such a younger age. Consequently, they ought to start work last the achievement gap in later years. Burris and Welner (2005) documented changes in training practice that closed the success gap between black and Latino college students and white and Asian students in center and high school within the diverse Rockville Centre school District in the big apple. The district instituted detracting (that is, a heterogeneous grouping of excessive- and coffee-achievers in all training) and improved getting to know by using steadily eliminating remedial instructions and offering all students rigorous classes in mathematics, worldwide records, international

Baccalaureate English, and records—training previously presented most effective to the best achievers.

Their five-year have look at observed a dramatic upward thrust in the charge of college students passing all eight New York state Regents checks to get hold of a Regents high school degree. earlier than detracting, the handiest 32% of the African American and Latino college students inside the graduating elegance of 2000 earned Regents diplomas, at the same time as 88 percent of white and Asian students did so. After detracting and increased mastering had been instituted for five years, 82% of African American and Latino students in the graduating elegance of 2003 earned Regents diplomas; 97 percent of white or Asian students did so. In reality, "The Regents degree fee for [detracted] minority students [eighty-two percentage] exceeded any kingdom's fee for white or Asian American students".

Burris and Welner (2005, p. 595) concluded that once "all students—the ones at the bottom in addition to those at the pinnacle of the [fulfillment] gap—have to get admission to best learning possibilities, all students' fulfillment can rise."

Hodgkinson (2003) highlighted every other version—the schools of the 21st Century—that appeared college students as whole men and women in their family context. This "is one of the most a hit fashions for putting together all of the factors ... that contribute to the superb academic, emotional, and social improvement of young children", which include (1) college-based applications; (2) sturdy links between early life and schools; (three) strong parental aid and involvement; (4) accepted get entry to; (5) a focal point on children's physical, social, emotional, and intellectual improvement; (6) robust personnel education and development; and (7) a commitment to serving operating families. Colleges of the 21st Century are now presented in over four hundred schools in a huge variety of groups across the US. Although the middle components simply referred to are usually gift, the program is bendy sufficient to maximize this system's fulfillment inside the particular "fingerprint" of each community placing.

Hodgkinson concluded: "although we do now not recognize a way to lessen poverty, research is abundant on the way to efficaciously lessen the consequences of poverty on our youngest kids".

Nowadays, as in the past, instructors are being challenged to develop their repertoire of teaching techniques to satisfy the needs and strengths of college students from a remarkable diversity of backgrounds and cultures. those learners—African people, American Indians, Asian people, Hispanics, and lots of others—face societal discrimination, stay in conditions of poverty, or each. The approaches wherein we train these younger humans to exert an effective have an impact on their linguistic, social, cognitive, and preferred instructional development.

Research shows, as an example, that powerful coaching acknowledges college students' gender variations and reaffirms their cultural, ethnic, and linguistic heritages. Many effective educational techniques construct on college students' backgrounds to in addition the improvement of their skills. Seriously vital is spotting that the use of effective instructional practices as tested using studies will improve achievement for all kids, such as folks that are not minorities or youngsters of poverty. The implementation of sound, research-based techniques that understand the advantages of variety can build a higher destiny for everybody.

Embracing variety

The large range of stories and views introduced to high school via culturally, linguistically, and ethnically diverse college students offer a powerful aid for all people to analyze extra—in different methods, in new environments, and with distinctive types of human beings. Every single person in this enormously numerous and ever-converting system has the electricity to serve as a useful resource for all others—students, teachers, and the community as an entire. As opposed to constituting trouble for college students and educators, the developing diversity in U.S. school rooms necessitates and encourages the improvement and use of diverse teaching strategies designed to respond to every student as a character.

The United States is fortunate, for it includes now not only immigrants but additionally political refugees, indigenous people, and descendants of humans (sometimes introduced towards their will) from every continent on the globe. This eternal variety has resulted in innovations, discoveries, ideas, literature, artwork, track, movies, exertions, languages, political systems, and foods that enrich American culture. Those equal resources additionally have the capacity for enriching the yank study room. Immigrant College students bring us possibilities to be explored and treasures to be appreciated, and that they help us challenge the fame quo.

Adopting an actually worldwide angle lets us view culturally and linguistically diverse college students and their parents or guardians as assets that provide unparalleled possibilities for enrichment. However, we want a more repertoire of procedures for coaching and gaining knowledge to cope with numerous styles of studying. Teachers and college students alike need to domesticate interpersonal abilities and appreciate other cultures. The new world financial system needs this global view. After all, our markets and monetary opposition are now global, and the capabilities of intercultural communication are essential in politics, international relations, economics, environmental control, the humanities, and different fields of human undertaking.

Surely, a numerous schoolroom is the best laboratory wherein to examine a couple of views required by using a global society and to place to apply information regarding numerous cultural styles. Students who discover ways to work and play collaboratively with classmates from diverse cultures are higher prepared for the arena they face now—and the arena they'll face in destiny. Coaching and gaining knowledge of techniques that draw on the social records and the everyday lives of students and their cultures can most effective assist this studying method.

Teachers sell crucial thinking once they make the policies of the classroom subculture explicit and allow college students to compare and contrast them with other cultures. College students can develop go-cultural competencies in culturally and linguistically diverse classrooms. For such studying to take region, however, teachers should have the attitudes, information, and abilities to make their school room's effective gaining knowledge of environments for all college students. Given the possibility, college students can participate in mastering groups within their colleges and neighborhoods and be equipped to assume optimistic roles as employees, circle of relatives participants, and citizens in a worldwide society. Zeichner (1992) has summarized the substantial literature that describes a successful teaching method for numerous populations. From his evaluation, he distilled twelve key factors for powerful coaching for ethnic- and language-minority students.

1.   Instructors have a clear experience of their personal ethnic and cultural identities.

2.   Teachers talk about excessive expectancies for the success of all college students and a belief that each college student can succeed.

3.   Instructors are individually devoted to reaching fairness for all college students and agree that they are capable of making a difference in their college students' mastering.

4.   Instructors have developed a bond with their students and stop seeing their college students as "the other."

5.   Faculties offer an academically challenging curriculum that includes attention to the improvement of better-stage cognitive capabilities.

6.   Coaching specializes in students' introduction of which means content material in interactive and collaborative getting to know surroundings.

7.   Instructors assist college students to see gaining knowledge of duties as significant.

8.   Curricula consist of the contributions and views of the distinctive ethno-cultural companies that compose the society.

9.   Instructors provide a "scaffolding" that links the academically challenging curriculum to the cultural sources that scholars bring to high school.

10.   Instructors explicitly teach college students the subculture of the college and seek to preserve college students' sense of ethnocultural pride and identification.

11.   Network contributors and parents or guardians are advocated to grow to be concerned in college students' education and are given a massive voice in making essential faculty decisions associated with programs (consisting of sources and staffing).

12.   Teachers are worried about political struggles outdoor the schoolroom which can be geared toward accomplishing a more just and humane society.

Educating numerous students

For the sake of clarity, this bankruptcy breaks the coaching techniques into important sections. The first phase, "techniques for culturally and ethnically diverse college students," carries techniques appropriate for children whose number one language can also or may not be English. The second section, "techniques for linguistically numerous college students," carries techniques that mainly address the unique desires of inexperienced persons of English as a second language. Every strategy includes a quick discussion of the method as well as examples of the method in use. Assets on the give up of every access allow the reader to discover additional facts and resources.

Strategies for culturally and ethnically numerous college students

Normally, U.S. schools provide college students of numerous backgrounds with training pretty exceptional from that provided to students of mainstream backgrounds. For example, poor youngsters and culturally and linguistically diverse students tend to obtain inferior practice due to the fact they're typically located inside the bottom analyzing organizations or dispatched out of the study room for remedial preparation.

Studies also show that schools tend to discriminate in opposition to students of various backgrounds through assessments that don't value their home language and thru using teaching procedures that fail to build on the strengths of their subculture or home languages. Nonetheless different research exhibit that many instructors fail to talk successfully with students from diverse backgrounds; common (and tough to exchange) instructional approaches regularly violate the behavior norms of those students' domestic cultures. Also, instructors may additionally have low expectations for students of diverse backgrounds and this reason fails to offer them hard and exciting classes.

Some researchers have found many identifiable factors associated with the level of young people's overall performance in college. Schools have to manage over a few factors but no longer others. If teachers recognize these factors and their consequences on young people who are newly arrived inside the United States, they will be better capable of verifying their desires and strengths and discover progressive ways of assisting them to regulate to their new schools and to live in a brand new tradition. a number of those important elements and their consequences encompass the following issues.

•	The level of the circle of relatives' socioeconomic sources is related to success in school however is conditioned by using different factors, including immigrant fame.

•	Prior training in the US of an origin is related to success in college.

• The age of front into the US influences success within the English language, in addition to other instructional areas, however, the diploma of success is also conditioned via literacy inside the home language. Those children who enter the US earlier than puberty may have an advantage in school.

• The longer the duration of life in the United States of America, the more the faculty success. Lamentably, this effect is offset by a reduction of motivation that comes via acculturation into the yank society.

• Intact own family and domestic aid systems are related to success in faculty. Now not extraordinarily, unaccompanied minors and college students from unmarried-discern families are at greater risk of failure in faculty.

In this context, it is important to understand how we define numerous ethnic businesses. As an instance, Asian Americans are often regarded incorrectly as an unmarried ethnic institution. There are, however, many wonderful subgroups of Asian people, each with its very own tradition, faith, and unique attitude. Generalization throughout such subgroups can lead to misperceptions and a failure to understand and address specific worries and needs. It's also vital to take into account that the general descriptor "Southeast Asian" commonly refers to folks that report their very own ethnic identification as Vietnamese, Laotian, Cambodian, or Hmong. The recent tendency to stereotype Asians as "high achievers" may mask full-size and unique instructional challenges and wishes.

Further, Hispanics or Latinos also are composed of many wonderful subgroups. Although the U.S. Census Bureau classifies all Spanish-speaking peoples below the overall heading "Hispanic starting place," this term consists of all persons who identify themselves as participants of households from Mexico, critical and Spanish-speaking South the united states, the Spanish-speaking Caribbean islands, or Spain. Moreover, people of Hispanic origin can be of any race.

Subsequently, it's far critical to be aware that companies coping with population facts confer with Alaskan Natives or American Indians as one group, even though the customs, languages, and cultures of the many tribes and countries of these businesses are vastly different.

U.S. Ethnic companies

The U.S. Census acknowledges 5 primary ethnic groupings within the United States of America: African Americans or blacks; American Indians and Alaskan Natives; Asian individuals; Hispanic Americans or Latinos; and local Hawaiians or Pacific Islanders.

African individuals or blacks refer to the ones of African ancestry who may additionally have lived for generations inside America. Blacks additionally include Afro-Caribbean's from the West Indies and Haiti and blacks from other islands, consisting of the Bahamas and Trinidad.

American Indians, also called native individuals, had been the original populations of North the US earlier than the arrival of the Spaniards, who had been observed through the English, French, and other Europeans. American Indian businesses often prefer to be called with the aid of their tribal association or the state to which they belong.

Alaskan Natives refers to indigenous Alaskans which

include Eskimos, Aleuts, and Inuits.

Asian individuals include all countrywide-origin organizations from Asia, some of whom come from technologically advanced nations like Japan. Others come from nations where some of the population have to get the right of entry to advanced generation and others do not, consisting of Korea, China, Vietnam, and India.

Hispanic Americans or Latinos are national-starting place agencies from the Spanish-speaking Caribbean, Mexico, important the United States, and Spanish-talking South the United States who are living inside America. Hispanics additionally consist of descendants from Spain, even as Latinos are those from the Americas residing in the United States of America. People of Mexican descent are the largest Hispanic group inside the US and many prefer to be referred to as using their particular country-wide foundation (such as Mexican American). Others can also pick terms they call themselves (which includes Chicanos). Local Hawaiians or Pacific Islanders refers to agencies of indigenous people who've lived for hundreds of years in the Hawaiian Islands or other Pacific Islands together with Fiji, Samoa, Tonga, the Marquesas, and Tahiti.

Huge proof supports this crucial end: the variations in success discovered among and among college students of culturally and ethnically diverse backgrounds and students of mainstream backgrounds aren't the result of differences in potential to research. Alternatively, they are the result of variations within the quality of the education those younger human beings have received in school. Furthermore, many college students who are vulnerable to failure in U.S. schools have types of studying which are at odds with traditional educational practices. A multitude of complicated elements contribute to college students' at-risk status; lots of these factors—crime, tablets, and poverty, amongst others—are past the manipulation of educators. However, educators do have the strength to update useless academic practices. The techniques that comply with had been validated to be powerful in growing scholar fulfillment. Keep excessive standards and demonstrate excessive expectations for all ethnically, culturally, and linguistically various students.

College students analyze extra while they're challenged with the aid of instructors who have high expectancies for them, encourage them to identify issues, involve them in collaborative activities, and boost up their studying. Teachers who specifically excessive expectancies deliver the notion that their college students have the potential to succeed in stressful activities. Such instructors keep away from repetitive rote gaining knowledge of; as an alternative, they involve younger humans in novel problem-fixing activities. They ask open-ended questions requiring students to use their judgment and form opinions. They pick sports wherein students need to use analytic capabilities, evaluate, and make connections. They count on college students to conduct research, entire their homework and manipulate their time efficaciously.

Now that detracting and improved gaining knowledge of with assist were proven to be powerful, instructors can confidently endorse for them. Hugh Mehan (2007, p. eleven) defines "detracting" as providing "a rigorous educational curriculum to all college students followed using an intensive gadget of instructional and social supports, or 'scaffolds.'" He notes that "detracting goes beyond simply technical or structural modifications, but entails a cultural exchange in teachers' beliefs, attitudes and values, modifications within the curriculum, and the company of coaching".

Consistent with Mehan (2007), research has shown that the schools' exercise of tracking neither provides students with identical instructional possibilities nor serves the needs of employers for a nicely-educated group of workers. Students from low-earnings and ethnic or linguistic minority backgrounds are disproportionately represented in low-music lessons and they seldom pass as much as high-song classes. College students located in low-track classes seldom acquire academic sources which are equivalent to college students who're located in excessive-music instructions. They regularly go through the stigmatizing outcomes of terrible labeling. They're now not organized properly for careers or college.

In a try to provide greater educational equity, educators in California schools were attempting an opportunity to monitoring since the Nineteen Eighties. In San Diego, one such software— achievement thru character dedication (AVID)—has remodeled the curriculum, path systems, and pedagogical techniques into "a couple of pathways" to university and career so that scholars are higher prepared and have greater alternatives after they whole excessive school. AVID "soundtracks" low-reaching ethnic and language-minority college students by placing both low- and high-reaching college students in the identical rigorous academic program. Students are taught explicitly a way to examine, how to work with instructors, and a way to write college applications. Those are skills regularly handed on by way of dad and mom who have attended university, however, they need to be trained to college students whose mother and father lack this shape of "cultural capital."

The AVID application has effectively organized underrepresented students for college. From 1988 to 1992, ninety-four percent of AVID students enrolled in college, compared to 56% of all excessive faculty graduates. African individuals and Latinos enrolled in college in numbers that passed each nearby and country-wide averages.

Lecture room examples

Jaime Escalante captured media interest together with his success in coaching calculus to Hispanic students. His excessive expectancies for his students and their subsequent accomplishments were the subject of the film Stand and supply. However, many teachers who will in no way be the challenge of a Hollywood film have stimulated and guided student achievement. Over and over, the research emphasizes the overwhelming importance of the trainer's notion that each student can study.

When instructors consider that scholars can learn, they talk about these expectancies explicitly, accordingly encouraging younger people, and in addition, they spend extra time creating challenging sports. They ask higher-order questions that require not most effective identity and categorization but also comprehension and analysis, utility to other situations, synthesis, and price judgments.

Heath and McLaughlin (1994) have determined that one of the reasons for the effectiveness of after-faculty teens programs organized with the aid of network-based corporations is that group of workers participants, regularly running on a shoestring budget, depend on college students to take some of the obligations for activities. Younger human beings plan, educate others and carry out a variety of duties critical to this system. Whilst students are added into the planning and become coaches for others, they're given "grownup" responsibilities and demanding situations; all of us should be capable of relying upon everybody else to expose up on time and do his or her element.

In addition, concerning college students inside the monetary elements of such operations (whether by fundraising or making requests of foundations) fosters involvement, responsibility, and the gaining knowledge of math capabilities. College students accumulate social competencies together with communication and overall performance talents. In such collaborative work, a variety of abilities is visible as an aid for the entire institution; all and sundry brings something unique to the desk. whilst journal writing is a required part of students' organization obligations, they mirror what they are studying, practice writing abilities, and preserve the group of workers knowledgeable of their man or woman progress and properly-being.

Students tend to want to take part and do their great whilst a teacher is nurturing and worrying. Nel Noddings (1995) advocates that when society around us concentrates on materialistic messages, "we must care more simple for our children and teach them to care". Of direction we need academic success for our college students, she notes, but "we can no longer gain even that unless our children consider they themselves are cared for and learn to care for others".

Noddings describes a practice known as "looping," in which instructors stay with an equal group of college students for 2 or greater years. Looping become referred to in excessive-acting schools in Oklahoma, Illinois, and New Jersey in the just for the youngsters have a look at of first-rate Practices in twenty States (countrywide middle for academic accountability. with the aid of following the same organization of college students for two or greater years, instructors get to realize their college students' desires and strengths better; accept as true with develops between teacher and students and among classmates. Looping additionally allows instructors to offer extra differentiated guidance, even tailoring training to character kids.

Classroom Examples

Noddings's definition of caring "implies a continuous look for competence." She observes "parents and teachers show being concerned through cooperating in kid's sports, sharing their own goals and doubts, and supplying cautiously for the steady boom of the children of their fee". Noddings indicates the usage of integrated curricular issues to educate caring to students.

within the area of "worrying for self," we would do not forget lifestyles degrees, spiritual increase, and what it method to broaden an admirable individual; in exploring caring for intimate others, we would include units on love, friendship, and parenting; underneath caring for strangers and worldwide others, we might take a look at conflict, poverty, and tolerance.

Younger college students also get excited when they examine that they can care for the surroundings thru recycling initiatives, becoming a member of others in cleansing and beautifying neighborhood parks, beginning a networking garden, or planting a tree. Those topics can be adapted for college kids from standard school thru high faculty.

Similarly, Noddings suggests alternative strategies of workforce employers in colleges. Standard students would gain from having the continuity of the same trainer or a strong group of specialists for two or extra years. Even at the high school degree, students might advantage if their instructor taught two subjects to the same thirty college students as opposed to one problem to sixty distinct students.

Using learning the strengths and demanding situations every student faces, teachers can refer kids and their families to community-based totally businesses that provide after-college homework assist and programs in sports and the humanities. high-appearing colleges also tend to have systems in the region to offer greater assistance for suffering novices or high-reaching college students taking hard coursework, consistent with the NCEA's just for the children high-quality Practices studies and Institutes.

Instructors need to assist in this work. Developing groups of teachers focused on scholar work became some other exercise noted by using the NCEA. Successful schools accomplish goals through collaboration. The academics in one Selma, California, high school maintain "attention lesson meetings" wherein educators from unique disciplines meet and provide feedback on one teacher's lesson plan, then strive out the revision in one of their classes and supply similar remarks. Others have "scoring events" to broaden not unusual ideas approximately what constitutes brilliant scholar work.

Educators should apprehend and appreciate the numerous unique methods of being a parent and expressing difficulty approximately the schooling of one's children. For instance, Gibson (1983, 1988) reviews that Punjabi immigrant parents in California accept as true with its miles the trainer's challenge to train and that mother and father have to now not be worried about what is going on at school. Punjabi parents aid their children's schooling via requiring that homework be carried out and ensuring that their children do not "hang out" with different college students however alternatively observe themselves to schoolwork. Even though the parents themselves may be pressured to take more than one process, they do no longer permit their children to work so that they have got time to finish their homework. As a result, Punjabi college students as a group have better prices of graduation and college popularity than different immigrant organizations.
Parental involvement is well installed as being correlated with scholar educational success. However, instructors can also have worries about the attitudes of "familism" among Mexican American students, which is defined as the "expressed identity with the hobbies and welfare of the circle of relatives". Valenzuela and Dornbusch venture "the dominant fantasy that academic achievement is obstructed via collective orientations." In sampling 492 adolescent college students of Mexican starting place, they discovered that neither parental schooling nor familism by

myself became related to educational fulfillment, however, the two variables operating together were related to academic achievement. They recommended that after younger people have relatives who've attended a U.S. excessive college, they have got get right of entry to more social capital. Also, being part of a dense social community of family complements the opportunity for "more than one option for academic support."

Schoolroom Examples

Searching for statistics about students' home cultures by asking them to interview their dad and mom approximately their lives as kids, the memories they consider, favored poems, and circle of relatives recipes. The outcomes of those interviews can tell the trainer about the wealth variety in his or her schoolroom. The interviews additionally can be made into booklets and, subsequently, studying materials for the entire magnificence to share.

Parent-trainer corporations can hold meetings at times convenient for parents to attend, and they could provide translators for those who do no longer talk English. A room within the college may be set apart for parents to satisfy and to talk about problems concerning their children's training or the faculty community. Instructors can visit dad and mom of their houses, or they could use figure-instructor conferences as a time to discuss homework and subject.

Mother and father who're welcomed into the school in methods which can be culturally appropriate for them become more accessible both as resources and as learners. Immigrant mothers and fathers can study both English as a second language (ESL) and survival skills for their new subculture. Dad and mom who're bilingual may be asked to translate for the ones who've no longer yet achieved fluency in a brand new language. Dad and mom who attend workshops can study family literacy and math activities that enhance their own talents to help their children gaining knowledge of these competencies. when students see that their parents are reputable by way of the college, there may be less of the conflict among home and school cultures that could motive a breakdown of discipline within the own family.

Mother and father and guardians are toddler's first teachers, but they may be no longer constantly aware of the approaches in which they mold children's language development and conversation capabilities. Kids analyze their language at domestic; the more interaction and communique they've at home, the greater kids analyze. Teachers can assist this vital function with the aid of sharing statistics about the hyperlink among domestic communication and kid's studying.

As an instance, teachers can act as "culture brokers" through speaking with mothers and fathers to emphasize the key position they play in their kid's education. Teachers can help mothers and fathers in know-how the expectations of the school and their lecture room as they elicit from parents their personal expectations of instructors and college students. Instructors also can endorse ways in which parents would possibly converse more frequently with their children to put together them for communication within the study room.

Mother and father won't be aware of how they help their children's instructional efforts when they speak the importance of education and take them to informal educational resources in the network. Teachers play a tremendously critical function in referring mother and father to community resources consisting of children's museums, artwork and technological know-how museums, and community-primarily based companies that offer homework help and humanities and sports applications. Instructors also may additionally recommend ESL and GED programs to mothers and fathers who want to continue their very own training.

Children learn the significance of language in expressing thoughts, feelings, and requests if dad and mom or guardians respond to them and renowned their thoughts. children also need steering in getting to know patterns of communication that are essential inside the study room, along with a way to make a request, ask a question, and respond to a question.

If dad and mom or guardians are literate in any language, they could read to their children in that language to encourage studying for pleasure and to assist children to begin to make the connection between oral language and analyzing. Although mother and father or guardians are not literate, they can use wordless books or create prose as they keep their youngsters and "read" with them.

Even the simplest evidence of being concerned approximately the significance of literacy will pay huge dividends in a young character's schooling. Parents or guardians can take time to talk with their youngsters approximately any interest they're doing collectively— eating a meal, for instance—thereby encouraging language development. These conversations among discerning and toddlers are useful whether they are in the home language or English. Parents or guardians can ask their youngsters questions on anything interest they're engaged in and the way it pertains to some other hobby, in addition, to asking how they sense about the interest or what they predict may also take place subsequently. They are as a result modeling the forms of conversation styles that younger human beings will use in college. On the identical time, of the route, in reality, giving children the presence of attention will pay large dividends.

Programs in family literacy can help dad and mom accumulate or enhance their very own literacy skills, making them better capable of assisting their children's development of literacy. The national center for the circle of relatives Literacy, with headquarters in Louisville, Kentucky, is a frontrunner in this attempt. Other techniques, consisting of the use of recorded books, permit adults and kids to study analyzing competencies collectively. Children are advocated to study once they see their mother and father analyzing and have their dad and mom examine them. Quite certainly, reading for a laugh encourages extra studying.

A sizable aid for instructors and PTAs is the country-wide network of Partnership Schools (NNPS) at Johns Hopkins College. Their materials assist with determining involvement in colleges; their website includes summaries of research on the circle of 'relatives' involvement. As an example, NNPS studies (Epstein, 2005) confirmed that Through excessive college, family involvement contributed to high-quality results for college students, along with better fulfillment, better attendance, more course credits earned, greater responsible preparation for class, and other signs of fulfillment in school analyzes indicated that scholars in neighborhoods with high concentrations of poverty had lower math success take a look at rankings, however, this impact became ameliorated by using on-going parental involvement in high college. NNPS research at the excessive faculty stage indicated that it is never too overdue to provoke applications of own family and network involvement, as the blessings accrue through grade twelve.

Research on "homework and targeted results toughen the importance of nicely-designed, concern-specific or goal-linked sports for own family and network involvement for a most powerful impact on pupil fulfillment and success in faculty". Sheldon and Epstein (2005a) documented that once teachers implement math homework requiring figure/child interactions and provide math materials for households to take domestic, "the proportion of students accomplishing math proficiency expanded from three hundred and sixty-five days to the following". In addition, Sheldon and Epstein (2005b) located that when teachers involve families in subject-particular interventions in studying and associated language arts, "college students' analyzing talents and scores are positively affected". Moreover, NNPS studies located "sizeable consequences of challenge-particular own family involvement [in homework] for college kids' technology document card grades and homework completion".

Students' shallowness and motivation are more desirable while teachers elicit their reports in study room discussions and validate what they have got to mention. Younger people come to be greater engaged in lessons when they are brought into the preliminary talk using being asked what they recognize approximately the subject and what they need to understand. If their questions are written down and used to form a guide for inquiry into the topic, college students are ways more likely to be interested in doing similar studies than if the questions truly pop out of textual content. The instructor also obtains better know-how of college students' previous understanding about a topic—a pre-evaluation, because it has been—which could manual the planning of the subsequent lesson.

One way wherein teachers can make certain recognition of college students' contributions is to use "semantic webbing." At the start of studying a brand new subject matter, the trainer asks students what they realize approximately that topic; the best manner to do that is to brainstorm a large number of institutions with the topic. For instance, the instructor or one of the students may put the subject "lifestyle" in a center circle on the chalkboard. Then, the recorder notes college students' associations in circles across the middle circle.

As a next step, the elegance can talk (and connect to traces) all of the associated aspects of the "way of life," making the internet of relationships on the board. This work may be accelerated by using categorizing the subtopics. The trainer also can ask students what they need to recognize about the subject handy. College students' questions, recorded for later use, can function as publications for studies. College students are more likely to be interested in getting to know a subject once they begin with their personal real questions. Those actual questions lead them in an ever-widening direction of the investigation.

Enforcing this method may be as easy as asking children to voice their questions on a given subject matter at the start of a lesson. After collecting scholarly questions, the teacher can ask whether or not any student already has data about the topic. Earlier than drawing on books and other assets, the scholars themselves can be assets with the aid of the usage of their personal understanding and previous reports.

Students' self-esteem is strengthened when they see and read about the contributions made by their very own racial or ethnic groups to the history and tradition of the United States. Whenever feasible, teachers adapt the curriculum to awareness instructions on topics that are meaningful to college students. This sort of recognition allows college students to practice language, wondering, reading, and writing competencies in actual, meaningful, and interactive situations. College students also come to understand that instructors cost and admire each child's lifestyle and language.

Teachers can pick out texts or if important, supplementary substances (inclusive of kid's literature written via diffusion of authors) that comprise the perspectives, voices, historical events, poetry, artwork, journals, and illustrations of the range of racial and ethnic businesses that make up U.S. society (and that may be represented inside the lecture room). Instructors can ask college students to interview their parents approximately their records, such as their lifestyle, poetry, song, recipes, novels, and heroes. The student can videotape, audiotape, or write the interview and percentage it with the relaxation of the elegance.

In interviews conducted by using the Latino fee, high faculty college students located that they sense neglected while the curriculum of the college incorporates nothing that relates to their own lifestyle. Conversely, they feel that each they and their subculture are valued when their tradition is protected in the curriculum. For more youthful college students, children's books approximately younger people in their own cultural context can provide avenues for dialogue and comparison of the similarities and differences among the lifestyle in their mother and father and that of the school or network in which they now stay.

If the instructor lets in sexist or racist language and stereotypes to skip unchallenged, students might be harmed in methods: (1) using the demeaning depiction of their organization, which can also become part of their self-idea, and (2) via the constraints they'll feel on their potential to live and work harmoniously with others of their classroom and their society.

Instructors can pick texts or supplementary materials to deal with the difficulty of stereotyping. The supplementary substances must be written by way of a selection of authors who comprise a wide variety of perspectives on historic activities, poetry, artwork, journals, music, and illustrations of women and men, as well as varied ethnic and racial corporations. Instructors also can point out sexist language and ethnic, racial, or gender stereotypes in regular instructional materials.

Weis and high-quality (2001) have documented the improvement of an experience of network and the contesting of stereotypes throughout the same old obstacles of race, class, and gender in unique faculty situations. inside the first, racial and class stereotypes dissolved in a ninth-grade literature elegance guided through two instructors in a racially incorporated public school in Montclair, New Jersey. The faculty has a range of socioeconomic corporations, from those dwelling in situations of excessive wealth to those residing in situations of dire poverty. The faculty is tracked academically, but the global literature class documented by using Michelle satisfactory becomes detracted. The lecturers requested questions that demanded taking a function and defending it. Students also were asked to broaden a brand new angle with the aid of getting inside the minds and feelings of the literary characters being studied and pronouncing what they might say. Instructors guided the students over the semester as they evolved a brand new attention to the variety of abilities in their classmates, no matter race.

Weis and great (2001) also documented an abstinence application amongst 8th-grade women within the Arts Academy, an urban magnet school in Buffalo, the big apple. The students differed only in racial identification; all lived in conditions of poverty. However, they advanced an identity as a set and distanced themselves from others in their identical heritage who had been taking a special path that they saw as unproductive (striking round men, smoking and drinking, and turning into pregnant at an early age). The organization got here to look that they shared commonplace issues and could proportion answers throughout racial traces. Through the facilitation of a workforce member from the gender-primarily based prevention outreach carrier Womanfocus, invited via the faculty guidance counselor, those ladies came to share many aspects in their personal lives over the course of the semester. Helping one another, they planned to graduate from excessive college, pass directly to college, and be successful. In doing so, they contested the notions of femininity, victimhood, and race prevailing in their neighborhoods.

Figuring out and dispelling stereotypes may be as simple as stating examples of sexist language in normal curriculum materials, inclusive of using "man" for "human" or using the pronoun "he" regarding each lady and man. The trainer can move past easy awareness of such stereotypes by asking students how such language makes them feel.

To encourage exploration of the way it feels to be in some other's footwear, the instructor also can ask students if they would really like to be classified "non-Japanese" because they live in the Western Hemisphere—just as many North individuals talk to those who live in the eastern Hemisphere as "non-Western." The trainer can also ask white and Asian college students whether or not they might prefer to be known as "nonblack," in an equal manner that blacks and Asians are regularly called "nonwhite."

The trainer can evaluate the dichotomy utilized in categorizations of racial groups in the US (i.e., black and white) with the continuum of racial and ethnic agencies in South America, in which there are more than twenty such categories or distinctions. Those hanging variations lend themselves to a discussion of the social creation or definition of racial companies; college students experience the opportunity to research the history and derivation of these definitions.

Research has shown that students learn more while their classrooms are compatible with their personal cultural and linguistic experiences. When the norms of interaction and communication in a classroom are very one of a kind from those to which students have been accustomed, they may revel in confusion and tension, be unable to take care of gaining knowledge of, and now not understand a way to appropriately seek the teacher's attention or take part in discussions. Through acknowledging college students' cultural norms and expectancies regarding conversation and social interplay, teachers can correctly manual pupil participation in instructional sports.

Studies on the effectiveness of culturally well-suited lecture rooms have been conducted with Hawaiian youngsters as well as with Navajo and African American kids. The aspects of the way of life that impact lecture room lifestyles maximum powerfully are those that affect the social company of gaining knowledge of and the social expectancies regarding verbal exchange.

The enterprise of the typical U.S. classroom is one in all whole-magnificence teaching in which the instructor as chief instructs, assigns texts, and demonstrates complete elegance. Such entire-elegance guidance is often accompanied with the aid of man or woman exercise and evaluation.

By evaluation, Jordan (1995) mentioned the outcomes amongst Hawaiian college students in public schools whose analyzing achievement advanced greatly after culturally compatible school rooms had been carried out through the Kamehameha Early education application (preserve). In an ethnographic study of the scholars' domestic existence, Jordan and colleagues within the Hawaiian community studies venture in the past due 1960s and early nineteen seventies found that older siblings have been responsible for looking after younger siblings and doing duties cooperatively in the home without direct parental supervision. Therefore, these educators structured their 3rd-grade lecture rooms into mastering centers. After direct guidance from the instructor, small blended-gender corporations of four or five students may want to help each other with tasks on the centers, without the direct supervision of teachers—much like their home state of affairs. Meanwhile, the academics worked with small groups of college students the usage of comprehension-orientated, direct instruction reading training the usage of specific sociolinguistic and cognitive styles, and a device for managing infant behavior which built on widespread contingency management to help the instructor in providing herself as someone who becomes each "hard and excellent," these being key attributes of adults that Hawaiian youngsters like and recognize.

In a collaboration with the tough Rock Demonstration faculty in Arizona, Jordan (1995) suggested that the same strategies had been tried with third grade Navajo college students, however, the strategies did now not work nicely with them. They discovered that during the Navajo lifestyle, boys and women were predicted to live in equal-gender corporations. Also, because their dwellings had been to this point aside, they didn't have studies with many children out of doors of the school in peer partner businesses because the Hawaiian children did. Thereafter, adjustments were made inside the lecture room company, and the Navajo children had been extra relaxed operating at getting to know centers with just one more baby of the equal gender.

In keeping with Tharp (1992), teaching and getting to know each other is more powerful when they may be contextualized in the stories, talents, and values of the community and while gaining knowledge of is a joint productive interest involving each friend and teachers.

Studying is furthered using "instructional conversations"—dialogues among instructors and freshmen about their not unusual learning activities.

A teacher notices that a Chinese American lady has a tendency no longer to raise her hand to participate in discussions. The instructor discovers that the kid is afraid to respond in front of the complete magnificence due to the fact she is still gaining knowledge of English and worries that others will snicker at her. The instructor divides the elegance into corporations of four to do collaborative research so that the lady can exercise talking in English in a smaller group.

Too regularly, while young humans speak a language other than English and are mastering English as a 2nd language, instructors of ESL or reading in English can also restrict their activities to the bottom degree of interpreting and phonics, degrees that do not project students intellectually. Most effective while college students have the possibility to maintain learning in their native language can they operate at their cognitive level and develop intellectually. After studying an eBook or article in their native language, they may be challenged with comprehension, utility, and evaluation questions—the better-order thinking skills. Moll, Diaz, Estrada, and Lopes (1992) found that the extent of wondering is a lot greater restrained in ESL analyzing groups than in native-language studying agencies. Jordan, Tharp, and Baird-Vogt (1992) determined that Hawaiian children's educational achievement expanded when certain elements of their home lifestyle were included in the primary study room. The use of a culturally suitable shape of communication referred to as "speak tale" engaged the scholars more fully. Similarly, Hawaiian college students were extra comfy in school when they had been recognized as being able to take obligation for retaining the order and cleanliness of their study room. In their homes, Hawaiian kids have many obligations for the care of younger siblings and cooperate in doing family chores. They felt more "at domestic" whilst they could come in early, straighten up the room, and set out other college students' work for the day. Instructors made the lecture room more culturally well suited with the aid of studying approximately the subculture of the house.

Use cooperative gaining knowledge of techniques.

One of the maximum difficult problems faced by instructors in multiethnic lecture rooms is that scholars, especially those from ethnic agencies suffering social discrimination, have a tendency to cluster in cliques based on ethnicity. College students can also take a look at that one peer institution draws itself apart and, in response, may come to experience that they should achieve this as well.

To break down this defensive withdrawal into ethnic agencies, instructors need to offer college students time to get to understand each different and to locate that they percentage commonplace floor, common issues, and commonplace feelings. One way to interrupt down synthetic limitations between college students is to encourage them to take part in a small institution over a prolonged time period, taking part in a shared pastime with a shared purpose that can best be achieved by working together.

Kids who have an opportunity to work in cooperations getting to know businesses with fellow students of other races and ethnicities get to understand the one's students as actual humans as opposed to as stereotypes. As college students analyze together and get to recognize each other, mutual respect and friendships can expand.

The teacher assigns students to corporations of 5 or six and gives every pupil a particular mission within the medical experiment they're to do collaboratively. One reads and units up the substances for the test; one plays the test. Another student information their effects, some other illustrates their findings, but any other reads the recorded revel into the relaxation of the elegance, and so on.

The social skills that guide such cooperative mastering must be trained. College students have to learn how to pay attention and deliver feedback, manipulate warfare, steer, contribute, and take obligation for a part of the task. Teachers want to allow groups sufficient time to "method" their own performance in an assignment by talking approximately about their interplay and how it can be advanced. obligations that consist of nice interdependence as part of the interest—this is, obligations requiring everyone inside the group to be depending on the entire institution's doing well a good way to achieve the intention—are much more likely to achieve success. In particular powerful is "jigsaw" obligations, which cannot be completed unless everybody allows or except every player learns one piece of the task and teaches the others. Cooperative mastering is extra than having students sit after every other; it entails structuring younger humans' want to talk, to get to recognize one another, and to work collectively.

Capitalize on college students' cultures, languages, and stories

Gaining knowledge is more likely to arise when young humans' expectations about the way to interact with adults and other kids shape the teachers' and administrators' expectancies for such interplay.

Saravia-Shore and Martinez (1992) observed that Puerto Rican high school dropouts who had succeeded in an alternative excessive school credited their accelerated achievement to the difference in the manner adults treated them in every school. They said that they felt they have been treated as kids inside the regular high college, however, the personnel contributors of the alternative school handled them as adults.

Mainly, their new instructors expected that they do their homework due to the fact they had enrolled so that it will bypass the GED examination. Instructors in the alternative excessive college confirmed numerous coaching strategies for numerous learners and information of the students' cultural norm of having households at an early age and being accountable for different individuals of their circle of relatives. Because they knew the scholars had certainly pressing obligations (which includes worrying for his or her families and running to assist them), they did no longer criticize students for being overdue to class, so long as their work was finished. Really put, the scholars felt that the lecturers within the alternative school understood their life stories and cared approximately their success.

Jordan, Tharp, and Baird-Vogt (1992) have shown that when teachers comprise the home culture's anticipated styles of interplay and discourse, college students sense more secure in college and participate more actively in gaining knowledge of situations. When college students are used to caring for different children at home, they have a foundation for cooperative gaining knowledge of and peer coaching. They can be triumphant with cooperative getting to know and peer teaching if they're given the possibility to use them and the aid of the teacher. If children are acquainted with having duties in being concerned for his or her bodily environment at home, they frequently sense at ease in caring for and handling the faculty environment as well.

Combine the arts in the curriculum

Not anything makes getting to know come alive greater than enticing students in arts activities that encourage communication on troubles which can be crucial to them. offering possibilities for students to express themselves through the visible and appearing arts enables them to learn about and expand their talents and a couple of intelligence: no longer most effective verbal and mathematical intelligence but additionally visual, spatial, musical, interpersonal, and intrapersonal intelligence.

Young children gain from being encouraged to make feel in their world and their relationships through drawing and portray image photos. Encouraging students to apply their imaginations and taking time to elicit their interpretations of visual arts through open-ended questions in a schoolroom putting is valuable in itself. Yet those conversations also permit students to apprehend, as they pay attention to other classmates, the multitude of interpretations that are feasible when viewing the identical work of art.

Parents may be invited to accompany their children as a set

to an artwork museum and to study the trainer asking children to explain what they see and what the artwork method to them. After they've made one of these go-to, dad and mom can be greater comfortable taking their kids again to the museum.

In addition, poetry can be a jumping-off place for discussions. The works of Billy Collins, Langston Hughes, Maya Angelou, and Bob Dylan often spark college students to write their very own poetry. Then, college students can learn how to perform their own work.

Researchers summarized the results of a hundred forty-five programs that incorporated the humanities in the curriculum in vital hyperlinks: gaining knowledge of in the Arts and scholar academic and social improvement. They agreed that "properly-crafted arts reports produce high-quality educational and social effects". One of the vital hyperlinks research mentioned the results of the Chicago Arts Partnerships in Education (CAPE) on college students' academic overall performance. In CAPE faculties, teams of teachers and teaching artists deliberate and taught curriculum gadgets that usually incorporated a visual artwork form with an academic situation (together with reading or social research). The consequences "established that the low SES youngsters in arts-integrated colleges carry out higher than those in evaluation schools in phrases of [standardized assessments of mathematics and analyzing] take a look at ratings".

DeMoss and Morris (2002) investigated the question of how the humanities help cognitive increase in students. They interviewed 30 students in CAPE colleges in ten lessons led via veteran teacher/artist partnerships. They located that "college students from all success levels displayed full-size will increase in their capability to analytically assess their own gaining knowledge of following arts-included devices," whilst "no such gains have been related to traditional instructional studies". Further, DeMoss and Morris documented those advantages of CAPE.

Observations of final performances inside the arts-included gadgets corroborated college students' own checks. College students who had problems controlling their behavior and staying on undertaking executed their elements on very last occasions with seriousness and competency. ... As college students throughout the board indicated in their interviews, the sorts of sports that the arts offer have interaction children more deeply in their gaining knowledge of by using growing an intrinsic obligation for the learning activities. This locating held especially authentic for those kids toughest to reach with the aid of traditional processes.

In this case, the humanities contributed to analytically deeper, experientially broader, and psychologically greater rewarding learning. These developments may want to have great high-quality consequences on college students' preferred cognitive increase through the years, particularly if students revel in arts-integrated learning of their school rooms on a normal foundation.

A more current examination demonstrating the benefits of integrating visual arts in the curriculum on young children's cognitive development became reported in the NY Times. Third-grade college students within the studying via artwork program backed with the aid of the Solomon R. Guggenheim Museum have been determined to have "finished better in six categories of literacy and crucial thinking talents—including thorough description, hypothesizing, and reasoning—than did college students who were now not within the software". On this program, the Guggenheim Museum sends teaching artists to the schools where they collaborate with the instructor for ninety minutes in step with a class at some point per week over a ten or twenty-week duration, helping college students and instructors learn about and make artwork. Companies of college students are also taken to the Guggenheim two or three instances in that period to see

Posters of artwork can enliven a study room and be a starting point for enriching conversations. If there are restrictions on displaying such work at the partitions, use inexpensive foam core panels that fold out and arise as the background for a lecture room gallery. Invite children to explain the artwork on the posters and create a story approximately what's taking place inside the pictures— what may have occurred before and what may show up next.
Children can learn how to mix number one colorings, discovering the secondary shades that are created while any number one colors are blended. They revel in painting, whether it's finger paint for the youngest students or tempera paint for the center and high college students. College students can do collaborative art projects, putting together character pieces into quilts, or developing works of art. Are seeking out illustrated children's paperback books, consisting of Jacob Lawrence's the exceptional Migration. Lawrence makes use of artwork to interpret the records of African Americans who migrated from the South to the North all through the early twentieth century.

Such visual references to historical events deliver social research to lifestyles.

Images are some other art form that children can research from a grownup, be it an instructor, an instructor's colleague, or a figure. Students can use disposable cameras to select locations, humans, and gadgets from their environment to photo; the snapshots can be published inside the classroom "gallery" and mentioned or used to construct a story, play, or poem. Photographic "essays" are another manner of sharing one's domestic subculture with others.

Center and excessive school college students experience "poetry slams" wherein they compete to be the fine performer of their personal poems. Mastering songs is some other manner to enjoy poetry. From the youngest kid's songs of Woody Guthrie to favorite global folks songs to the songs of social justice within the Civil Rights movement, the track illuminates the human circumstance and makes social research more memorable. Students may even study performs aloud in the study room, and later the scholars themselves can write and carry out plays for the magnificence.

Worrying for college students includes positively influencing their decisions associated with their physical well-being. Congress exceeded the child nutrients Act in June 2004, requiring faculty districts to craft "well-being" policies. Such rules have to include desires for nutrition schooling and methods to grow the physical interest of all college students.

Educators who're aware of the growing epidemic of adolescent weight problems and diabetes are alarmed. In line with Kleinfield, "One in 3 children born in the US [in 2001] is predicted to end up diabetic of their lifetimes, according to a projection through the centers for disease manage and Prevention. The forecast for Latinos is even bleaker: one in each two."

Nationally, the growing trouble of obese children influences minority students disproportionately. Adolescence Type 2 diabetes, the maximum commonplace form, is often related to obesity. Being overweight has ended up a first-rate scientific problem among Latino/Hispanic households. Within the 2003–04 baby developments take a look at, 25.3% of Mexican American men from a while six to eleven were obese as defined by the centers for ailment control and Prevention—the highest price in that age organization. Evaluate their price to the figure for black males (17.5%) and white males (18.5%) of the equal age institution. among girls ages six to eleven, the highest percentage (26.5) of obese children turned into black females, accompanied via 19.4% of Mexican American women and 16.9% of white women. within the twelve to nineteen age range, black women were the highest percentage of obese children at 25.4%. furthermore, "Asians, particularly those from a long way jap international locations like China, Korea, and Japan, are acutely liable to Type 2 diabetes, the maximum commonplace form of the disease". Similarly, they expand type 2 diabetes at a ways decrease weights than people of different races; at any weight, they may be 60% more likely than whites to settlement the sickness.

Teachers can assist to counteract television advertisements for fast food, large portions, sodas, sugary snacks, and sedentary existence that feeds childhood obesity and frequently cause diabetes, especially amongst Asians, Latinos, and African people. The big apple instances take a look at East Harlem in the big apple city found a 31% fee of diabetes a few of the 90% Latino and African American population there. Alas, "whilst fitness government mentioned obesity a countrywide trouble, day by day participation in fitness center classes dropped to 28% in 2003 from 42% in 1991, according to the facilities for disorder manage and Prevention". To promote more healthy eating conduct, teachers can assign studies initiatives evaluating the calories in fast ingredients in numerous eating places, smooth beverages (which includes weight loss program sodas), breakfast meals, and snacks (fried as opposed to baked chips, the nutrients facts about various styles of microwave popcorn). If every baby researches one product, the elegance can create a chart evaluating them all. A similar class undertaking could ask college students to behave as detectives, uncovering the quantity of high-fructose corn syrup in diverse products with the aid of investigating and recording the facts at the ingredients label. Teachers of older college students can display the film excellent size me, which places a human face at the consequences of fast ingredients and also includes data on approximately nutritious foods.

Instructors inquisitive about making health a part of the curriculum can integrate units at the health advantages of meals with complicated carbohydrates (beans and multigrain or whole grain bread) as compared to fantastically refined carbohydrates (which includes white bread and maximum pasta). they also may assist college students to inspect why ingesting apples and other fruits as snacks are healthful as well as scrumptious; the fitness blessings of leafy green greens; making sandwiches or wraps of roasted greens; the better degrees of mercury in large fish in comparison to smaller fish; and the blessings of olive oil in comparison to butter and margarine.

One faculty district in Texas used the Get in shape (households in schooling) application for a nine-week summertime intervention camp for his or her college students who had been obese. For five days every week, students exercised ate healthy snacks and lunches, and learned approximately excellent nutrition; their mother and father got here to the school one night per week to learn about vitamins to assist their children. The program, developed using Peggy Visio, a dietitian and adjunct professor, additionally added the hundred thirty fifth-graders to dancing, kickboxing, yoga, swimming, and volleyball. The benefits of concerning dad and mom are clear: they could guide a healthier lifestyle within the home and advice for healthy lunches and snacks in faculty.

Instructors can also encourage college students to take gain of sports applications offered using network businesses like ladies and Boys Clubs, the YMCA, and the Police Athletic League. Community-primarily based groups regularly sponsor summer season camps and after-college programs. Taking component in sports activities; yoga; tai chi; or simple deep, slow breathing also allows lessen strain. Even inviting a well-knowledgeable parent or a trainer or a fitness professional from a local health center to proportion data on healthful vitamins, exercise, and pressure reduction will positively have an impact on college students in this vicinity.

Instructors can explore network schools as fashions for an academic method that places kids in the middle and addresses cognitive, social, emotional, and physical desires and strengths. The latest file from the ASCD fee on the entire baby (clean & Berg, 2006) presents examples of successful community colleges. Community colleges purpose to expand college students who are "academically gifted and physically and emotionally wholesome and respectful, responsible, and caring; who can make contributions to the community and the arena". Network faculties additionally provide "based enrichment activities and renowned college students' want for preference, manage, competence, and belonging".

Network faculties open their classrooms to network-primarily based corporations and resources that aid kids through after-faculty homework help and enrichment programs as well as supportive applications for dad and mom, including ESL, GED practice, parenting guides, and parent and network leadership workshops in the evening. a few network schools have dental clinics on the website; others have nurseries so that teenage mothers can complete faculty. Some schools in excessive allergies regions have clinics inside the faculty so students can get help and leave out less college.

Network faculties make an array of network assets accessible to guide children and families in attaining their potential. Whilst schools, mother and father, and network corporations pool their resources, they can offer "supportive environments that nurture students' social, emotional, physical, ethical, civic and cognitive improvement".

The ASCD fee recognized numerous non-school factors that have an impact on instructional fulfillment which includes nutrients, determine the participation of their toddler's college, time looking television, mobility, and mothers' academic stage. Essential, too, is research by way of McLaughlin and co-workers (1994) showing that adolescents who take part regularly in network-primarily based teens improvement packages—along with arts, sports activities, and community provider—have better instructional and social consequences in addition to better instructional and profession aspirations than other teens. The concept is to "build on kid's learning styles ... and guide the basic needs of kids and their households, together with health, nutrients, and monetary and social properly-being".

Chicago, Illinois, has been considered one of the most important network college projects inside the US. Of Chicago's six hundred and thirteen schools, one hundred and two now operate as network faculties. They serve a median of fifteen thousand students and their families every year. A have a look at by way of blank and Berg (2006, p.16) confirmed that "eighty-one percent of community faculties arc showing development in instructional fulfillment as compared to seventy-four percent of normal public faculties". In Indianapolis, Indiana, a community high faculty commenced in 2000 now has forty-nine network partners. These businesses provide intellectual and bodily health consultation, day-care and after-faculty packages, university guidance, and person training programs. Their college students' standardized test rankings have risen ten to fifteen points every year for the reason that application started. The sophomores examined in 2003 outscored the ones in all of the traditional excessive faculties in Indianapolis.

Comprise a couple of kinds of assessment

In latest years, standardized checking out has been used to drive faculty reform, with decidedly blended results. The Coalition for proper Reform in education (CARE) shows that instead of relying on a single standardized check for excessive-stakes selections inclusive of promoting to the following grade, actual evaluation of pupil work (including student exhibitions, portfolios, merchandise, and overall performance responsibilities) is most well-known. A couple of signs of academic performance and development on schoolwork for the duration of the year have to be a part of this technique.

Valenzuela and colleagues endorse a method that could remember: "1) enter (the adequacy of resources), 2) process (the first-class of guidance), and 3) output (what college students have learned as measured via tests or other signs)". The usage of standardized checking out alone tends to focus on output, neglecting the alternative two dimensions. College students who stay in groups of poverty regularly do not have the get entry to resources or distinctly certified instructors that scholars in wealthier districts do. For this reason, they are a long way from experiencing identical academic possibilities.

Amongst many others, Hodgkinson (2003) has suggested that the point of interest of the current excessive-stakes standardized trying out system is too slender:

An additional hassle entails the heavy preoccupation with studying and math readiness skills and talents in the early years of training. Even as those competencies are glaringly important, factors that are much less targeted on academics, which includes self-belief, resilience, being concerned, emotional development, and supportive family individuals may be just as vital. ... Given the national preoccupation with "excessive-stakes trying out" as the only degree of scholar, faculty, district, state, and possibly countrywide instructional fulfillment, and the steady checking out of those areas that are maximum effortlessly measured, including studying and math sub-skills, a preschool program that has also emphasized social/emotional development may be visible as "smooth" or "afraid to face data."

Even though it seems overdone, primary faculties right all the way down to kindergarten in a few cases are being assessed by way of scholar scores at the NAEP, Iowa tests of simple abilities, IQ, or the state fulfillment tests. (One of the hidden agendas here is that instructional achievement might be described by way of the student's ability to take standardized multiple-desire exams.) 1/2 of the simple colleges in Fairfax County, Virginia, are comparing their kindergartners the use of an 11-web page report card, assessing language, studying, writing, math, science, social research, fitness, motion, art, and track in addition to social and emotional improvement. in place of checkmarks for "once in a while," "commonly," and "continuously," mother and father are encountering terms which include "pre early emergent," "early emergent," "emergent," and "novice." a few mother and father may additionally have a tough time greedy those evaluation results. They'll need a few assists to understand the difference between seeing an "A" on their toddler's report card and searching at a toddler's degree of development, irrespective of the benefit of having a higher feeling of what students are truly learning. Unless parents are prepared for this modification, the ideal shift to look studying as boom, using a ramification of scientific and statistical measures, won't trap on.

The just for the children observe of first-class Practices (NCEA, 2006) also noted that "all the high-appearing faculties we visited draw statistics from a couple of tests and use those statistics to inform each choice."

Similar to the outcome talents of analyzing and arithmetic, maximum folks need our students to develop such behavior of mind as thinking, gazing intently, making connections, developing that means, valuing their experience, identifying patterns, displaying empathy, and evaluating their own work. College students emerge as greater awareness of those capacities when they may be recognized, discussed, and assessed.

Lincoln middle Institute has developed an assessment tool to evaluate habits of mind that aren't measurable thru standardized tests. Seeking the 30-yr history of philosophy and practice at the institute, Madeleine Fuchs Holzer advanced definitions for nine capacities for innovative studying. As an example, she defined "growing meaning" as developing interpretations on the idea of previous capacities (which include questioning, noticing deeply, figuring out styles, and making connections), seeing these in light of others in the network, developing a synthesis, and expressing it on your own voice.

Holzer shared the capacities with colleges from at least eight schools and several primary and excessive faculties during the Lincoln middle Institute summer Institute. She advocated and acquired feedback about them and revised the capacities via several iterations. The institute posted the definitions of the capacities after which requested a consultant, Drew Dunphy, to work with a set of instructors from the excessive faculty for arts, creativeness, and Inquiry in New York town to increase rubrics for the capacities.

There are several blessings to working as a group to expand rubrics. Instructors can spot gaps in colleagues' efforts and work to reinforce them. In addition, while teachers broaden and own an evaluation tool, college students' dreams and consequences become more consistent. By identifying the improvement of those capacities as their aim, instructors allow students to understand that they cost the expression of these innate features of thought and emotion.

Any other evaluation that engages college students within the process is the usage of portfolios. Instructors and college students can expand portfolios containing samples in their classwork and instructor-made exams over the year. Asking college students to check their portfolios bimonthly and pick the great examples in their work for that time period coaches them in self-evaluation and enables them to peer their development. The instructor can share those portfolios on dad and mom's night to show how students are doing. Further, if students don't carry out properly on a standardized take a look at used in an excessive-stakes occasion, including advertising to the subsequent grade, their work samples could also be used to reveal that they're ready for the following grade.

Strategies for Linguistically diverse students

The term "linguistically and culturally numerous students" encompasses a good-sized array of younger humans. As President John F. Kennedy famously recommended, the US is a "state of immigrants." students who come to high school talking a local language apart from English—from homes and groups wherein English is not the language of verbal exchange—have often been perceived by the English-talking majority as the most educationally vulnerable. Now that so many dual-language bilingual programs were in the vicinity for the beyond twenty years, but, we can see that coming to a school that helps to turn into bilingual and bi-literate can truly be an advantage.

As the sector will become greater economically interdependent, the advantages of bilingualism and cross-cultural know-how are better understood. in line with the Yankee Council on the coaching of overseas Languages, the variety of excessive faculty students who are enrolled in foreign language packages in public high schools has grown step by step from 1978—while 3.2 million (23% of the general public high school population) had been enrolled in such classes—to the year 2000, when five, eight hundred and ninety-nine, four hundred were enrolled in such lessons.

The latest research has redefined the character of how we apprehend the instructional vulnerability of linguistically and culturally diverse students. Stereotypes and myths have started to present way, laying a foundation on which to conceptualize current instructional practices.

Present-day questioning emphasizes the fee of speaking more than one language. Rather than being taken into consideration "disadvantaged" as speakers of a language aside from English, such students are actually being considered potentially bilingual and bi-literate. The primary language (L1) is now taken into consideration as a base on which English language newcomers (ELLs) can build "additive" bilingualism (getting to know a second language [L2] while becoming literate of their first language and eventually literate in both).

Teachers wishing to look evidence of the effectiveness of numerous applications for ELLs have to be aware of the work of Thomas and Collier (2002), who carried out the maximum comprehensive longitudinal studies look at thus far at the lengthy-time period academic effectiveness of 8 one of a kind ok–12 packages for language-minority students, in addition to English monolingual students who take part in -manner immersion (also called twin-language) packages.

Thomas and Collier researched English as a second language (ESL), transitional bilingual education, developmental bilingual education (DBE), one-manner (one organization learning bilingually), and two-manner (two agencies studying each different language as a second language) bilingual programs, in addition to the location of ELLs in mainstream classes. Their 2002 record in their take a look at (from 1985 to 2001) covers six sites inside the United States. In discovering extra than two hundred thousand student records each year, they transformed standardized test ratings into ordinary curve equivalents and probabilities. They observed the following highlights.

Enrichment 90-10 [90 percentage training in L1 and 10% in L2] and 50-50 one-manner and -way developmental bilingual training (DBE) programs (or dual-language, bilingual immersion) are the simplest applications … observed … that help [English language novices] to absolutely attain the fiftieth percentile in both L1 and L2 in all subjects and to maintain that degree of excessive success, or reach even higher degrees through the give up of education. The fewest dropouts come from those packages.

Parents who refuse bilingual/ESL services for their youngsters have to be informed that their children's lengthy-term academic achievement will possibly be tons lower as a result and that they should be strongly suggested in opposition to refusing bilingual/ESL services while their infant is eligible. The study's findings of this study indicate that ESL or bilingual offerings, as required by using Lau v. Nichols, boost college students' success ranges with the aid of extensive quantities.

Every other full-size finding: ELL students who attend remedial, segregated programs do no longer near the fulfillment hole after being positioned in mainstream training. Educational gains are finely executed in an enrichment, not a remedial, software, Thomas and Collier determined. They suggested against brief-time period bilingual training (one to three years). They discovered that it takes at least four years of bilingual training or four years of education in a scholar's L1 inside the home us of a and four years in bilingual packages for college students to attain grade-level overall performance in English (the 50th percentile at the subtest of reading in English).

As a result, the maximum efficient training is in twin-language programs wherein both L1 and L2 are found out concurrently and college students have the opportunity to talk with college students fluent in that L2. Thomas and Collier determined that the most powerful predictor of student achievement in English (L2) turned into formal L1 education in either the home US or the host (United States of America). "The greater L1 grade-level schooling, the better L2 success," they cited.

A thrilling finding turned into that "bilingually schooled college students outperform similar monolingually schooled students in academic fulfillment in all subjects, after four to seven years of twin language education." The authors also mentioned

An enrichment bilingual/ESL software needs to meet students' developmental needs: linguistic (L1–L2), instructional, cognitive, emotional, social, bodily. colleges need to create a natural mastering environment in school, with plenty of herbal, rich language (L1, L2), each oral and written, utilized by students and instructors; meaningful, "actual world" hassle-solving; all college students working collectively; media-rich studying (video, computers, print); difficult thematic devices that get and keep students' hobby; and the usage of students' bilingual-bicultural knowledge to bridge to new know-how throughout the curriculum.

Due to the fact, one of the goals of bilingual applications within the twenty-first century is to put together college students to be gifted bilingually inside the workplace, Thomas and Collier (2002, p.5) also researched the achievement of local Spanish audio system in Spanish and local English audio system in a twin-language bilingual software.

The local-English audio system in two-way bilingual immersion applications maintained their English, added a 2nd language to their understanding base, and done well above the fiftieth percentile in all concern regions on norm-referenced tests in English. Those bilingually schooled college students equaled or outperformed their contrast groups being schooled monolingually, on all measures.

The number of years of primary language schooling, either in the domestic USA or in host us of a, had a greater impact than socioeconomic fame when the number of years of training becomes four or greater years. in addition, the L2 instructional achievement of older immigrant arrivals with sturdy grade-level training completed in L1 in the domestic united states become much less stimulated by low socioeconomic repute and more dependent on a range of years completed. Likewise, students of low socioeconomic reputation who have been born inside the U.S. or arrived at a completely young age finished at high tiers in L2 while grade-degree training became furnished in both L1 and L2 in the U.S.

These days, educators pick that students develop linguistic facility in each English and their domestic language, in preference to learn English simplest and lose the home language, handiest to must relearn a second language later of their college years. research suggests that scholars' cognitive development proceeds more with ease in their local language and that scholars research content material more effortlessly inside the native language at the same time as they are getting to know English as a second language.

An interdisciplinary method to the curriculum—breaking from many decades of separation among the numerous disciplines—is a powerful ally in teaching culturally and linguistically various children. Rather than coaching reading as a separate problem, as an example, instructors now view reading as a process for studying concepts and exploring topics and their connections. Cooperative mastering corporations and peer tutoring work well on the side of PC-mediated language mastering. And dad and mom are companions of their children's education, in addition to assets for instructors in expertise young humans' cultural styles of communique and interaction.

Set up, in reality, bilingual lecture rooms

Students who come to high school with a domestic language aside from English study extra from applications wherein their local language is one of the languages of education. By using persevering to examine problem content material in their native language, the scholars do no longer fall in the back of their educational subjects at the same time as acquiring English. Potentially bilingual students who are in developmental or late-exit bilingual programs for five years appear to progress at a faster fee in subjects presented in English than do their counterparts in early-exit bilingual packages.

When potentially bilingual students retain to analyze in their domestic language while learning English, they maintain to develop cognitively and acquire talents (along with studying) that can later be transferred to English. Once they have found out vocabulary in English, they could realize what they decode. The context of mastering is more difficult if the practice is completely in a scholar's second language. College students taught totally within the second language additionally threaten to lose the possibility to turn out to be bilingual and bi-literate.

A college that respects the language and tradition of its ethnically and linguistically diverse college students (and their dad and mom or guardians) develops instructional conditions that maximize the resources these students bring to school. In preference to being stressed and distressed via looking to cope in a language they cannot understand, college students continue to learn content material and abilities and expand a feeling of efficacy in addition to belonging to their new college. If the faculty context does not permit this linguistic and cultural range, students are much more likely to feel alienated and burdened.

Whilst the range of students in a school who speak the same language merits the establishment of bilingual software, encouraging younger human beings to study the content of their native language while gaining knowledge of English as a second language is possible to grow standard mastering. College students can examine topics that include arithmetic, technology, and social research in their local language until they have found out sufficient English to observe the instructional content material in English.

With the help of such programs as logo-author, college students can use computers to do programming and word processing in their local language. In one sixth grade lecture room, for instance, new immigrant college students in comparison dwellings around the sector. They saw snapshots of different sorts of dwellings and found out that cultural responses to exclusive ecological systems were one of the reasons for differences among earlier cultures. Igloos have been variations to their surroundings simply because the adobe "apartments" of native people within the southwestern United States of America had been adaptations to theirs. The developers of each form of dwellings used available assets. With the use of Spanish, college students discovered software geometrical shapes to symbolize igloos and Anasazi dwellings. Additionally, they wrote about the systems in Spanish.

Include dual-language strategies

Students gifted in languages aside from English examine more efficaciously in twin-language mastering conditions. They hold to examine content material in their native language at the same time as learning English as a second language using interacting with monolingual English-speaking college students who also are gaining knowledge of a second language.

This approach is treasured for numerous motives. First, young humans' native language is affirmed and revered whilst it becomes a topic being taught to their English-talking friends. Second, potentially bilingual college students can share their native-language expertise as peer tutors to English-speaking students who are getting to know a second language for enrichment; within the system, the advantage revel in running in English as nicely. 0.33, the lengthy-term profits are greater because, on this additive bilingual approach, students talented in languages other than English become bilingual and bi-literate. Fourth, college students aren't segregated into classes for potentially bilingual students or monolingual English-speaking students; all are incorporated and become bilingual over a length of five or six years.

In a few faculties, college students spend half the day in an immersion situation, gaining knowledge of content in English, and the opposite 1/2 immersed in learning content material of their local language. In other colleges, college students first of all research precise topics which include math, art, song, or physical training in English, their second language. Now and then, monolingual English-speaking students are immersed in a second language, consisting of Spanish, with a local Spanish audio system.

Based on many years of running with scores of -manner immersion programs, Howard and Christian (2002) have unique suggestions for imposing two-manner immersion bilingual packages. They observe Thomas and Collier (2002) and others in suggesting a minimum of four to six years of bilingual preparation. They suggest possible approaches:

• Fifty percentage of coaching in L1 and fifty percent in L2 from kindergarten thru middle faculty, or

• Ninety percentage inside the local language with ten percentage in L2 for grades k–1, eighty percentage in the local language, and twenty percent in L2 for grades 2–3, and 50/50 using 4th grade and beyond.

They stress that educational coaching desires to be of excessive pleasant and that there be "finest language input that is comprehensible, exciting, and of enough amount, and opportunity for output … along with explicit language arts instruction" in both L1 and L2 so that scholars emerge as bilingual and bi-literate.

To accomplish these practices, teachers' use of the sheltered training remark Protocol (SIOP) is usually recommended. Howard and Christian (2002) also advocate different teaching practices along with constructivist, infant-focused, lively discovery learning. At the side of August and Hakuta (1998), they advocate a coaching technique called "academic verbal exchange," which "affords college students with possibilities for extended communicate in areas that have educational value in addition to relevance for them". Cooperative mastering offers students possibilities for conversations in both languages if the groups are established to consist of the same numbers of native speakers of both L1 and L2. Cooperative mastering is also an opportunity to increase go-cultural expertise.

Instructors can decorate the mastering of a second language via structuring informal conditions wherein students who are proficient in languages aside from English act as peer tutors for monolingual English-speaking college students learning a second language and vice versa. Second-language learning for both organizations is stronger when they can talk informally at certain instances at some stage in the school day in their second language. This alternative social business enterprise of getting to know a second language does no longer depends entirely on the trainer as the locus of coaching. Students emerge as instructors and assets for each other; second-language studying is reciprocal.

College students studying Spanish as a second language, for example, maybe encouraged to apply the language in functional conditions. Younger students can research elements of Latino cultures by way of the usage of recipes in Spanish to prepare dinner Mexican, Dominican, and Puerto Rican dishes. Or they could find out about the track of each subculture by studying to sing songs in Spanish. Older students can find out about the rain forests in vital and south the United States; they might, as one example, graph the range of drug treatments derived from plants in this environment.

Rote drill and practice are uninteresting and absent meaning for young human beings; holistic reviews are lots more enticing. For example, students can use language-revel methods to research technological know-how in English. In doing so, they connect doing and looking at an experiment to speaking, writing, and reading. Because their oral language is written down for later reading, they can apprehend what they read, and their analyzing has which means.

Studies at the mastering of second languages show the cost of an improved emphasis on "communicative competence". To be ready in communicating, students want to head beyond sincerely gaining knowledge of the regulations of grammar. Additionally, they need to learn how to practice social and cultural policies. Students learning a second language ought to learn, for example, that the informal language used with friends and friends might not be suitable in more formal situations, together with creating a request of a teacher or answering questions during a task interview. College students must discover ways to take turns in a communique, whilst to talk and preserve still, how to "exhibit" listening, and while to be direct or oblique. Those culturally suitable approaches of talking may be found out whilst students listen to stories, see dramas, read books to communicating, and write and act outperforms.

"Coaching via communication" is some of the five requirements for powerful Pedagogy proposed by using Tharp, Estrada, Dalton, and Yamauchi (2000) to improve mastering effects for all students—however especially the ones of numerous ethnic, cultural, linguistic, or monetary backgrounds. Different researchers additionally support the technique of attracting students through instructional conversation. As previously mentioned, the educational conversation is a prolonged talk this is educational and relevant to students' lives. Tharp and colleagues advise a holistic approach that employs all five requirements, which includes: instructors and college students producing together, developing language and literacy throughout the curriculum, connecting faculty to students' lives, coaching complex questioning, and coaching through an educational communique.

The instructor starts evolved studying a children's story by first showing the illustrations and asking the scholars to explain them. After analyzing the tale, the instructor asks a pupil to retell it. Subsequently, the teacher can also ask the students to write the tale as a play with a specific ending or to jot down a continuation of the tale. This technique enables younger humans to see the relationship between writing and reading.

The instructor asks students to interrupt into organizations of five. Every group is responsible for writing and illustrating a tale. Group individuals must first negotiate who will do which responsibilities in English, then which events to demonstrate. They ought to agree on the series of events and variety them sequentially. One way of structuring this hobby is to offer pages categorized as "predominant characters," "problem to be solved," "first event," "second event," "0.33 occasion," and "resolution of the trouble."

High school college students can be assigned to observe one scene of a play that takes vicinity within the tradition they may be gaining knowledge of approximately. They then shape agencies and write the scene as they keep in mind it. After the businesses respond to one another's efforts and refine the speaking (possibly by relating to the video of the play), they act out the scene. A next undertaking might name on them to change the function and status of one of the characters and determine how that individual would speak: What would possibly he or she say differently? How might the other characters reply? The scholars can then act out the scene, using the same fundamental content however especially announcing matters to a person with a distinctive social function.

College students also can imagine real-existence conditions wherein they may find themselves and act out the parts of various audio systems, alternating in social roles. They can get feedback from friends who are members of the linguistic institution they're studying.

The mastering of language cannot be separated from what's being found out. Too frequently, college students with constrained proficiency in English are required to study the abstract or grammatical components of language in preference to the functional and communicative elements. Those more important practical capabilities are finely advanced at the side of the studying of content.

While students examine a second language in a functional manner (similar to the manner they learned their first language), the procedure has real meaning. Getting to know makes sense and is extra thrilling. College students additionally benefit by studying move-cultural competencies. Learning greetings in a second language, for example, in addition to the "well mannered" conduct associated with that language permits young humans to talk more effortlessly in a brand new way of life. Mastering the way to request meals at a dinner table requires basic grammar and well-mannered conduct. College students can pass on to talk about how polite conduct differs in one-of-a-kind cultures and what "polite" manner inside the study room among buddies, in a

In place of getting rid of students from a content material lesson in mathematics because they're not but proficient in English, the teacher can pair bilingual and monolingual college students in small companies and offer math-related tasks within those organizations. Bilingual students will assist the monolingual students in finishing those responsibilities while offering herbal fashions of language development inside the content material domain.

Pairs of students may carry out a simple experiment of their lecture room: they may be to discover "what is going to take place if?" Labels at the items they use guide their inquiry. College students write the steps in their test inside the shape of an enjoy chart and tell what took place after they observed the stairs. If they're stuck, they can ask any other pair of students for help. The series of steps is then written and may be illustrated with photos. Every other day, they could use the enjoy chart to exercise studying aloud in English.

For older students who've discovered the methods of arithmetic (addition, subtraction, multiplication, department) of their native language, and specifically for individuals who already know the Arabic variety system, an overview of the mathematics method in English is an effective manner of studying purposeful English. Whilst younger humans understand a procedure in numerical shape, they could research the vocabulary and the guidelines for asking questions and pointing out answers. Regularly, faculties cannot shape bilingual classrooms due to the fact their students are so linguistically various that the wide variety of children talking any one language is inadequate for a separate magnificence. In these settings, pullout packages should be prevented; they stigmatize children. Yet sheltered English and content material-embedded ESL programs advantage college students who are proficient in languages apart from English. Such programs make certain that scholars have adequate time to apply English themselves rather than sitting as a passive target market for the instructor.

The Sheltered instruction observation Protocol becomes evolved to help teachers in the usage of sheltered English strategies. SIOP was constructed by way of short and Echevarria (1999) based totally on the studies concerning excellent practices, in addition to on the studies of middle school instructors and researchers who collaborated in growing the statement device. The taking part teachers used sheltered guidance in conventional ESL training, content-primarily based ESL training, and sheltered content material lessons. SIOP presents concrete examples of sheltered preparation that teachers can use to guide ELL college students' expertise in tutorial content material. Numerous teachers would possibly use SIOP as the premise for helping every different as a learning community while they are trying out new strategies and speak their exercise, sharing questions and answers.

The sheltered English method makes getting to know content material greater comprehensible to English language freshmen. The approach consists of

•	Speaking at a fee and stage of complexity suitable to the proficiency degree of students.

•	The usage of visual aids and picture organizers in

addition to math manipulative.

- Constructing on previous know-how.
- Providing frequent possibilities for interaction amongst L1 and L2 audio systems.
- Modeling educational tasks.
- Reviewing key content and vocabulary.

In sheltered English school rooms, instructors offer many examples and hands-on activities so college students can understand abstracts in addition to concrete academic substances. This method won't be complex. As an example, the instructor may additionally reveal activity and describe in easy terms what she is doing. As she attracts a face, she tells the youngsters, "I am drawing eyes," and "I'm drawing a mouth," and "these are tooth." The visible references make comprehension faster and simpler, and the modeling of language permits children to examine new grammatical structures. Even using drawing as a teaching device may additionally model for students the effectiveness of nonverbal manner of mastering their new language and new culture; this activity may additionally lead to the usage of drawing as a tool for peer tutoring.

College students proficient in languages other than English analyze extra through being actively engaged in cooperative gaining knowledge of than by way of listening passively. College students whose native language is aside from English advantage from running in cooperative mastering groups with native English audio system due to the fact they can listen to a native version of English and exercise their English in proper communicative conditions. Instructors who structure cooperative gaining knowledge of situations for ELLs enable their college students to emerge as greater actively engaged in mastering.

Doubtlessly bilingual college students want to practice generating and rehearsing their second language. Small agencies in which every toddler has a specific role and precise responsibilities allow youngsters to research greater than if they're simply passive listeners. For this reason, cooperative mastering businesses are greater effective than whole-class preparation due to the fact small agencies (three or four students) challenge children to use language extra often. However, the scholars need to be grouped around significant responsibilities so that they use language for work-associated communique. Cooperative techniques were established to work nicely with Chicano, Laotian, Cambodian, Hmong, and Jap college students.

In a junior excessive technology class, college students discover some of the troubles of their neighborhood. They then collaboratively increase a questionnaire to use to interview people within the community to find out what they pick out as community problems. If their community has many citizens who speak a language other than English, they'll want a second version of the questionnaire in that language. After forming teams to interview community members about the neighborhood issues, college students return to high school, record the responses, and graph them by way of frequency. They could then speak about whether or not there is a hassle that they could work together to clear up, what sources they want to clear up it, and the pros and cons of diverse guidelines for reaching a solution.

In every other example, more youthful students may be assigned to investigate one in all two local American groups: the Algonquin or the Iroquois. Their purpose is to discover the adaptive strategies each group used to take advantage of the environment for his or her dwellings, apparel, meals, and transportation. The students are assigned to one-of-a-kind roles, which include researcher, recorder, reporter, illustrator, or graph maker (to graph the effects of the studies).

The trainer gives each organization a coloring eBook containing line drawings of humans from the Algonquin and Iroquois international locations pursuing sports of daily lifestyles. The students can interpret the drawings to discover a manner of transportation, materials from which dwellings had been made, and so forth. They display their findings on a chart, and they also write a short narrative describing the drawing.

Instructors have a foundation on which to construct go-age peer tutoring whilst their college students' cultures emphasize the care of more youthful children using older siblings (Puerto Rican, Hawaiian, and Chicano cultures, for instance). Studies show that go-age tutoring enhances studying for people who are tutored and for the tutors themselves. Heterogeneous move-capacity grouping promotes scholar tutoring via the sharing of different skills in extraordinary contexts. As an instance, a scholar who is nonetheless learning English may be robust in math and might help an English-talking classmate with a mathematics undertaking.

Teachers can offer to gain knowledge of possibilities for college students who're gifted in languages other than English with the aid of organizing their classroom to consist of cross-age tutoring and peer tutoring. College students who're gifted in any other language, together with

Spanish, can provide language models and practice for monolingual English audio systems gaining knowledge of Spanish. In some mastering situations, Spanish can be used to speak approximately a shared activity. In every other state of affairs wherein English is the primary language, the tuition roles can be reversed.

College students are analyzing a variety of structures. The use of the chalkboard, a scholar who speaks best English demonstrates the use of zero in the Arabic range gadget to a local Spanish speaker with the aid of showing math troubles after which running with the alternative student to resolve them. After learning the Mayan quantity system, the local Spanish speaker then demonstrates, in Spanish, the Mayan number system and its use of place and 0 to the English-speaking student, explaining that the Mayans had been the primary world way of life to use an image for zero.

Setting up verbal exchange is the most critical attention in coaching. In lots of bilingual populations, language alternation (or code-switching) is frequently used for greater powerful conversation. In conversations, either teacher or student may exchange the language in midstream to capture the listener's interest, to emphasize something, to clarify, to intricate, or to address those in a group who might also apprehend the second language greater without difficulty. Therefore, college students and teachers need to be capable of simply use these evidently taking place alternations to gain conversation inside the schoolroom.

In discussing the entire language technique, in which

language is taught clearly as it takes place within any social environment, Goodman (1986) has noted, "complete language applications respect the novices—who they're, wherein they arrive from, how they talk, what they read, and what stories they have already had." both Edelsky (1986) and Huerta-Macias and Quintero (1992) encompass code-switching as a part of this whole language method.

In an analyzing exercise carried out in English, a pupil hesitates in answering a comprehension query posed by using the instructor. The instructor rephrases the query in the child's native language, and the kid proudly responds to the query in her local language. In this scenario, the teacher specializes in the aim of story comprehension and alternates the language used to achieve this purpose.

In an own family literacy program, five families come together for ninety minutes as soon as per week after college. Their instructor conducts the lessons in Spanish and English, alternating in line with the linguistic abilities and alternatives of dad and mom and children. This approach permits parents and youngsters to experience ease in expressing themselves in both languages. Their activities encompass conversing, studying, writing, and creating artwork initiatives. The mother and father tend to apply Spanish to explicit themselves; the trainer alternates between talking Spanish with the parents and English with the youngsters. The children also use each language freely as they communicate to their mother and father, their brothers and sisters, and the trainer.

In developing literacy, the particular language used isn't as critical as encouraging verbal exchange among dad and mom and their children. The motive right here is to apply the language abilities of the mother and father as a resource to continue supporting their youngsters with analyzing and writing abilities at domestic. This verbal exchange—and the improvement of leisure of reading and writing collectively—are the primary desires. Other outcomes encompass growing to admiration for the dad and mom's local language, supporting the pupil to develop biliteracy, and developing the native language as an aid whilst acquiring literacy in English.

Linguistically diverse students had been proven to gain from interdisciplinary methods. Students proficient in languages apart from English can learn content with more comprehension if their mastering is interdisciplinary.

For college kids learning English as a second language, thematic techniques beautify getting to know and comprehension due to the fact the brand new gaining knowledge of is incremental and added to a topic that the students already apprehend. Having a base vocabulary associated with the theme presents college students a context wherein to suit new gaining knowledge of from the various disciplines. Vocabulary is bolstered via its use in exceptional problem contexts.

Specializing in a subject and referring to diverse disciplines to that subject matter allows college students to higher understand each new area when you consider that it's far linked to an acknowledged center. When there may be a subject, the vocabulary and talents can be evolved in connection with the content material. This method affords coherence to college students who are gifted in languages aside from English. Rather than looking to study several separate and distinct regions with diverse vocabularies simultaneously, they can work inside a huge, unifying subject matter.

The bilingual technological know-how program Descubrimiento is an instance of an interdisciplinary program that integrates technological know-how content material and processes, overseas language mastering, and English as a second language. because college students set up, behavior, examine, report, and write up the experiments as institution contributors, they analyze a second language, either English or Spanish, even as they may be obtaining technology competencies and content. Additionally, they learn to work cooperatively. All the abilities of verbal exchange in every language are used on distinct days to analyze, question, file, and percentage what has been learned from the technology experiment.

Instructors can create situations in which two potentially bilingual college students use a commonplace computer to greater effortlessly examine English as a second language. while sharing a word processing program, second-language learners have the possibility to generate language, create dialogues, interview every other, assist each different with corrections, and act as an audience for the other's writing. But, one computer shared through a whole class of students does not permit an awful lot of language exercise as does pairing students who've to to to get entry to a computer laboratory.
The varieties of software used for language learning additionally make a distinction. Some language-gaining knowledge of programs simply translates drill and practice into laptop formats. different programs—desktop

publishing software program, as an instance—motivate students to write down in their second language, when you consider that they recognize that their writing might be edited collaboratively and then posted, to be examined by way of classmates and parents or guardians.

The net can also be used to correspond with "sister faculties" in the same city, every other kingdom, or maybe another USA character correspondence or bilingual newsletters written via college students can increase their writing and literacy capabilities in each their local and second languages.

With the aid of the usage of computer systems, teachers can task college students to offer greater of their personal interpretation and to generate their very own textual content, in preference to certainly perform rote drill-and-exercise activities. For example, an instructor can display a photo of two human beings interacting with a couple of college students on the PC. Their task is to imagine the identity of everybody and to increase a dialogue wherein every one one one of them assumes the voice of one of the people inside the photo. Each response to the opposite and gives remarks if she or he is "out of character" or desires help.

The trainer can also structure conditions in which college students use computer systems to bolster writing talents in their second language by using offering assignments that have an immediate communicative motive. As an instance, instructors assign two students to a computer and ask every to provide peer tutoring to the opposite. Students can interview each different thru the computer—one asking questions through the laptop and the other writing the solutions.

Writing a play or an information story collectively can be exciting and rewarding. Whilst writing a news tale, one scholar can act because the correspondent and interview the "newsmaker" or "informant." students also can interview each other approximately their diverse countries of foundation and write an eBook for the whole class using combining their man or woman accounts.

On the excessive school level, as an ongoing school room venture, bilingual students can learn to use a laptop publishing software program to collaboratively produce a bilingual month-to-month publication that they can change with a bilingual magnificence in a sister faculty in every other district. The publication might also include poems; jokes; network surveys; methods of handling issues at faculty; or interviews with battle mediators, college members, or parents, all telling about their jobs. By exchanging newsletters with a sister faculty (and probable such as a column that allows students from the other faculty to inform how they cope with concerns and troubles), college students are using language to find out about actual-lifestyles issues.

Cummins, Brown, and Sayers (2007) suggest similar bilingual strategies with students the usage of both L1 and L2 and laptop applications to create films, audio CDs, and net pages. Students can proportion the consequences in their projects aimed at producing new information, developing literature, doing motion studies, and addressing the social realities of their community in both languages. When they alternate their work with other training, students can use computers and other generations to create and share literature and art and discover problems of social relevance to them and their communities (tasks like "Voices of Our Elders" or "The Social history of our network").

Cummins additionally suggests that bilingual college students from kindergarten can bring in words in either L1 or L2 and explore their meanings in each language with friends and instructor, incorporating their words into a technology-supported bilingual dictionary developed by the whole class.

For older college students in bilingual or L2 immersion training, Cummins indicates developing vital literacy by using comparing the way that the identical information occasions and troubles are mentioned in L1 and L2 at the net.

At the same time as college students with college-educated dad and mom generally have a network of social relationships to facilitate instructional fulfillment (a shape of social capital), students whose mother and father did not attend college frequently lack these styles of networks.

Gibson and Bejinez's (2002) ethnography documented how adult worrying and constructing social capital prompted the staying power of Mexican migrant college students in faculty. They studied the federally funded Migrant schooling software (MEP) at Hillside, California, an integrated high school with about equal proportions of white (45%) and Mexican (42%) students. Gibson and Bejinez tested how the MEP staff "facilitated student engagement by using growing worrying relationships with college students, presenting them with get entry to institutional guide, and implementing activities that construct from and serve to validate students' home cultures". MEP instructors who came from migrant backgrounds and have been college knowledgeable provided role fashions for the migrant college students and explicitly assisted them with tutoring and the university utility procedure. They mounted a workplace wherein students should socialize as well as discover statistics and guide.

Gibson and Bejinez additionally drew on the literature on being concerned as "a precondition for college kids to experience agree with and belonging within the school surroundings so that you can set up beneficial school-based totally relationships". They "observed caring relationships between migrant instructors and college students to be on the very heart of the [MEP] application's success in attractive college students academically and retaining them in faculty".

Sooner or later, Gibson and Bejinez constructed on the research at the school structures and employees facilitating "the minority students' potential to withstand the assimilationist pressures of faculty." Minority students who felt there has been a secure location for them to speak Spanish in addition to English and to construct upon their lifestyle—bringing their a couple of identities to high school rather than concealing them—had any experience of belonging rather than marginalization and alienation. This feeling of belonging in school has been correlated with engagement with schoolwork and perseverance within the face of barriers.

In the Gibson and Bejinez (2002) observe, one MEP trainer noted, "We have a desirable conversation, and we keep on pushing them. It really is why our work is continually packed. They know we've got high expectations, and that I assume that they're truly looking to meet them".

The dual-language packages discussed right here enable all college students to construct their local language while studying a second. College students also recognize that in reciprocal dating they're both teaching and mastering. As did Weis and high-quality (2001), Gibson and Bejinez located that anti-Mexican, anti-immigrant, anti-Spanish stereotypes were contested both in the MEP workplace and by the faculty's Mexican students' affiliation, wherein students may want to take management in organizing, fund-raising, and celebrating their local way of life. They did so by way of retaining a commencement ceremonial dinner at which they honored their dad and mom. Gibson has known as this "additive acculturation," this is, acculturation without assimilation.

Instructors can inspire students to proportion elements in their local cultures through assignments in social studies in which a particular US's records and way of life is researched using a small organization of college students and then supplied to the entire magnificence to help scholar pride in their subculture and mastering approximately others. Different sports encompass building a lecture room library of autobiographies and children's books in diverse languages, assigning internet websites where college students can study their culture, or hosting international days that commemorate college students' cultures.